Advance Praise for
Poetry: A Pocket Anthology, *Third Edition*

"I find the Introduction clear and concise and I think that it makes the book versatile enough for courses of many levels."

Margaret Noel Sipple
Northern Virginia Community College

"Since this anthology contains such a fine survey of older and contemporary works, students always find it easy to select poems that speak to them."

Robin Woods
Ripon College

"I applaud your inclusion of a wide range of living poets."

James Hirsh
Georgia State University

"Yes, I like the book. My students, in their course evaluations, were UNANIMOUS in their favorable comments. They were tired of huge anthologies that are difficult to use and just represent 'overkill' in the classroom."

Dan Sheridan
University of North Dakota

"I think Gwynn's anthology is excellent, and as pedagogy instructor at the University of Michigan I have supervised a number of graduate students who have used the book and told me it teaches very well."

Porter Shreve
University of Michigan

"This book is surprisingly inclusive for such a short book, and its apparatus is excellent."

Janet McCann
Texas A&M University

"The material on quoting and documentation is fabulous."

Terry Rasmussen
Casper College

"Gwynn has managed to make many (if not all) of the points that larger, more unwieldy anthologies make. . . ."

Carol Ann Davis
College of Charleston

"The strengths of Gwynn's anthologies are the price, the selection of contemporary works, and the introductory/background material."

Kathleen Dale
University of Wisconsin, Milwaukee

R. S. Gwynn has edited several other books, including *Literature: A Pocket Anthology; Drama: A Pocket Anthology; Fiction: A Pocket Anthology, The Longman Anthology of Short Fiction* (with Dana Gioia), and two volumes of *The Dictionary of Literary Biography.* He has also authored five collections of poetry, including *No Word of Farewell: Selected Poems: 1970–2000.*

Professor Gwynn teaches at Lamar University in Beaumont, Texas

Poetry

A Pocket Anthology

(*Formerly* A Longman Pocket Anthology)

THIRD EDITION

Edited by

R. S. Gwynn
Lamar University

PENGUIN ACADEMICS

New York San Francisco Boston
London Toronto Sydney Tokyo Singapore Madrid
Mexico City Munich Paris Cape Town Hong Kong Montreal

Editor-in-Chief: Joseph Terry
Acquisitions Editor: Erika Berg
Marketing Manager: Melanie Craig
Production Manager: Donna DeBenedictis
Project Coordination and Electronic Page Makeup: The Clarinda Company
Senior Cover Designer/Manager: Nancy Danahy
Text Designer: Keithley and Associates, Inc.
Cover Photo: © Tony Stone Images
Manufacturing Buyer: Lucy Hebard
Printer and Binder: R.R. Donnelley & Sons Company/Harrisonburg
Cover Printer: Phoenix Color Corp.

For permission to use copyrighted material, grateful acknowledgment is made
to the copyright holders on pp. 437–442, which are hereby made part of this
copyright page.

Library of Congress Cataloging-in-Publication Data

Poetry : a pocket anthology / edited by R. S. Gwynn — 3rd ed.
   p. cm.
   "Penguin Academics."
   Includes indexes.
   ISBN 0-321-08720-8 (pbk.)
   1. Poetry—Collections.

PN6101.P52   2002
821.008—dc21

2001038004

Please visit our website at http://www.ablongman.com/gwynn

For more information about the Penguin Academics series, please contact us by
mail at Longman Publishers, attn. Marketing Department, 1185 Avenue of the
Americas, 25th Floor, New York, NY 10036, or by e-mail at www.ablongman.com

ISBN 0-321-08720-8

1 2 3 4 5 6 7 8 9 10—DOH—04 03 02 01

Contents

Preface

When the Pocket Anthology series first appeared almost a decade ago, our chief aim was to offer a clear alternative to the anthologies of fiction, poetry, and drama that were available at the time. *Poetry: A Pocket Anthology*, now in the Penguin Academics series (previously titled *Poetry: A Longman Pocket Anthology*), is in its third edition. *Poetry* is designed to be used in a wide range of courses. This brief anthology can be bundled with one or more of a rich selection of the most popular Penguin titles, which Longman offers at significantly reduced prices. Also, *Poetry* has been published concurrently with two companion volumes, *Fiction* and *Drama*, and in a combined edition, *Literature*. Your Longman representative can supply full details about these books and available Penguin titles.

    Poetry addresses the four wishes and concerns most commonly expressed by both instructors and students. First, of course, is the variety of selections it contains. Admittedly, a pocket anthology has to be very selective in its contents, so we are especially proud that the over three hundred poems in this book include both a generous selection of works by poets from past centuries and a large number of contemporary poems that reflect the diversity of authorship, subject matter, and form that is essential to the study of contemporary poetry. Approximately one third of the poems in *Poetry* are by women and minority writers, including such important contemporary voices as Julia Alvarez, Rita Dove, and Cathy Song. More important, the contents of *Poetry* have profited both from the advice of experienced instructors who have cited poems that possess appeal to students and from the editor's own long experience as a poet, critic, and teacher of literature and creative writing. A strong effort has been made to include a number of poems that reflect contemporary social questions and thus will easily stimulate classroom discussion;

also, *Poetry* contains examples (many of them by contemporary poets) of virtually every traditional poetic form used in English-language poetry, ranging from the haiku and the cinquain to the rondeau redoublé and the sestina. These examples help to make *Poetry* invaluable for courses that emphasize analysis of poetic meter and form or composition of poems in formal patterns. Among the features *Poetry* are two useful appendices, one grouping poems thematically and another grouping them by form, which provide students and instructors a quick way to locate poems of comparable types for discussion, analysis, and emulation.

Our second aim was flexibility. We wanted a book that could be used as both a primary and supplemental text in a wide range of courses, ranging from introduction to poetry courses to advanced classes in poetic analysis to creative writing workshops. When combined with one of its companion volumes, *Fiction* or *Drama*, or with novels, collections of short stories or poems by individual authors, or plays available from Penguin, *Poetry* may also be used in introductory literature courses. *Poetry* contains, in addition to its generous selection of poems, biographical headnotes for authors, an introduction that covers the techniques and terminology of the genre, and a concise section on writing about poetry and research procedures. As a further aid to instructors and students, our website at **http://www.ablongman.com/gwynn** provides discussion questions, suggestions for writing topics, links to other useful websites, and commentary on the poems, much of which has been provided by instructors and students themselves.

Third, we wanted an affordable book. Full-sized introductory literature books now cost upwards of sixty dollars, and many of the comprehensive anthologies of poetry are in the same price range. Longman is committed to keeping the price of the Pocket Anthology series reasonable without compromising on design or typeface. We believe that readers will find the attractive layout of *Poetry* preferable to the cramped margins and minuscule fonts found in many literature textbooks. Because of its low cost, *Poetry* may be easily supplemented in individual courses with works of criticism, handbooks of grammar and usage, or with manuals of style. The price of *Poetry* remains low, and we believe that earlier editions' claims that the book represents "a new standard of value" remain accurate.

Finally, we stressed portability. Many instructors expressed concern for students who must carry large literature books, many of which now approach 2000 pages, across large campuses in backpacks already laden with books and materials for other courses. A semester is a short time, and few courses can cover more than a fraction of the material that many full-sized collections contain. Because most instructors focus on a single genre at a time, *Poetry* and its companion volumes, *Fiction* and *Drama*, remain compact yet self-contained editions that, if a snug fit in most pockets, are still easy to handle and carry. We trust that sympathetic instructors and their students will be grateful for a book that does not add a physical burden to the already heavy intellectual one required by college courses.

In closing, we would like to express our gratitude to the instructors who reviewed our preliminary materials and offered invaluable recommendations for improvements. They are: Herman Asarnow, University of Portland; Francis Burch, St. Joseph's University; Kathleen Dale, University of Wisconsin, Milwaukee; Carol Ann Davis, College of Charleston; James Hirsh, Georgia State University; Edward H. Hoeppner, Oakland University; Jennifer Maier, Seattle Pacific University; Janet McCann, Texas A&M University, College Station; Terry Rasmussen, Casper College; Daniel Sheridan, University of North Dakota; Porter Shreve, University of Michigan, Milwaukee; Margaret Sipple, Northern Virginia Community College; and Robin Woods, Ripon College.

These instructors reviewed the second edition: Shireen Carroll, Davidson College; Tracy Case, Yakima Valley Community College; Bill Clemente, Peru College; Michel de Benedictis, Miami-Dade Community College; Allen Kupser, Nassau Community College; Dwight McCawley, West Chester University of Pennsylvania; Robert L. McDonald, Virginia Military Institute; Jim Papworth, Ricks College; Frank Rooney, Wentworth Institute of Technology; John Ruszkiewicz, University of Texas; Charles Schuster, University of Wisconsin–Milwaukee; Deborah Sutton, Jefferson College; John Walsh, Saint Peter's College; and David Williams, San Francisco State University.

We are also grateful to the professors who commented on the first edition: Marsha Aldrich, Michigan State University; Herman L. Asarnow, University of Portland; Lea Baechler, Columbia University; Paul Bodmer, Bismark State College; Peggy F. Broder, Cleveland State University; William Covino, University of Chicago; Dwight Eddins, University of Alabama; Wil Gehne, State University of New York,

Binghamton; Cheryl Glenn, Oregon State University; Julia Hamilton, Inver Hills Community College; Jennie Harrison, North Harris College; Mary Hojnacki, University of Massachusetts, Lowell; Jim Holte, East Carolina University; Aija Hoover, Odessa College; John Morris, Cameron University; Lee Patterson, Duke University; Marco Portales, Texas A&M University; Lawrence Rainey, Yale University; Kim Roberts, University of Maryland; Danny Robinson, Bloomsburg University; Pam Schirmeister, New York University; James Schuttemeyer, Thomas More College; Shirely Simpson, Nicholls State University; Michael Steinman, Nassau Community College; Kathleen Thornton, State University of New York, Albany; and Clifford Dale Whitman, Southern Arkansas University.

R. S. Gwynn
Lamar University

Introduction

An Anecdote: Where Poetry Starts

The room is not particularly grand—a large lecture hall in one of the old buildings on the college campus—and the small group of first-year students whose literature class has been dismissed so that they can attend the poetry reading have taken seats near the back of the room. They have been encouraged to come by their instructor, and when she enters she looks around the room and nods in their direction, smiling.

The seats gradually fill. The crowd is a mixed one—several men and women known by sight as senior faculty members; a scattering of other older visitors, many of them apparently from the community; a large contingent of instructors and graduate students from the English Department sitting in the front rows; and small clusters of undergraduates scattered throughout the room.

One of the students scans the crowd, wondering aloud which is the poet. On the walk to the reading, the class's consensus has been that the poet, a cadaverous gray-haired man wrapped in a black cloak, would recite his poems in a resonant monotone, preferably with a strong breeze tossing his hair. Speculation on how the wind effect might be managed inside a lecture hall makes them laugh.

Now the crowd grows quiet as the instructor steps to the podium and adjusts the microphone. She makes a few complimentary remarks about the strong turnout and thanks several benefactors for their financial support of poetry at the university. Then she introduces the guest. Her students know most of this information, for they have studied several of his poems in class that week, but they are still slightly surprised when he rises to polite applause and takes the lectern. The

balding middle-aged man wearing a chambray shirt and loosely knot-
ted tie could be taken for a professor in any campus department, and
when he adjusts his glasses and clears his throat, blinking at the audience, there is little about him that would fit anyone's romantic stereo-
type of a poet.

Surprisingly, he does not begin with a poem. Instead, in a relaxed
voice he tells an anecdote about his young daughter and an overdue science project. When he moves from the background story into the poem
itself, there is little change in his volume level, and his tone remains
conversational. The students find that the poem, which they had discussed in class only a couple of days before, takes on new meaning
when its origins are explained by the poet himself. They find themselves
listening attentively to his words, even laughing out loud several times.
The hour goes by quickly, and at its end their applause, like that of the
rest of the audience, is long and sincere.

At the next class meeting, the instructor asks for reactions to the
reading. While some of the class members are slightly critical, faulting
the speaker for his informal manner and his failure to maintain eye contact with the room, most of the remarks are positive. The comments
that surface most often have to do with how much more meaningful the
poems in the textbook become when the poet explains how he came to
write them, how one poem is actually spoken in the voice of his dead father, how another is addressed to a friend who was paralyzed in an au-
tomobile accident. While these things could perhaps be inferred from
the poems alone, the students are unanimous in their opinion that
knowing the details beforehand adds a great deal to the first impression
a poem makes. As one student puts it, "It's just that a poem makes a lot
more sense when you know who's talking and when and where it's supposed to be taking place."

"It always helps to know where poetry starts," adds one of her
classmates.

Speaker, Listener, and Context

The situation just described is hardly unique. Instructors have long encouraged, even begged, their students to attend events like this one, and
the college poetry reading has become, for many Americans, the closest
encounter they will have with this complex and often perplexing art

form. But what students often find at such readings, sometimes to their amazement, is that poetry need not be intimidating or obscure, thus providing a gentle reminder that the roots of poetry, like those of all literature, were originally part of the **oral tradition**—stories and poems that were passed down from generation to generation in ancient societies and recited for audiences that included all members of the tribe, from the wizened elders to the youngest children. For most of its long history, poetry has been a popular art form aimed at *audiences* (remember that the word means "hearers"), and it is only recently that its most visible signs of life are to be found on college campuses. The reasons for this academic retreat are too complicated to go into here, but it is perhaps worth noting that we are daily exposed to a great deal of poetry in oral form, primarily through the medium of recorded song lyrics, and that the unique qualities of poetry throughout the ages—its ability to tell stories or summarize complicated emotions in a few well-chosen words—are demonstrated whenever we memorize the lines of a popular song and sing them to ourselves.

Of course, poetry written primarily for the page is usually more demanding than song lyrics. Writers of popular songs aim at a wide commercial audience, and this simple fact of economics, added to the fact that the lyrics are not intended primarily for publication but for being recorded with all the resources of studio technology, tends to make many song lyrics relatively uninteresting when they appear in print. A poem, on the other hand, will primarily exist as a printed text, although certainly its effect may be greatly enhanced through a skillful oral performance in which the poet can also explain the background of the poem, its setting and speaker, and the circumstances under which it was written. In general, these details, which are so crucial to understanding a poem yet are often only implied when the poem appears in print, are called the **dramatic situation** of a poem. Reduced to its simplest formulation, dramatic situation can be summed up in a question: *Who is speaking to whom under what circumstances?* If the poet fails to provide us with clues or if we are careless in picking up the information that is provided, then we may begin reading with no sense of reference and, thus, may go far astray. Even such words as "on," "upon," or "to" in titles can be crucial to our understanding of dramatic situation, telling us something about an event or object that provided the stimulus for the poem or about the identity of the "you" addressed in the poem.

An illustration may be helpful. Suppose we look at what is unquestionably the most widely known poem ever written by an American. It is a poem which virtually all Americans can recite in part and, in fact, do so by the millions every week. Yet if we were told that this poem is unusual in that its best-known section is a long, unanswered question addressed by the speaker to a companion about whether or not the object named in the title even exists, then it is likely that most of us would be confused. Before going further, let's look at the poem.

The Star-Spangled Banner

O say, can you see, by the dawn's early light,
    What so proudly we hailed at the twilight's last gleaming?
Whose broad stripes and bright stars thro' the perilous fight,
    O'er the ramparts we watched, were so gallantly streaming!
And the rockets' red glare, the bombs bursting in air,
    Gave proof through the night that our flag was still there:
O say, does that star-spangled banner yet wave
    O'er the land of the free and the home of the brave?

On the shore, dimly seen thro' the mists of the deep,
    Where the foe's haughty host in dread silence reposes,
What is that which the breeze, o'er the towering steep,
    As it fitfully blows, now conceals, now discloses?
Now it catches the gleam of the morning's first beam,
    In full glory reflected now shines on the stream:
'Tis the star-spangled banner! O long may it wave
    O'er the land of the free and the home of the brave!

And where is that band who so vauntingly swore
    That the havoc of war and the battle's confusion
A home and a country should leave us no more?
    Their blood has washed out their foul footsteps' pollution.
No refuge could save the hireling and slave
    From the terror of flight, or the gloom of the grave:
And the star-spangled banner in triumph doth wave
    O'er the land of the free and the home of the brave!

Oh! thus be it ever, when freemen shall stand
    Between their loved homes and the war's desolation!

Blest with victory and peace, may the heav'n-rescued land
   Praise the Pow'r that hath made and preserved us a nation.
Then conquer we must, when our cause it is just,
   And this be our motto: "In God is our trust."
And the star-spangled banner in triumph shall wave
   O'er the land of the free and the home of the brave!

"Now wait a minute!" you may be complaining. "'The Star-Spangled Banner' is a *song*, not a poem. And what's this *question* business? Don't we always sing it while facing the flag? Besides, it's just a patriotic song. Nobody really worries about what it *means*."

In answer to the first comment, "The Star-Spangled Banner" *was* in fact written as a poem and set to music only after its composition. Most of us probably will agree that the words are not particularly well-suited to the melody (which was taken, curiously, from a popular British barroom ballad) and the song remains notoriously difficult to sing, even for professional performers. Garth Brooks, the popular country singer, once remarked before attempting it at a Super Bowl game that it "is one of the hardest songs to sing," implying that the audience at such an event always seems ready to witness a failure. In its original form, "The Star-Spangled Banner" (or "The Defense of Fort McHenry," the title under which it was first published) is an example of **occasional verse,** a poem that is written about or for an important event (or *occasion*), sometimes private but usually of some public significance. While poems of this type are not printed on the front pages of newspapers as often they once were, they are still being written. Enough poems appeared after the assassination of President John F. Kennedy in 1963 to fill a book, *Of Poetry and Power,* and the Challenger disaster of 1985 stimulated a similar outpouring of occasional poems, one of them by Howard Nemerov, who served as poet laureate of the United States (1988–1990). More recently, Maya Angelou recited "On the Pulse of Morning" at the first inauguration of President Bill Clinton, and Miller Williams read "Of History and Hope" at the second. The author of "The Star-Spangled Banner," Francis Scott Key (1779–1843), wrote poetry as an avocation. Yet like many men and women who are not professional writers, Key was so deeply moved by an event that he witnessed that occasional poetry was the only medium through which he could express his feelings.

Now let's go back to our question about dramatic situation, taking it one part at a time: *Who is speaking?* A technical word that is often used to designate the speaker of a poem is **persona** (plural: **personae**), a word that meant "mask" in ancient Greek. Even though the persona of "The Star-Spangled Banner" never uses the word "I" in the poem, the speaker seems to be Key himself, a fact that can be verified by biographical research. Still, it is probably safer to look at poems carefully to see if they give any evidence that the speaker is someone other than the poet. Poems like "Ulysses" by Alfred, Lord Tennyson or "Porphyria's Lover" by Robert Browning have titles that identify personae who are, respectively, a character from ancient epic poetry and an unnamed man who is confessing the murder of his lover, Porphyria. In neither case should the persona be identified with the poet himself. Other poems may be somewhat more problematic. Edgar Allan Poe's "The Raven," like many of Poe's short stories, is spoken by a persona who should not be identified with the author, even though he shares many of the same morbid preoccupations of Poe's other characters; even Sylvia Plath, a poet usually associated with an extremely candid form of autobiographical poetry known as **confessional poetry,** identified the persona of her masterpiece "Daddy" as an invented character, "a girl with an Electra complex." Sometimes poems have more than one persona, which is the case with Thomas Hardy's "The Ruined Maid" and Robert Frost's "Home Burial," two poems which consist almost entirely of dialogue. In other poems, the voice may simply be a third-person **narrator** such as we might find in a short story or novel. While it is perhaps true that many poems (including the majority of those included in this text) are in fact spoken by the poet out of his or her most private feelings, it is not a good idea to leap too quickly to the assumption that the persona of a poem is identical to the poet and shares his or her views. Conclusions about the degree to which a poem is autobiographical can be verified only by research and familiarity with a poet's other works.

To return to our question: Who is speaking *to whom?* Another useful term is **auditor,** the person or persons being spoken to in a poem. Some poems identify no auditor; others clearly do specify an auditor or auditors, in most cases identified by name or by the second-person pronoun "you" (or "thee/thou" in older poetry). Again, the title may give clues: Poe's "To Helen" is addressed to the famous beauty of Homeric legend;

Robert Herrick's "To the Virgins, to Make Much of Time" is addressed to a group of young women; William Cullen Bryant's "To the Fringed Gentian" is addressed to a common New England wildflower. (The figure of speech **apostrophe** is used when a nonhuman, inanimate, or abstract thing is directly addressed.) Relatively few poems are addressed directly to the reader, so when we read the opening of William Shakespeare's Sonnet 18 ("Shall I compare thee to a summer's day?") we should keep in mind that he is not addressing us but another individual, in this case a young male friend who is referred to in many of the sonnets. A powerful poem like Claude McKay's "If We Must Die" begins in this manner:

> If we must die, let it not be like hogs
> Hunted and penned in an inglorious spot,
> While round us bark the mad and hungry dogs,
> Making their mock at our accursed lot.

Later in the poem McKay identifies his auditors as "Kinsmen." Without outside help, about all we can say with certainty at first glance is that the poet seems to be addressing a group of companions who share his desperate situation; when we learn, possibly through research, that McKay was an African-American poet writing about the Harlem race riots of 1919, the symbolic nature of his exhortation becomes clearer.

Now the final part of the question: Who is speaking to whom *under what circumstances?* First, we might ask if there is a relationship, either implied or stated, between persona and auditor. Obviously many love poems take the form of verbal transactions between two parties and, because relationships have their ups and downs, these shifts of mood are reflected in the poetry. One famous example is Michael Drayton's sonnet "Since There's No Help," which begins with the persona threatening to end the relationship with the auditor but ends with an apparent reconciliation. Such "courtship ritual" poems as John Donne's "The Flea" and Andrew Marvell's "To His Coy Mistress" are witty arguments in favor of the couple's engaging in sexual relations, no more, no less. An example from poetry about marital love is Matthew Arnold's "Dover Beach," which ends with the plea "Ah, love, let us be true/To one another" as the only hope for stability the persona can find in a world filled with uncertainty and fear. Even an age disparity between persona and auditor can lend meaning to a poem, which is the case with the Herrick poem mentioned earlier and a dialogue poem like John Crowe Ransom's "Piazza Piece," a classic example of the debate between innocence and experience.

Other questions relating to circumstances of the dramatic situation might concern the poem's physical setting (if any), time (of day, year, historical era), or even such matters as weather. Thomas Hardy's "Neutral Tones" provides a good example of a poem in which the setting—a gray winter day in a barren, outdoor place—symbolically reinforces the persona's memory of the bitter end of a love affair. The shift in setting from the springtime idyll to the "cold hillside" in John Keats's "La Belle Dame sans Merci" cannot be overlooked in discussing the persona's disillusionment. Of course, many poems are explicitly occasional and may even contain an **epigraph** (a brief explanatory statement or quotation) or a **dedication,** which explains the setting. Sometimes footnotes or even outside research may be necessary. John Milton's "On the Late Massacre in Piedmont" will make little sense to readers if they do not know that the poet is reacting to the massacre of a group of Protestants by Roman Catholic soldiers and that Milton, an English Puritan, uses the occasion to attack the papacy as a "triple tyrant" and the "Babylonian woe."

To return, then, one final time to "The Star-Spangled Banner," let's apply our question to the poem. We have already determined that Key is the persona. Who is the "you" mentioned four words into the poem? It seems clear that Key is addressing an auditor standing close to him, either a single individual or a group, as he asks the auditor if he can see the flag that they both observed for the last time the previous day at sundown. Key tells us that it is now just at the moment of dawn, and that even though the flag could be glimpsed periodically in the "rockets' red glare" of the bombardment throughout the night, it cannot be clearly seen now. It is a crucial question, for if the flag is no longer flying "o'er the ramparts," it will mean that the fort has fallen to the enemy. The tension mounts and moves into the second stanza, where at last, "thro' the mists of the deep," the flag can be discerned, "dimly seen" at first, then clearly as it "catches the gleam" of the full sunlight.

The full story of how Key came to write the poem is fairly well known and supports this reading. The events that the poem describes took place on September 13 and 14, 1814, during the War of 1812. Key, a lawyer, came aboard a British warship anchored off Baltimore to argue for the release of a client and friend who had been taken hostage by the British. Key won his friend's release, but the British captain, fearing that he might reveal information he had learned on board, kept Key overnight, releasing him and his client in the morning. It was during that night that Key witnessed the bombardment and, with it, the failure of the British to take Baltimore. The final half of the poem celebrates the American victory and offers a hopeful prayer that God will continue to smile on America "when our cause . . . is just." One might well argue that Key's phrase "conquer we must" contradicts the spirit of the earlier parts of the poem, but few people have argued that "The Star-Spangled Banner" is a consistently great poem. Still, it is an effective piece of patriotic verse that has a few moments of real drama, expressed in a vivid manner that lets its readers become eyewitnesses to an incident from American history.

Lyric, Narrative, Dramatic

The starting point for all literary criticism in Western civilization is Aristotle's *Poetics*, a work dating from the fourth century B.C. While Aristotle's remarks on drama—tragedy, in particular—are more complete than his analysis of other types of literature, he does mention three main types of poetry: lyric, epic, and dithyrambic. In doing so, Aristotle outlines for the first time a theory of literature based on **genres,** or separate categories delineated by distinct style, form, and content. This three-fold division remains useful today, although in two cases different terminology is employed. The first genre, **lyric poetry,** originally comprised brief poems that were meant to be sung or chanted to the accompaniment of a lyre. Today we still use the word "lyrics" in a specialized sense when referring to the words of a song, but lyric poetry has become such a large category that it includes virtually all poems that are primarily *about* a subject and contain little narrative content. The subject of a lyric poem may be the poet's emotions, an abstract idea, a satirical insight, or a description of a person or place. The persona in a lyric is usually closely identified with the poet himself or herself; because we tend to identify the essence of poetry with personal, subjective expression of feelings or ideas, lyric poetry remains the largest genre, with a number of subtypes. Among them are the **epigram,** a short, satirical lyric usually aimed at a specific person; the **elegy,** a lyric on the occasion of a death; and the **ode,** a long lyric in elevated language on a serious theme.

Aristotle's second genre, the **epic,** has been expanded to include all types of **narrative poetry,** that is, poetry whose main function is to tell a story. Like prose fiction, a narrative poem has a plot, characters, a setting, and a point of view, and may be discussed in the same terms as, say, a short story. The epic is a long narrative poem about the exploits of a hero. **Folk epics** like *The Iliad* or *Beowulf* were originally intended for public recitation and existed in oral form for a long period of time before they were transcribed. Little or nothing is known about the authors of folk epics. **Literary epics,** like Dante's *The Inferno* or Henry Wadsworth Longfellow's *The Song of Hiawatha,* differ in that they are the products of known authors who *wrote* their poems for publication. **Ballads** are generally shorter narratives with song-like qualities that often include rhyme and repeated refrains. **Folk ballads,** like folk epics, come from the oral tradition and are usually published anonymously; "Bonny Barbara Allan" and "Sir Patrick Spens" are typical examples. **Art ballads** or **literary ballads,** on the other hand, are conscious imitations of the ballad style by later poets and are generally somewhat more sophisticated than folk ballads in their techniques. Examples of this popular genre include Keats's "La Belle Dame sans Merci," a recent specimen like Marilyn Nelson's "Ballad of Aunt Geneva," and Samuel Taylor Coleridge's famous long art ballad, "The Rime of the Ancient Mariner." There are also other types of narrative poetry that have been popular through the centuries. **Metrical romances,** verse tales of the exploits of knights, were a popular genre of the Middle Ages and Renaissance; Edmund Spenser's *The Faerie Queene* is one of the most ambitious examples of the type. At the opposite extreme are **mock-heroic narratives** like John Dryden's *MacFlecknoe* or Lord Byron's *Don Juan,* which spoof the conventions of epic poetry for comic or satirical effect. **Realistic narratives** of medium length (under 1000 lines) like Robert Frost's "Home Burial" or, more recently, B. H. Fairchild's "Body and Soul" and Leon Stokesbury's "Evening End," have been popular since the early nineteenth century and are sometimes discussed as "poetic novellas" or "short stories in verse."

There is no exact contemporary analogue for Aristotle's third category, **dithyrambic** poetry. This type of poem was composed to be chanted at religious rituals by a chorus and was the forerunner of tragedy. Today the third category is called **dramatic poetry,** because it has perhaps as much in common with the separate genre of drama as with lyric and narrative poetry. In general, the persona in a dramatic poem is an invented character not to be identified with the poet. The poem is presented as a speech or dialogue that might be acted out like a soliloquy or a scene from a play. The **dramatic monologue** is a speech by a single character, usually delivered to a silent auditor; notable examples are Tennyson's "Ulysses" and Browning's "My Last Duchess." A dramatic monologue sometimes implies, in the words of its persona, a distinct setting and an interplay between persona and auditor. At the close of "Ulysses," the aged hero urges his "mariners" to listen closely and to observe the ship in the harbor waiting to take them off on a final voyage. Dramatic poetry can also take the form of **dialogue poetry,** in which two personae speak alternately. Examples are Christina Rossetti's "Up-Hill" and Hardy's "The Ruined Maid." In the past, a popular type of dialogue poem was the *débat*, or mock-debate, in which two characters, usually personified abstractions like the Soul and the Body, argued their respective merits.

While it is easy enough to find examples of "pure" lyrics, narratives, and dramatic monologues, sometimes the distinction between the three major types may become blurred, even in the same poem. "The Star-Spangled Banner," for example, contains elements of all three genres. The opening stanza, with its vivid recreation of a question asked at dawn, is closest to dramatic poetry. The second and third stanzas, which tell of the outcome of the battle, are primarily narrative. The final stanza, with its patriotic effusion and religious sentiment, is lyrical. Still, the three-fold division is useful in discussing a single author's various ways of dealing with subjects or in comparing examples of one type by separate authors. To cite three poems by the same poet in this collection, we might look at William Blake's "The Tyger," "A Poison Tree," and "The Chimney Sweeper." The first of these is a descriptive lyric, dwelling primarily on the symbolic meaning of the tiger's appearance; the second is a narrative that relates, in the allegorical manner of a parable, the events leading up to a murder; the third is a short dramatic monologue spoken by the persona identified in the title.

The Language of Poetry

One of the most persistent myths about poetry is that its language is artificial, "flowery," and essentially different from the language that people speak in going about their daily lives. While these beliefs may be true of some poetry, one can easily find numerous examples that reveal the opposite side of the coin. It is impossible to characterize poetic language narrowly, for poetry, which is after all the art of language, covers the widest range of linguistic possibilities. For example, here are several passages from different poets, all describing birds:

Hail to thee, blithe Spirit!
   Bird thou never wert—
That from Heaven, or near it,
   Pourest thy full heart
In profuse strains of unpremeditated art.

Higher still and higher
   From the earth thou springest
Like a cloud of fire;
   The blue deep thou wingest,
And singing still dost soar, and soaring ever singest.

Percy Bysshe Shelley, "To a Skylark"

I caught this morning morning's minion, king-
dom of daylight's dauphin, dapple-dawn-drawn Falcon, in his riding
Of the rolling level underneath him steady air, and striding
High there, how he rung upon the rein of a wimpling wing
In his ecstacy!

Gerard Manley Hopkins, "The Windhover"

When the lilac-scent was in the air and Fifth-month grass was
   growing,
Up this seashore in some briers,
Two feather'd guests from Alabama, two together,
And their nest, and four light-green eggs spotted with brown,
And every day the he-bird to and fro near at hand,
And every day the she-bird crouch'd on her nest, silent, with bright
   eyes,

And every day I, a curious boy, never too close, never disturbing
   them,
Cautiously peering, absorbing, translating.

Walt Whitman, "Out of the Cradle Endlessly Rocking"

At once a voice arose among
   The bleak twigs overhead
In a full-hearted evensong
   Of joy illimited;
An aged thrush, frail, gaunt, and small,
   In blast-beruffled plume,
Had chosen thus to fling his soul
   Upon the growing gloom.

Thomas Hardy, "The Darkling Thrush"

There is a singer everyone has heard,
Loud, a mid-summer and a mid-wood bird,
Who makes the solid tree trunks sound again.
He says that leaves are old and that for flowers
Mid-summer is to spring as one to ten.

Robert Frost, "The Oven Bird"

The blue booby lives
on the bare rocks
of Galápagos
and fears nothing.
It is a simple life:
they live on fish,
and there are few predators.

James Tate, "The Blue Booby"

Of these quotes only the oldest, from the early nineteenth century,
possesses the stereotypical characteristics of what we mean when we use
the term "poetic" in a negative sense. Poetry, like any other art form,
follows fashions that change over the years; by Shelley's day, the use of
"thee" and "thou" and their related verb forms ("wert" and "wingest")
had come full circle from their original use as a familiar form of the second person employed to address intimates and servants to an artificially

heightened grammatical form reserved for prayers and poetry. Hopkins's language, from a poem of the 1870s, is artificial in an entirely different way: here the poet's **idiom,** the personal use of words that marks his poetry, is highly idiosyncratic; indeed, it would be hard to mistake a poem by Hopkins with one by any other poet. Whitman, on the other hand, should present few difficulties; the only oddities here are the spelling of "briers" and the use of "Fifth-month" instead of "May," a linguistic inheritance, perhaps, from Whitman's Quaker mother. Of course, one might argue that Whitman's "naturalness" results from his use of his free verse, but both Hardy and Frost, who use rhymed, metrical verse, are hardly less natural. When we move to the contemporary period, we can find little difference between the language of many poems and conversational speech, as Tate's lines indicate.

Still, in reading a poem, particularly one from the past, we should be aware of certain problems that may impede our understanding. **Diction** refers to the individual words in a poem and may be classified in several ways. A poem's **level of diction** can range from slang at one extreme to formal usage at the other, although in an age in which most poems use a level of diction that stays in the middle of the scale, ranging between conversational and standard levels, these distinctions are useful only when a poet is being self-consciously formal (perhaps for ironic effect) or going to the opposite extreme to imitate the language of the streets. In past eras, the term **poetic diction** was used to indicate a level of speech somehow refined above ordinary usage and, thus, somehow superior to it; today the same term would most likely be used as a way of condemning a poet's language. Still, we should keep in mind that the slang of one era may become the standard usage of another.

A good dictionary is useful in many ways, particularly in dealing with **archaisms** (words that are no longer in common use) and other words that may not be familiar to the reader. Take, for example, the opening lines of Edgar Allan Poe's "To Helen":

> Helen, thy beauty is to me
>   Like those Nicean barks of yore,
> That gently, o'er a perfumed sea,
>   The weary, way-worn wanderer bore
>   To his own native shore.

Several words here may give trouble to the average contemporary reader. First, "o'er," like "ne'er" or similar words such as "falt'ring" and "glimm'ring," is simply a contraction; this dropping of a letter, called **syncope,** is done for the sake of maintaining the poem's meter; in the third stanza of "The Star-Spangled Banner," the words "Pow'r" and "heav'n" are contracted for the same reason. "Barks of yore" will probably send most of us to the dictionary, for our sense of "bark" as either the outer surface of a tree or the noise that a dog makes does not fit here; likewise, "yore" is unfamiliar, possibly archaic. Looking up the literal sense of a word in a dictionary discloses its **denotation,** or literal meaning. Thus, we find that "barks" are small sailing ships and that "yore" refers to the distant past. Of course, Poe could have used "ships of the past" or a similar phrase, but his word choice was perhaps dictated by **connotation,** the implied meaning or feel that some words have acquired; it may be that even in Poe's day "barks of yore" had a remote quality that somehow evoked ancient Greece in a way that, say, "ancient ships" would not. But what are we to make of "Nicean," a proper adjective that sounds geographical but does not appear in either the dictionary or gazetteer? In this case we have encountered an example of a **coinage** or **neologism,** a word made up by the poet. Speculation on the source of "Nicean" has ranged from Nice, in the south of France, to Phoenician, but it is likely that Poe simply coined the word for its exotic sound. Similarly, we might note that the phrase "weary, way-worn wanderer" contains words that seem to have been chosen primarily for their alliterative sounds.

When we put a poem into our own words, we **paraphrase** it, a practice that is often useful when passages are hard to understand. Other than diction, **syntax** (the order of words in a sentence) may also give readers problems. Syntax in poetry, particularly in poems that use rhyme, is likely to be different from that of both speech and prose; if a poet decides to rhyme in a certain pattern, word order must be modified to fit the formal design, which may present difficulties to readers in understanding the grammar of a passage. Here is the opening of a familiar piece of American patriotic verse: "My country, 'tis of thee, / Sweet land of liberty, / Of thee I sing." What is the subject of this sentence? Would you be surprised to learn that the subject is "it" (contained in the contraction '*tis*)? The passage from Poe presents few difficulties of this order but does contain one example of **inversion,** words that fall out of their expected order (a related syntactical problem lies in **ellipsis,** words that are consciously omitted by the poet). If we do not allow for inverted syntax we are likely to be confused by "the weary, way-worn wanderer bore / To his own native shore." The wanderer bore *what?* A quick mental sentence diagram shows that "wanderer" is the direct object of "bore," not its subject. A good paraphrase should simplify both diction and syntax: "Helen, to me your beauty is like those Nicean (?) ships of the ancient past that carried the weary, travel-worn wanderer gently over a perfumed sea to his own native land." In paraphrasing, only the potentially troublesome words and phrases should be substituted, leaving the original language as intact as possible. Paraphrasing is a useful first step toward unfolding a poem's literal sense, but it obviously takes few of a poet's specific nuances of language into account. "Poetry," Robert Frost famously remarked, "is what is lost in translation." He might have extended the complaint to include paraphrase as well.

Several other matters relevant to poetic language are worth mentioning. **Etymology,** the study of the sources of words, is a particularly rewarding topic in English literature because our language has such an unusually rich history—compare the size of an unabridged French dictionary to its English counterpart. Old English (or Anglo-Saxon), the ancient language of the British Isles, was part of the Germanic family of languages. When the Norman French successfully invaded Britain in 1066 they brought with them their own language, part of the Romance language family (all originally derived from Latin). By the time of Geoffrey Chaucer's death in 1400, these two linguistic traditions had merged into a single language, Middle English, which can be read today, despite its differences in spelling, pronunciation, and vocabulary. We can still, however, distinguish the words that show their Germanic heritage from those of Latinate origin, and despite the fact that English is rich in synonyms, the Germanic and Latinate words often have different connotations. "Smart" is not quite the same as "intelligent," and a "mapmaker" is subtly different from a "cartographer." A poet's preference for words of a certain origin is not always immediately clear, but we can readily distinguish the wide gulf that separates a statement like "I live in a house with my folks" from "I abide in a residence with my parents."

A final tension exists in poems between their use of **concrete diction** and **abstract diction.** Concrete words denote that which can be perceived by the senses, and the vividness of a poem's language resides primarily in the way it uses **imagery,** sensory details denoting specific details of experience. Because sight is the most important of the five senses, **visual imagery** ("a dim light"; "a dirty rag"; "a golden daffodil") predominates in poems, but we should also be conscious of striking examples of the other types of imagery: **auditory** ("a pounding surf"), **tactile** ("a scratchy beard"), **olfactory** ("the scent of apple blossoms"), and **gustatory** ("the bitter tang of gin"). The use of specific imagery has always been crucial for poetry; think, for example, of the way Chaucer uses brilliantly chosen concrete details—a nun's coral jewelry, a monk's hood lined with fur, a festering sore on a cook's shin—to bring his pilgrims to life in the prologue to *The Canterbury Tales.* In the early twentieth century, a group of poets led by Americans Ezra Pound and H. D. (Hilda Doolittle) pioneered a poetic movement called **imagism,** in which concrete details predominate in short descriptive poems (see H. D.'s "Sea Rose"). "Go in fear of abstractions," commanded Pound, and his friend William Carlos Williams modified the remark to become a poetic credo: "No ideas but in things."

Still, for most poets abstract words remain important because they carry the burden of a poem's overall meaning or theme. William Butler Yeats's "Leda and the Swan" provides a good example of how concrete and abstract diction may coexist in a poem. In reading this account of the myth in which Zeus takes the form of a swan, impregnates a mortal woman, and thus sets in motion the chain of events that leads to the Trojan War (Leda was the mother of Helen of Troy), we will probably be struck at first by the way that tactile imagery ("a sudden blow"; fingers attempting to "push / The feathered glory" away; "A shudder in the loins") is used to describe an act of sexual violation. Even though some abstract words ("terrified"; "vague"; "glory"; "strange") appear in the first eight lines of the poem, they are all linked closely to concrete words like "fingers," "feathered," and "heart." In the last two lines of the poem, Yeats uses three large abstractions—"knowledge," "power," and "indifferent"—to state his theme (or at least ask the crucial rhetorical question about the meaning of the myth). More often than not, one can expect to encounter the largest number of abstract words near the conclusions of poems. Probably the most famous abstract statement in English poetry—John Keats's "Beauty is truth, truth beauty,'—that is all / Ye know on earth, and all ye need to know."—appears in the last two lines of a fifty-line poem.

Two other poetic devices sometimes govern a poet's choice of words. **Onomatopoeia** refers to individual words like "splash" or "thud" whose meanings are closely related to their sounds. Auditory imagery in a poem can often be enhanced by the use of onomatopoeic words. In some cases, however, a whole line can be called onomatopoeic, even if it contains no single word that illustrates the device. Hardy uses this line to describe the pounding of distant surf: "Where hill-hid tides throb, throe on throe." Here the repetition of similar sounds helps to imitate the sound of the ocean. A second device is the **pun,** the use of one word to imply the additional meaning of a similar-sounding word (the formal term is **paranomasia**). Thus, when Anne Bradstreet compares her first book to an illegitimate child, she addresses the book in this manner: "If for thy Father asked, say thou had'st none; / And for thy Mother, she alas is poor, / Which caused her thus to send thee out of door." The closeness of the interjection "alas" to the article and noun "a lass" is hardly coincidental. Poets in Bradstreet's day considered the pun a staple of their repertoire, even in serious poetry, but contemporary poets are more likely to use it primarily for comic effect:

> They have a dozen children; it's their diet,
> For they have bread too often. Please don't try it.
>
> *Anonymous*

More often than not, puns like these will elicit a groan from the audience, a response that may be exactly what the poet desires.

Figurative Language

We use figurative language in everyday speech without thinking of the poetic functions of the same devices. We can always relate experience in a purely literal fashion: "His table manners were deplorable. Mother scolded him severely, and Dad said some angry words to him. He left the table embarrassed and with his feelings hurt." But a more vivid way of saying the same thing might employ language used not in the literal but in the figurative sense. Thus, another version might run, "His table manners were swinish. Mother jumped on his back about them, and Dad scorched his ears. You should have seen him slink off like a scolded puppy." At least four comparisons are made here in an attempt to describe one character's table manners, his mother's scolding, his father's words, and the manner in which the character retreated from the table. In every case, the thing being described, what is called the **tenor** of the figure of speech, is linked with a concrete image or **vehicle.** All of the types of figurative language, what are called **figures of speech** or **tropes,** involve some kind of comparison, either explicit or implied. Thus, two of the figures of speech in the above example specifically compare aspects of the character's behavior to animal behavior. The other two imply parental words that were delivered with strong physical force or extreme anger. Some of the most common figures of speech are:

Metaphor: a direct comparison between two unlike things. Metaphors may take several forms.

> His words were sharp knives.
>
> The sharp knife of his words cut through the silence.
>
> He spoke sharp, cutting words with his knife-edged voice.
>
> His words knifed through the still air.
>
> "I will speak daggers to her. . . ." (*Shakespeare*, Hamlet)

Implied metaphor: a metaphor in which either the tenor or vehicle is implied, not stated.

> The running back gathered steam and chugged toward the endzone. (Compares the player to a steam locomotive without naming it explicitly.)
>
> "While smoke on its chin, that slithering gun
> Coiled back from its windowsill" *(X. J. Kennedy).*

Simile: a comparison using *like, as,* or *than* as a connective device.

> "My love is like a red, red rose . . ." *(Robert Burns)*
>
> My love smells as sweet as a rose.
>
> My love looks fresher than a newly budded rose.

Conceit: an extended or far-fetched metaphor, in most cases comparing things that apparently have almost nothing in common.

"Make me, O Lord, thy spinning wheel complete. . . ."

(Edward Taylor)

(The poem, "Huswifery," draws an analogy between the process of salvation and the manufacture of cloth, ending with the persona attired in "holy robes.")

The **Petrarchan conceit,** named after the first great master of the sonnet, is a clichéd comparison usually relating to a woman's beauty (see Thomas Campion's "There Is a Garden in Her Face"; Shakespeare's Sonnet 130 parodies this type of trope). The **metaphysical conceit** refers to the extended comparisons favored by such so-called metaphysical poets as John Donne, George Herbert, and Edward Taylor. The conceit in the final three stanzas of Donne's "A Valediction: Forbidding Mourning" compares the poet and his wife to a pair of drafting compasses, hardly an image that most people would choose to celebrate marital fidelity.

Hyperbole: overstatement, a comparison using conscious exaggeration.

He threw the ball so fast it caught the catcher's mitt on fire.

"And I will love thee still, my dear,
Till a' the seas gang dry." *(Robert Burns)*

Understatement: the opposite of hyperbole.

"I don't think we're in Kansas anymore, Toto."

(Dorothy, in *The Wizard of Oz*)

I had to spend a moment or two filling out my tax forms before I mailed them to the IRS.

"The space between [birth and death] is but an hour,
The frail duration of a flower." *(Philip Freneau)*

Allusion: metaphor making a direct comparison to a historical or literary event or character, a myth, a biblical reference, etc.

He is a Samson of strength but a Judas of duplicity.

"He dreamed of Thebes and Camelot,
And Priam's neighbors." *(Edwin Arlington Robinson)*

Metonymy: use of a related object to stand for the thing actually being talked about.

> It's a white-collar street in a blue-collar town.
> "And O ye high-flown quills [that is, literary critics] that soar the skies,
> And ever with your prey still catch your praise." *(Anne Bradstreet)*

Synecdoche: use of a part for the whole, or vice versa.

> The crowned heads of Europe were in attendance.
> "Before the indifferent beak could let her drop."
> *(William Butler Yeats)*

Personification: giving human characteristics to nonhuman things or to abstractions.

> Justice weighs the evidence in her golden scales.
> The ocean cursed and spat at us.
> "Of all her train, the hands of Spring
> First plant thee [a yellow violet] in the watery mould."
> *(William Cullen Bryant)*

Apostrophe: variety of personification in which a nonhuman thing, abstraction, or person not physically present is directly addressed as if it could respond.

> "Milton! Thou shouldst be living at this hour."
> *(William Wordsworth)*
> "Is it, O man, with such discordant noises,
>   With such accursed instruments as these,
> Thou drownest Nature's sweet and kindly voices,
>   And jarrest the celestial harmonies?"
> *(Henry Wadsworth Longfellow)*

Paradox: an apparent contradiction or illogical statement.

> I'll never forget old what's-his-name.

"His [God's] hand hath made this noble work [the universe] which
  Stands,
His Glorious Handiwork not made by hands." *(Edward Taylor)*

Oxymoron: a short paradox, usually consisting of an adjective and
noun with conflicting meanings.

The touch of her lips was sweet agony.
"Progress is a comfortable disease" *(e. e. cummings)*
"A terrible beauty is born." *(William Butler Yeats)*

Synesthesia: a conscious mixing of two different types of sensory experience.

A raw, red wind rushed from the north.
"Leaves cast in casual potpourris
Whisper their scents from pits and cellar-holes." *(Richard Wilbur)*

Transferred epithet: strictly speaking, not a trope; it occurs when an
adjective is "transferred" from the word it actually modifies to a nearby
word. In this example, the plowman is weary, not the path ("way") he
walks upon.

"The plowman homeward plods his weary way." *(Thomas Gray)*

Allegory and Symbol

Related to the figurative devices are the various types of symbolism that
may occur in poems. We have already discussed how symbolism works
in fiction, but its use in poetry is perhaps even more complex. In many
cases, a poem may seem so simple on the surface that we feel impelled
to read deeper meanings into it; Robert Frost's "Stopping by Woods on a
Snowy Evening" is a classic case in point. There is nothing wrong with
searching for larger significance in a poem, but the reader should perhaps
be wary of leaping to conclusions about symbolic meanings before
fully exhausting the literal sense of a poem. Both allegory and symbolism
require that the reader supply abstract or general meanings to the
specific concrete details of the poem.

The simplest form taken by this substitution occurs in **allegory.** An allegory is usually a narrative that exists simultaneously on at least two levels, a literal level and a second level of abstract meaning. Throughout an allegory a consistent sequence of parallels exists between the literal and the abstract. Sometimes allegories may imply third or fourth levels of meaning as well, especially in long allegorical poems like Dante's *The Divine Comedy*, which has been interpreted in personal, political, ethical, and religious (Christian) terms. The characters and actions in an allegory explicitly signify the abstract level of meaning, and generally this second level of meaning is what the poet primarily intends to convey. For example, Robert Southwell's "The Burning Babe" is filled with fantastic incidents and paradoxical speech that are made clear in the poem's last line: "And straight I callèd unto mind that it was Christmas day." The literal burning babe of the title is revealed to be the Christ child, who predicts his own future to the amazed watcher. Thus, in interpreting the poem the reader must substitute theological terms like "redemption" or "original sin" for the literal details it contains.

Two types of prose allegories, the fable and the parable, have been universally popular. A fable is a short, nonrealistic narrative that is told to illustrate a universal moral concept. A parable is similar, but generally contains realistic characters and events. Thus, Aesop's fable of the tortoise and the hare, instead of telling us something about animal behavior, illustrates the virtue of persistence against seemingly unbeatable competition. Jesus's parable of the Good Samaritan tells the story of a man who is robbed and beaten and eventually rescued by a stranger of another race in order to define the concept of "neighbor" for a questioning lawyer. Poetic allegories like George Herbert's "Redemption" or Rossetti's "Up-Hill" can be read in Christian terms as symbolic accounts of the process of salvation. Robert Burns's witty ballad "John Barleycorn" tells on the literal surface the story of a violent murder, but the astute reader quickly discovers that the underlying meaning involves the poet's native Scotland's legendary taste for strong drink.

Many poems contain symbolic elements that are somewhat more elusive in meaning than the simple one-for-one equivalences presented by allegory. A **symbol,** then, is any concrete thing or any action in a poem that implies a meaning beyond its literal sense. Many of these things or actions are called **traditional symbols,** that is, symbols that hold roughly the same meanings for members of a given society. Certain flowers, colors, natural objects, and religious emblems possess meanings that we can generally agree upon. A white lily and a red rose suggest different occasions, mourning and passion. In Western societies, few would associate black with gaiety or red with innocence, and dawn and rainbows are traditional natural symbols of hope and new beginnings. It would be unlikely for a poet to mention a cross without expecting readers to think of its Christian associations.

Other types of symbols can be identified in poems that are otherwise not allegorical. A **private symbol** is one that has acquired certain meanings from a single poet's repeated use of it. Yeats's use of "gyres" is explained in some of his prose writings as a symbol for the turning of historical cycles, and his use of the word in his poems obviously goes beyond the literal level. Some visionary poets like Yeats and William Blake have devised complicated private symbolic systems, a sort of alternative mythology, and understanding the full import of these symbols becomes primarily the task of the specialist. Other poets may employ **incidental symbols,** things that are not usually considered symbolic but may be in a particular poem, or symbolic acts, a situation or response that seems of greater than literal import. As noted earlier, one of the most famous poems using these two devices is Frost's "Stopping by Woods on a Snowy Evening." In this poem, some readers see the "lovely, dark and deep" woods as inviting but threatening, and want to view the persona's rejection of their allure ("But I have promises to keep / And miles to go before I sleep") as some sort of life-affirming act. Frost himself was not particularly helpful in guiding his readers, often scoffing at those who had read too much metaphysical portent into such a simple lyric, although in other of his poems he presents objects—a rock wall between neighboring farms, an abandoned woodpile—that obviously possess some larger significance. There are many modern poems that remain so enigmatic that readers have consistently returned to them looking for new interpretations. Poems like these were to a degree influenced by the French symbolists, a group of poets of the late nineteenth century, who deliberately wrote poems filled with vague nuances subject to multiple interpretations. Such American attempts at symbolist experiments as Wallace Stevens's "Anecdote of the Jar" or "The Emperor of Ice-Cream" continue to perplex and fascinate readers, particularly those who are versed in recent schools of interpretation that focus on the indeterminacy of a poetic text.

Tone of Voice

Even the simplest statement is subject to multiple interpretations if it is delivered in several different tones of voice. Consider the shift in emphasis between saying "*I* gave you the money," "I *gave* you the money" and "I gave *you* the money." Even a seemingly innocent compliment like "You look lovely this morning" takes on a different meaning if it is delivered by a woman to her obviously hung-over husband. Still, these variations in **tone,** the speaker's implied attitude toward the words he or she says, depend primarily on vocal inflection. Because a poet only rarely gets the opportunity to elucidate his tone in a public performance, it is possible that readers may have difficulties in grasping the tone of a poem printed on the page. Still, many poems should present few tonal problems. The opening of Milton's sonnet "On the Late Massacre in Piedmont" ("Avenge, O Lord, thy slaughtered saints . . .") establishes a tone of righteous anger that is consistent throughout the poem. Keats's initial apostrophe in "Ode on a Grecian Urn" ("Thou still unravished bride of quietness, / Thou foster-child of silence and slow time . . .") strikes the reader as both passionate and reverent in the poet's response to an undamaged artifact of the ancient past. Thus, in many cases we can relate the tone of voice in poems to the emotions we employ in our own speech, and we would have to violate quite a few rules of common sense to argue that Milton is being flippant or that Keats is speaking sarcastically.

Irony is the element of tone by which a poet may imply an attitude that is in fact contrary to what his words appear to say. Of course, the simplest form of irony is **sarcasm,** the wounding tone of voice we use to imply exactly the opposite of what we say: "That's really a *great* excuse!" "What a *wonderful* performance!" One is almost tempted to add a firm "Not!" after such deliberately insincere bits of praise. **Verbal irony** is the conscious manipulation of tone by which the poet's actual attitude is the opposite of what he or she says. In a poem like Hardy's "The Ruined Maid," it is obvious that one speaker considers the meaning of "ruined" to be somewhat less severe than the other, and the whole poem hinges on this ironic counterpoint of definitions and the different moral and social attitudes they imply. Consider the opening lines of Oliver Wendell Holmes's "Old Ironsides," a piece of propaganda verse which succeeded in raising enough money to save the U.S.S. *Constitution* from the scrap yard: "Ay, tear her tattered ensign down! / Long has it waved on high, / And many an eye has danced to see / That banner in the sky. . . ." Because Holmes's poetic mission is to *save* the ship, it is obvious that he is speaking ironically in the opening line; he emphatically *does not* want the ship's flag stripped from her, an attitude that is made clear in the third and fourth lines. Verbal irony is also a conspicuous feature of verse satire, poetry that exists primarily to mock or ridicule, although often with serious intent. One famous example, in the form of a short satirical piece, or **epigram,** is Sarah N. Cleghorn's "The Golf Links," a poem written before the advent of child-labor laws:

> The golf links lie so near the mill
> > That almost every day
> The laboring children can look out
> > And see the men at play.

Here the weight of the verbal irony falls on two words, "laboring" and "play," and the way each is incongruously applied to the wrong group of people.

"The Golf Links," taken as a whole, also represents a second form of irony, **situational irony,** in which the setting of the poem (laboring children watching playing adults) contains a built-in incongruity. One master of ironic situation is Thomas Hardy, who used the title "Satires of Circumstances" in a series of short poems illustrating this sort of irony. Hardy's "Ah, Are You Digging on My Grave?" demonstrates a similar ironic situation, a ghostly persona asking questions of living speakers who can offer little comfort to the dead. **Dramatic irony,** the third type of irony, occurs when the persona of a poem is less aware of the full import of his or her words than is the reader. Blake's "The Chimney Sweeper" is spoken by a child who does not seem to fully realize how badly he is being exploited by his employer, who has apparently been using the promises of religion as a way of keeping his underage workers in line. A similar statement could be made of the persona of Walter Savage Landor's "Mother, I Cannot":

Mother, I cannot mind my wheel;
　My fingers ache, my lips are dry:
Oh! if you felt the pain I feel!
　But oh, who ever felt as I?

No longer could I doubt him true;
　All other men may use deceit:
He always said my eyes were blue,
　And often swore my lips were sweet.

The young woman speaking here apparently has not realized (or is deliberately unwilling to admit) that she has been sexually deceived and deserted by a scoundrel; "All other men may use deceit" gives the measure of her tragic naïvete. Dramatic irony, as the term implies, is most often found in dramatic monologues, where the gap between the speaker's perception of the situation and the reader's may be wide indeed.

Repetition: Sounds and Schemes

Because poetry uses language at its most intense level, we are aware of the weight of individual words and phrases to a degree that is usually lacking when we read prose. Poets have long known that the meanings that they attempt to convey often depend as much on the sound of the words as their meaning. We have already mentioned one sound device, onomatopoeia. Consider how much richer the experience of "the murmuring of innumerable bees" is than a synonymous phrase, "the low sound of a lot of bees." It has often been said that all art aspires to the condition of music in the way that it affects an audience on some unconscious, visceral level. By carefully exploiting the repetition of sound devices, a poet may use some of the same effects that the musical composer does.

Of course, much of this sonic level of poetry is subjective; what strikes one listener as pleasant may overwhelm the ear of another. Still, it is useful to distinguish between a poet's use of **euphony**, a series of pleasant sounds, and **cacophony**, sounds that are deliberately unpleasant. Note the following passages from Alexander Pope's "An Essay on Criticism," a didactic poem which attempts to illustrate many of the devices poets use:

Soft is the strain when Zephyr gently blows,
And the smooth stream in smoother numbers flows; . . .

The repetition of the initial consonant sounds is called **alliteration,** and here Pope concentrates on the *s* sound. The vowel sounds are generally long: str*ai*n, bl*ow*s, sm*oo*th, and so on. Here the description of the gentle west wind is assisted by the generally pleasing sense of euphony. But Pope, to illustrate the opposite quality, follows this couplet with a second:

But when loud surges lash the sounding shore,
The hoarse, rough verse should like the torrent roar.

Now the wind is anything but gentle, and the repetition of the *r* sounds in su*r*ges, sho*r*e, hoa*r*se, *r*ough, ve*r*se, to*r*rent, and *r*oar force the reader's voice into the back of the throat, making sounds that are anything but euphonious.

Repetition of sounds has no inherent meaning value (although some linguists might argue that certain sounds do stimulate particular emotions), but this repetition does call attention to itself and can be particularly effective when a poet wishes to emphasize a certain passage. We have already mentioned alliteration. Other sound patterns are **assonance,** the repetition of similar vowel sounds (st*ee*p, *e*ven, rec*ei*ve, v*ea*l), and **consonance,** the repetition of similar consonant sounds (du*ck*, tor*que*, stri*ke*, tri*ck*le). It should go without saying that spelling has little to do with any sound pattern; an initial *f* will alliterate with an initial *ph*.

Rhyme is the most important sound device, and our delight in deftly executed rhymes (consider the possibilities of rhyming "neighbor" with "sabre," as Richard Wilbur does in one of his translations) goes beyond mere sound to include the pleasure we take when an unexpected word is magically made to fit with another. There are several types of rhyme. **Masculine rhyme** occurs between single stressed syllables: *fleece, release, surcease, Nice* (a city in France), and so on. **Feminine rhyme,** also called **double rhyme,** matches two syllables, one stressed and one usually unstressed: *stinging, upbringing, flinging.* **Triple rhyme** goes further: *slithering, withering.* **Slant rhyme** (also called **near rhyme** and **off rhyme**) contains hints of sound repetition (sometimes related to assonance and consonance): *chill, dull, sale* are possibilities, although poets often grant themselves considerable leeway in counting as rhyming words pairs that often have only the slightest similarity. When rhymes fall in a pattern in a poem and are **end rhymes,** occurring at the end of lines, then it is convenient to assign letters to the matching sounds and speak of a **rhyme scheme.** Thus, a stanza of four lines ending with *heaven, hell, bell, eleven* is said to have a rhyme scheme of *abba.* Rhymes may also occasionally be found in the interior of lines, what is called **internal rhyme.**

More complicated patterns of repetition involve more than mere sounds but whole phrases and grammatical units. Ancient rhetoricians, in teaching the art of public speaking, identified several of these, and they are also found in poetry. **Parallel structure** is simply the repetition of grammatically similar phrases or clauses; for example, Tennyson's "To strive, to seek, to find, and not to yield." **Anaphora** and **epistrophe** are repeated words or phrases at, respectively, the beginnings and ends of lines. Whitman uses these schemes extensively, often in the same lines. This passage from *Song of Myself* illustrates both anaphora and epistrophe:

> If they are not yours as much as mine they are nothing, or next to nothing,
> If they are not the riddle and the untying of the riddle they are nothing,
> If they are not just as close as they are distant they are nothing.

Antithesis is the matching of parallel units which contain contrasting meanings, such as Whitman's "I am of old and young, of the foolish as much as the wise, / Regardless of others, ever regardful of others, / Maternal as well as paternal, a child as well as a man. . . ." While the rhetorical schemes are perhaps more native to the orator, the poet can still make occasional effective use of them. Whitman's poetry was influenced by many sources but perhaps by none so powerfully as the heavily schematic language of the King James Bible.

Meter and Rhythm

The subject of poetic meter and rhythm can be a difficult one, to say the least, and it is doubtless true that such phrases as *trochaic octameter* or *spondaic substitution* have an intimidating quality. Still, discussions of meter need not be limited to experts, and even beginning readers should be able to apply a few of the metrical principles that are commonly found in poetry written in English.

First, let's distinguish between two terms that are often used synonymously: **poetry** and **verse.** Poetry refers to a whole genre of literature and thus stands with fiction and drama as one of the three major types of writing. Verse, on the other hand, refers to a mode of writing in lines of a certain length; thus, many poets still retain the traditional practice of capitalizing the first word of each line to indicate its integrity as a unit of composition. Virtually any piece of writing can be versified (and sometimes rhymed as well). Especially useful are bits of **mnemonic verse,** in which information like the number of days in the months or simple spelling rules ("I before E / Except after C . . .") is cast in a form that is easy to remember. Although it is not strictly accurate to do so, many writers use verse to denote metrical writing that somehow does not quite measure up to the level of true poetry; phrases like **light verse** or **occasional verse** (lines written for a specific event, like a birthday or anniversary) are often used in this way.

If, on the other hand, a writer is unconcerned about the length of individual lines and is governed only by the width of the paper being used, then he or she is not writing verse but **prose.** All verse is metrical writing; prose is not. Surprisingly enough, there is a body of writing called **prose poetry,** writing that uses language in a poetic manner but avoids any type of meter; see Carolyn Forché's "The Colonel" for one example. Perhaps the simplest way to think of **meter** in verse is to think of its synonym, **measure** (think of the use of meter in words like odometer or kilometer). Thus, meter refers to the method by which a poet determines line length.

When we talk about meter in poetry, we ordinarily mean that the poet is employing some kind of consistent **prosody** or system of measurement. There are many possible prosodies, depending on what the poet decides to count as the unit of measurement in the line, but only three of these systems are common in English-language poetry. Perhaps the simplest is **syllabic verse.** In verse of this type, the length of the line is determined by counting the total number of syllables the line contains (see Sylvia Plath's "Metaphors" for one example). Much French poetry of the past was written in twelve-syllable lines, or **Alexandrines,** and a word like **octosyllabic** denotes a line of eight syllables. Because English is a language of strong stresses, most of our poets have favored other prosodic systems, but syllabic poetry has been attempted by many poets, among them Marianne Moore, Richard Wilbur, and Dylan Thomas. Moore, in particular, often wrote in **quantitative syllabics,** that is, in stanzas containing the same number of lines with identical numbers of syllables in the corresponding lines of different stanzas.

More natural to the English language is **accentual** verse, a prosodic system in which only accented or strongly stressed syllables are counted in a line, which can also contain a varying number of unaccented syllables. Much folk poetry, intended perhaps to be recited to the beat of a percussion instrument, retains this stress-based pattern, and the oldest verse in the British tradition, Anglo-Saxon poetry like *Beowulf,* is composed in four-stress lines which were recited to musical accompaniment. Many of the verses we recall from nursery rhymes, children's chanting games ("Red rover, red rover, / Send [any name from one to up to four syllables can be substituted here—*Bill, Susan, Latisha, Elizabeth*] right over") and sports cheers ("Two bits, four bits, six bits, a dollar! / All for the [*Owls, Cowboys, Cardinals, Thundering Herd*] stand up and holler!") retain the strong sense of rhythmical pulse that characterizes much accentual verse, a fact we recognize when we clap our hands and move rhythmically to the sound of the words. Indeed, the lyrics to most current rap music are actually composed in a four-stress accentual line, and the stresses or "beats" can be heard plainly when we listen or dance. Gerard Manley Hopkins, attempting to recapture some of the flavor of Anglo-Saxon verse, pioneered a type of accentual prosody that he called **sprung rhythm.** Accentual meters still supply possibilities for contemporary poets; indeed, what often appears to be free verse is revealed, on closer inspection, to be a poem written in accentual meter. Richard Wilbur's "The Writer," for example, is written in a stanza containing lines of three, five, and three strong stresses, respectively, but the stresses do not overwhelm the reader insistently. Wilbur's "Junk" employs Anglo-Saxon meter, and his strong alliteration helps the reader hear the four strong stresses in each line.

Accentual-syllabic verse is the most important prosodic system in English, dominating our poetry for the five centuries from Chaucer's time down to the early twentieth century. Even though in the last fifty years free verse has become the prevailing style in which poetry is written, accentual-syllabic verse still has many able practitioners. An accentual-syllabic prosody is somewhat more complicated than the two systems we have mentioned, for it requires that the poet count both the strongly stressed syllables and the total number of syllables in the line. Because stressed and unstressed syllables alternate fairly regularly in this system, four **metrical feet,** representing the most common patterns, designate the subdivisions of rhythm that make up the line (think of a yardstick divided into three feet). These feet are the **iamb** (or **iambic foot**), one unstressed and one stressed syllable; the **trochee** (or **trochaic foot**), one stressed and one unstressed syllable; the **anapest** (or **anapestic foot**), two unstressed syllables and one stressed syllable; and the **dactyl** (or **dactylic foot**), one stressed and two unstressed syllables. The first two of these, iambic and trochaic, are called **double meters;** the second two, **triple meters.** Iambic and anapestic meters are sometimes called **rising meters** because they "rise" toward the stressed syllable; trochaic and dactylic meters are called **falling meters** for the opposite reason. Simple repetition of words or phrases can give us the sense of how these lines sound in a purely schematic sense. The **breve** (˘) and **ictus** (´) are used to denote unstressed and stressed syllables, respectively.

Iambic:

 release / release / release

 to fall / into / despair

 Marie / discov / ers candy

Trochaic:

 melting / melting / melting / melting

 Peter / disa / greed en / tirely

 clever / writing / filled the / page

Anapestic:

 to the top / to the top

 a retriev / er appeared

 and a ter / ri ble thunder

Dactylic:

> shívering / shívering / shívering / shívering / shívering
>
> térribly / íll with the / sýmptoms of / víral pneu / mónia
>
> nóte how the / mínister / whíspered at / Émily's / gráve

Because each of these lines contains a certain number of feet, a second specialized term is used to denote how many times a pattern is repeated in a line:

one foot	monometer
two feet	dimeter
three feet	trimeter
four feet	tetrameter
five feet	pentameter
six feet	hexameter
seven feet	heptameter
eight feet	octameter

Thus, in the examples above, the first set of lines is iambic trimeter; the second, trochaic tetrameter; the third, anapestic dimeter; and the fourth, dactylic pentameter. The third lines in the iambic and anapestic examples are **hypermetrical;** that is, they contain an extra unstressed syllable or **feminine ending.** Conversely, the third lines in the trochaic and dactylic examples are missing one and two unstressed final syllables, respectively, a common practice called **catalexis.** Although over thirty combinations of foot type and number of feet per line are theoretically possible, relatively few are ordinarily encountered in poetry. The iambic foot is most common, followed by the anapest and the trochee; the dactylic foot is relatively rare. Line lengths tend to be from three to five feet, with anything shorter or longer used only sparingly. Still, there are famous exceptions like Poe's "The Raven," which is composed in trochaic octameter or Southwell's "The Burning Babe," in iambic heptameter.

Meter denotes regularity, the "blueprint" for a line from which the poet works. Because iambic pentameter is the most common meter used in English, our subsequent discussion will focus on poems written in it. But most good poets quickly learn that a metronomic regularity, five iambic feet marching in lockstep line after line, is not a virtue and quickly becomes predictable. Thus, there are several ways by which poets can add variety to their lines so that the actual **rhythm** of the line, what is actually heard, plays a subtle counterpoint against the regularity of the meter. One way is to vary the placement of the **caesura** (∥) or pause within a line (usually indicated by a mark of punctuation). Another is by mixing **end-stopped lines,** which clearly pause at their conclusion, with **enjambed** lines, which run on into the next line with no pause. The following lines from Tennyson's "Ulysses" illustrate these techniques:

> This is my son, mine own Telemachus,
> To whom I leave the scepter and the isle,
> Well-loved of me, discerning to fulfill
> This labor, by slow prudence to make mild
> A rugged people, and through soft degrees
> Subdue them to the useful and the good.

Lines two and six have no caesurae; the others do, after either the third, fourth, or fifth syllable. Lines one, two, and six are end-stopped; the others are enjambed (or use *enjambment*).

Another technique of varying regularity is **metrical substitution,** where feet of a different type are substituted for what the meter calls for. In iambic meter, trochaic feet are often encountered at the beginnings of lines, or after a caesura. Two other feet, the **pyrrhic** (⌣ ⌣), consisting of two unstressed syllables, and the **spondee** (′ ′), consisting of two stressed syllables, are also commonly substituted. Here are Tennyson's lines with their scansion marked.

> This is / my son, ∥ / mine own / Telem / achus,
> To whom / I leave / the scep / ter and / the isle,
> Well-loved / of me, ∥ / discern / ing to / fulfill
> This la / bor, ∥ by / slow pru / dence to / make mild
> A rug / ged peo / ple, ∥ and / through soft / degrees
> Subdue / them to / the use / ful and / the good.

Even though these are fairly regular iambic pentameter lines, it should be observed that no single line is without some substitution. Still, the dominant pattern of five iambic feet per line should be apparent (out of thirty total feet, about twenty are iambs); there is even a strong tendency on the reader's part to "promote" the middle syllable of three unstressed syllables ("Subdue / them *to* / the use / ful *and* / the good") to keep the sense of the iambic rhythm.

How far can a poet depart from the pattern without losing contact with the original meter? That is a question that is impossible to answer in general terms. The following scansion will probably strike us at first as a far departure from regular iambic pentameter:

$$/ \ || \ / \ / \ \cup \ || \ / \ / \ \cup \ \cup \ || / \ / \ \cup \ / \ \cup \ /$$

Yet it is actually the opening line of one of Shakespeare's most frequently quoted passages, Mark Antony's funeral oration from *Julius Caesar:*

Friends, || Ro´ / mans, || coun / trymen, || / lend me / your ears

Poets who have learned to use the full resources of meter do not consider it a restraint; instead, they are able to stretch the pattern to its limits without breaking it. A good analogy may be made between poetry and dance. Beginning dancers watch their feet and count the steps while making them; after considerable practice, the movements become second nature, and a skillful pair of partners can add dips and passes without losing the basic step of the dance.

Free Verse, Open Form, and Closed Form

Nothing has been so exhaustively debated in English-language poetry as the exact nature of **free verse.** The simplest definition may be the best: free verse is verse with no consistent metrical pattern. In free verse, line length is a subjective decision made by the poet, and length may be determined by grammatical phrases, the poet's own sense of individual "breath-units," or even by the visual arrangement of lines on the page. Clearly, it is easier to speak of what free verse is not than what it is, and free verse (a term, incidentally, that few poets, even its practitioners, seem very happy with) offers a wide variety of possibilities. Extensive use of free verse is a fairly recent phenomenon in the history of poetry. Even though there are many examples of free verse from the past (the Psalms, Ecclesiastes, and the Song of Solomon from the King James Bible), the modern history of free verse begins in 1855 with the publication of Walt Whitman's *Leaves of Grass.* Whitman, influenced by Ralph Waldo Emerson's statement that "it is not meters but meter-making argument that makes a poem," created a unique variety of long-line free verse based on grammatical units—phrases and clauses. Whitman's free verse is so distinctive that he has had few direct imitators (Robinson Jeffers is one from the twentieth century), and subsequent poets who have used free verse have written lines that vary widely in syllable count. Good free verse, as T. S. Eliot remarked, still contains some kind of "ghost of meter," and its rhythms can be as terse and clipped as those of Philip Levine or as lushly sensuous as those of Pattiann Rogers. The poet who claims that free verse is somehow easier to write than metrical verse would find many arguments to the contrary. As Eliot said, "No verse is free for the poet who wants to do a good job."

All poems have form, the arrangement of the poem on the page that differentiates it from prose. Sometimes this arrangement indicates that the poet is following a preconceived plan—a metrical pattern, a rhyme scheme, a purely visual design like that of **concrete** or **spatial poetry,** or a scheme like that of **acrostic verse,** in which the first letters of the lines spell a message. An analysis of poetic form notes how the lines are arranged, how long they are, and how they are grouped into blocks or **stanzas.** Further analysis might reveal the existence of types of repetition, rhyme, or the use of a **refrain,** or a repeated line or groups of lines. A large number of the poems composed in the last 100 years have been written in **open form,** which simply means that there is no strict pattern of regularity in the elements mentioned previously; in other words, there is no consistent meter and no rhyme scheme. Still, even a famous poem in open form, such as William Carlos Williams's "The Red Wheelbarrow," can be described in formal terms:

so much depends
upon

a red wheel
barrow

glazed with rain
water

beside the white
chickens.

Here we observe that the eight-line poem is divided into **uniform stanzas** of two lines each (or couplets). Line length varies between four and two syllables per line. The odd-numbered lines each contain three words; the even, one. While there is no apparent use of rhyme or repetition here, many poems in open form contain some rhyme and metrical regularity at their conclusions. Alan Dugan's "Love Song: I and Thou" falls into regular iambic tetrameter in its final lines, and Naomi Shihab Nye's "The Traveling Onion," a typical contemporary example of an open form poem, concludes with a closing rhyme on "career" and "disappear."

    Closed form, on the other hand, denotes the existence of some kind of regular pattern of meter, stanza, rhyme, or repetition. **Stanza forms** are consistent patterns in the individual units of the poem (*stanza* means "room" in Italian); **fixed forms** are patterns that encompass a complete poem, for example, a sonnet or a villanelle. **Traditional forms** are patterns that have been used for long periods of time and thus may be associated with certain subjects, themes, or types of poems. **Nonce forms** are patterns that originate in an individual poem and have not been widely used by other poets. Of course, it goes without saying that every traditional form was at first a nonce form; the Italian poet (now lost to memory) who first wrote a lyric consisting of fourteen rhymed eleven-syllable lines could not have foreseen that poets the world over in subsequent centuries would produce literally millions of sonnets that are all variations on the original model. Some of the most common stanza and fixed forms are briefly discussed herein.

Stanza Forms

Blank verse is not, strictly speaking, a stanza form because it consists of individual lines of iambic pentameter that do not rhyme. However, long poems written in blank verse may be arranged into **verse paragraphs** or stanzas with a varying number of lines. Blank verse originally appeared in English in the fifteenth century with the Earl of Surrey's translation of the *Aeneid*; such verse has been used extensively for narrative and dramatic purposes since, particularly in epics like

Milton's *Paradise Lost* and in Shakespeare's plays. Also written in stanzas of varying lengths is the **irregular ode,** a poem which employs lines of varying lengths (although usually of a regular rhythm that is iambic or matches one of the other feet) and an irregular rhyme scheme.

Paired rhyming lines *(aabbcc . . .)* are called **couplets,** although they are only rarely printed as separate stanzas. **Short couplets** have a meter of iambic tetrameter (and are sometimes called **octosyllabic couplets**). If their rhymes are predominantly feminine and seem chosen for comic effect, they may be called **Hudibrastic couplets** after Samuel Butler's satirical poem *Hudibras* of the late 1600s. **Heroic couplets** have a meter of iambic pentameter and take their name from John Dryden's translation of the *Aeneid* (1697) and Alexander Pope's hugely successful translation of Homer's *Iliad* and *Odyssey* (1720–1726), all three of these being "heroic" or epic poems. Heroic couplets have also been used effectively in satirical poems like Pope's "mock epic" *The Dunciad* (1728–1743) and even in dramatic monologues like Browning's "My Last Duchess," where the rhymes are so effectively buried by enjambment that the poem approximates speech. Two other couplet forms, both rare, are **poulter's measure,** rhyming pairs of alternating lines of iambic hexameter and iambic heptameter, and **fourteeners,** pairs of iambic heptameter (fourteen-syllable) lines, which, because there is generally a caesura after the fourth foot, closely resemble common meter (see below).

A three-line stanza is called a **tercet.** If it rhymes in an *aaa bbb . . .* pattern, it is a **triplet;** sometimes triplets appear in poems written in heroic couplets, especially at the end of sections or where special emphasis is desired. Iambic pentameter tercets rhyming *aba bcb cdc . . .* are called **terza rima,** a pattern invented by Dante for *The Divine Comedy.*

A four-line stanza is known as a **quatrain.** Alternating lines of tetrameter and trimeter in any foot, rhyming *abcb* or *abab,* make up a **ballad stanza;** if the feet are strictly iambic, the quatrain is called **common meter,** the form of many popular hymns like "Amazing Grace." **Long meter,** also widely used in hymns, consists of iambic tetrameter lines rhyming *abcb* or *abab;* **short meter** has a similar rhyme scheme but contains first, second, and fourth lines of iambic trimeter and a third line of iambic tetrameter. The *In Memoriam* **stanza,** named after Tennyson's long poetic sequence, is iambic tetrameter rhyming *abba.* The *Rubaiyat* **stanza,** an import from Persia, consists of lines of either iambic tetrameter or pentameter, rhyming *aaba* *bbcb* . . . ; Edward FitzGerald's translation *The Rubaiyat of Omar Khayyam* employs this form. Four lines of iambic pentameter rhyming *abab* are known as an **English quatrain,** also known as the **elegiac stanza** (after Thomas Gray's "Elegy Written in a Country Churchyard"). Lines of the same meter rhyming *abba* make up an **Italian quatrain.** One other unusual quatrain stanza is an import from ancient Greece, the **Sapphic stanza,** named after the poet Sappho. The Sapphic stanza consists of three **hendecasyllabic** (eleven-syllable) lines of this pattern:

$$ \prime \cup / \prime \cup / \prime \cup \cup / \prime \cup / \prime \cup $$

and a fourth line called an **Adonic,** which is five syllables long and consists of one dactylic foot and one trochaic foot. The Sapphic stanza is usually unrhymed. The quatrain stanza is also used in another import, the **pantoum,** a poem in which the second and fourth lines of the first stanza become the first and third of the second, and the second and fourth of the second become the first and third of the fourth, and so on. Pantoums may be written in any meter and may or may not employ rhyme.

A five-line stanza is known as a **quintet** and is relatively rare in English poetry. The **sestet,** or six-line stanza, can be found with a number of different meters and rhyme schemes. A seven-line stanza is called a **septet;** one septet stanza form is **rime royal,** seven lines of iambic pentameter rhyming *ababbcc.* An eight-line stanza is called an **octave;** one widely used stanza of this length is **ottava rima,** iambic pentameter lines rhyming *abababcc.* Another octave form is the **Monk's Tale stanza,** named after one of Chaucer's tales; it is iambic pentameter and rhymes *ababbcbc.* The addition of a ninth line, rhyming *c* and having a meter of iambic hexameter, makes a **Spenserian stanza,** named after Edmund Spenser, the poet who invented it for *The Faerie Queene,* a long metrical romance.

Fixed Forms

Fixed forms are combinations of meter, rhyme scheme, and repetition that make up complete poems. One familiar three-line fixed form is the **haiku,** a Japanese import consisting of lines of five, seven, and five syllables, respectively. Related to the haiku is the **tanka,** which adds two additional seven-syllable lines.

Two five-line fixed forms are the **limerick** and the **cinquain.** The limerick consists of anapestic trimeter in lines one, two, and five, and anapestic dimeter in three and four. The rhymes, *aabba,* are usually double rhymes used for comic effect. English poet Wendy Cope wittily reduced T. S. Eliot's complex modernist classic "The Waste Land," a long poem that contains phrases in foreign languages and the poet's own explanatory footnotes, to a set of five limericks. Here is the final one:

> No water. Dry rocks and dry throats,
> Then thunder, a shower of quotes
> From the Sanskrit and Dante.
> Da. Damyata. Shantih.
> I hope you'll make sense of the notes.

A cinquain, the invention of American poet Adelaide Crapsey, consists of five unrhymed lines of two, four, six, eight, and two syllables, respectively.

The most important of the fixed forms is the **sonnet,** which consists of fourteen lines of rhymed iambic pentameter. The original form of the sonnet is called the **Italian sonnet** or the **Petrarchan sonnet** after the fourteenth-century poet who popularized it. An Italian sonnet is usually cast in two stanzas, an octave rhyming *abbaabba* and a sestet with a variable rhyme scheme; *cdcdcd, cdecde, cddcee* are some of the possible patterns. A **volta** or "turn," usually a conjunction or conjunctive adverb like "but" or "then," may appear at the beginning of the sestet, signifying a slight change of direction in thought. Many Italian sonnets have a strong logical connection between octave and sestet—problem/solution, cause/effect, question/answer—and the volta helps to clarify the transition. The **English sonnet,** also known as the **Shakespearean sonnet** after its prime exemplar, was developed in the sixteenth century after the sonnet was imported to England and employs a different rhyme scheme that takes into consideration the relative scarcity of rhymes in English (compared with Italian). The English sonnet has a rhyme scheme of *ababcdcdefefgg* and is usually printed as a single stanza. The pattern of three English quatrains plus a heroic couplet often forces a slightly different organizational scheme on the poet, although many of

Shakespeare's sonnets still employ a strong volta at the beginning of the ninth line. Other English sonnets may withhold the turn until the beginning of the closing couplet. A third sonnet type, relatively rare, is the **Spenserian sonnet,** named after Edmund Spenser, author of *Amoretti,* one of the earliest sonnet sequences in English. The Spenserian sonnet rhymes *ababbcbccdcdee.* There are many other sonnets written over the years which have other rhyme schemes, often hybrids of the Italian and English types. These are usually termed **nonce sonnets;** Shelley's "Ozymandias," with its unusual rhyme scheme of *ababacdcedefef,* is one notable example. In "Ode to the West Wind," Shelley also employs a fourteen-line stanza rhyming *aba bcb cdc ded ee,* which has been called a **terza rima sonnet.**

Several other fixed forms, all French imports, have appeared frequently in English poetry. The **rondeau** has fifteen lines of iambic tetrameter or pentameter arranged in three stanzas: *aabba aabR aabbaR;* the *R* here stands for the unrhymed refrain, which repeats the first few words of the poem's first line. A maddeningly complex variation is the thirty-one line **rondeau redoublé,** through which Wendy Cope wittily maneuvers in her poem of the same name. The **villanelle** is a nineteen-line poem, usually written in iambic pentameter, employing two refrain lines, A_1 and A_2, in a pattern of five tercets and a final quatrain: A_1bA_2 abA_1 abA_2 abA_1 abA_2 abA_1A_2. A related form, also nineteen lines long, is the **terzanelle,** which uses several more repeating lines (capitalized here): A_1BA_2 bCB cDC dED eFE f A_1FA_2. The **ballade** is twenty-eight lines of iambic tetrameter employing a refrain that appears at the end of its three octaves and final quatrain, or **envoy:** *ababbcbC ababbcbC ababbcbC bcbC.* Obviously the rhyming demands of the villanelle, the terzanelle, and the ballade pose serious challenges to English-language poets. A final fixed form is the thirty-nine-line **sestina,** which may be either metered or in free verse and which uses a complicated sequence repeating, in different order, the six words that end the lines of the initial stanza. The sequence for the first six sestets is *123456 615243 364125 532614 451362 246531.* A final tercet uses three words in the interior of the lines and three at the ends in the pattern *(2)5(4)3(6)1.* Many sestinas hinge on the poet's choice of six end words that have multiple meanings and can serve as more than one part of speech.

There are many other less familiar types of stanza forms and fixed forms; Lewis Turco's *The Book of Forms* and Miller Williams's *Patterns of Poetry* are two reference sources useful in identifying them.

Literary History and Poetic Conventions, and Theory

What a poet attempts to do in any given poem is always governed by the tension that exists between originality and convention, in other words, between the poet's desire, in Ezra Pound's famous phrase, to "make it new" and the various stylistic devices that other poets and readers are familiar with through their understanding of the poetic tradition. If we look at some of the most obscure passages of Pound's *Cantos* we may think that the poet has departed about as far from conventional modes of expression as possible, leaving his audience far behind him. Yet it is important to keep two facts in mind. First, this style was not arrived at overnight; Pound's early poetry is relatively traditional and should present little difficulty to most readers. He arrived at the style of the *Cantos* after a twenty-year apprenticeship to the styles of writers as different as Li-Po, Robert Browning, and William Butler Yeats. Second, by the time Pound was writing his mature poetry the modernist movement was in full flower, forcing the public not only to read poems but also to look at paintings and sculpture and to listen to music in ways that would have been unimaginable only a decade or two earlier. When we talk about the stylistic conventions of any given literary period, we should keep in mind that poets are rarely willing to go much beyond what they have educated their audiences to understand. This mutual sense of agreement is the essence of poetic convention.

One should be wary of making sweeping generalizations about "schools" of poetry or the shared conventions of literary periods. In any era, there is always a significant amount of diversity among individual poets. Further, an anthology of this limited scope, which by its very nature must exclude most long poems, is likely to contribute to a misleading view of literary history and the development of poetry in English. When we read Shakespeare's sonnets or Milton's shorter poems, we should not forget that their major reputations rest on poetry of a very different sort. The neoclassical era in English poetry, stretching from the late seventeenth century until almost the end of the eighteenth century, is poorly represented here because the satires of Dryden and Pope and long philosophical poems like Pope's *An Essay on Man* do not readily lend themselves to being excerpted. Poe once claimed that a long poem is "simply a contradiction in terms," but the continued high reputations of *The Faerie Queene, Paradise Lost, Don Juan*, and even a modern verse-novella like Robinson Jeffers's "The Roan Stallion" demonstrate that Poe's was far from the last word on the subject.

The earliest poems in this volume, all by anonymous poets, represent poetry's links to the oral folk tradition. The American folk songs that children learn to sing in elementary school represent our own inheritance of this rich legacy. The poets of the Tudor (1485–1558) and Elizabethan (1558–1603) eras excelled at lyric poetry; Sir Thomas Wyatt and Henry Howard, Earl of Surrey, had imported the sonnet form from Italy, and the form was perfected during this period. Much of the love poetry of this period is characterized by conventional imagery, so-called Petrarchan conceits, which even a later poet like Campion employs in "There Is a Garden in Her Face" and which Shakespeare satirizes brilliantly in his Sonnet 130 ("My mistress' eyes are nothing like the sun").

The poetry of the first half of the seventeenth century has several major schools: a smooth lyricism influenced by Ben Jonson that can be traced through the work of Herrick, Waller, and Lovelace; a serious body of devotional poetry by Donne, Herbert, and Milton; and the metaphysical style, which uses complex extended metaphors or meta-physical conceits—Donne and Herbert are its chief exemplars, followed by the early American poets Bradstreet and Taylor. Shortly after the English Restoration in 1660, a profound period of conservatism began in the arts, and the neoclassical era, lasting through most of the eigh-teenth century, drew heavily on Greek and Roman models. Poetry dur-ing this period—the age of Swift, Pope, and Gray—was dominated by one form, the heroic couplet; the genres of epic and satire; and an em-phasis on human reason as the poet's chief guide. Never has the private voice been so subordinated to the public as in this period when, as Pope put it, a poet's highest aspiration should be to utter "What oft was thought, but ne'er so well expressed."

The first inklings of the romantic era coincide with the American and French revolutions, and poets of the latter half of the eighteenth century like Freneau and Blake exhibit some of its characteristics. But it was not until the publication of *Lyrical Ballads* (1798), a book contain-ing the best early work of Wordsworth and Coleridge, that the romantic era can be said to have truly flowered. Wordsworth's famous formulation of a poem as "the spontaneous overflow of powerful feeling recollected in tranquillity" remains one of romanticism's key definitions, with its emphasis on emotion, immediacy, and reflection; Wordsworth's own poetry, with its focus on the natural world, was tremendously influential. Most of the English and American poets of the first half of the nineteenth century have ties to romanticism in its various guises, and even a poet as late as Whitman (b. 1819) inherits many of its liberal, democratic attitudes. Poets of the Victorian era (1837–1901) continued to explore many of the same themes and genres as their romantic forebears, but certainly much of the optimism of the early years of the nineteenth century had dissipated by the time poets like Hardy, Housman, and Yeats, with their omnipresent irony and pessimism, came on the scene in the century's last decades.

The twentieth century and the beginning of the twenty-first century have been ruled by the upheavals that modernism caused in every art form. If anything characterized the first half of the twentieth century, it was its tireless experimentation with the forms of poetry. There is a continuum in English-language poetry from Chaucer through Frost and Robinson, but Pound, Williams, and Cummings, to mention only three chief modernists, published poetry that would have totally mystified readers of their grandparents' day, just as Picasso and Matisse produced paintings that represented radical breaks with the forms of the past. Although many of the experiments of movements like imagism and surrealism seem quaint today, they parallel the general direction taken by most of the other arts during the same period.

For the sake of convenience more than anything else, it has been useful to refer to the era following the end of World War II as the postmodern era. Certainly many of the hard-won modernist gains—open form and increased candor in language and subject matter—have been taken for granted by poets writing in the contemporary period. The confessional poem, a frankly autobiographical genre that reveals what poets in earlier ages might have striven desperately to conceal, surfaced in the late 1950s in the works of Lowell, Snodgrass, Plath, and Sexton, and remains one of the chief post-modern genres. Still, as the selections here will attest, considerable variety exists in the contemporary scene, and it will perhaps be many years before critics have the necessary historical distance to assess the unique characteristics of the present period.

Writing About Poetry

Writing assignments vary widely and your teacher's instructions may range from general ("Discuss any two poems in your text which contain an effective use of imagery") to very specific ("Write an explication, in not less than 1000 words, of one of Edwin Arlington Robinson's sonnets, focusing on his use of form and his psychological insights into character"). Such processes as choosing, limiting, and developing a topic; "brainstorming" by taking notes on random ideas and refining those ideas further through group discussion or conferences with your instructor; using the library and the Internet to locate supporting secondary sources; and revising a first draft in light of critical remarks are undoubtedly techniques you have practiced in other composition classes. Basic types of organizational schemes learned in "theme-writing" courses can also be applied to writing about poetry. Formal assignments of these types should avoid contractions and jargon, and should be written in a clear, straightforward style. Most literary essays are not of the personal experience type, and you should follow common sense in avoiding the first person and slang. It goes without saying that you should carefully proofread your rough and final drafts to eliminate errors in spelling, punctuation, usage, and grammar.

Writing assignments on poetry usually fall into two categories: explication (or close reading) of single poems and analysis of poetic techniques in one or more poems. Because explication involves the careful "unfolding" of individual poems on a line-by-line basis, an assignment of this type will usually focus on a single short poem or a passage from a longer one. Some poems yield most of their meaning on a single reading; others, however, may contain complexities and nuances that deserve close inspection of how the poet utilizes the elements discussed in this introduction. A typical explication might examine both form and content. Because assignments in analysis usually involve many of the same techniques as explication, we will look at explication more closely. The following is a checklist of questions that you might ask yourself before explicating a poem; the sample passages of analysis apply to a poem from this book, Edwin Arlington Robinson's "Firelight."

Form

1. How many lines does the poem contain? How are they arranged into stanzas? Is either the whole poem or the stanza an example of a traditional poetic form?

> "Firelight" is an Italian sonnet. It is divided into two stanzas, an octave and sestet, and there is a tonal shift, or what is known in sonnets as a "turn" or <u>volta</u>, at the beginning of line nine, though here there is no single word that signals the shift.

2. Is there anything striking in the visual arrangement of the poem—indentation, spacing, etc.? Are capitalization and punctuation unusual?

> Capitalization and punctuation are standard in the poem, and Robinson follows the traditional practice of capitalizing the first word of each line.

3. In what meter, if any, is the poem written? Does the poet use any notable examples of substitution in the meter? Are the lines primarily end-stopped or enjambed?

> The meter is fairly regular iambic pentameter ("Her thoughts / a mo / ment since / of one / who shines") with occasional substitution of trochees ("Wiser / for si / lence") and spondees ("their joy / recalls / No snake, || / no sword").
> Enjambment occurs at the ends of lines two, five, six, seven, nine, ten, twelve, and thirteen; this has the effect of masking the regular meter and rhymes and enforcing a conversational tone, an effect that is assisted by the caesurae in lines six, seven,

nine, and (most importantly) fourteen. The caesura in this last line calls attention to "Apart," which ironically contrasts with the poem's opening phrase: "Ten years together."

4. What is the rhyme scheme, if any, of the poem? What types of rhyme are used?

The rhyme scheme of this poem is <u>abbaabba</u> <u>cdecde.</u> Robinson uses exact masculine rime; the only possible exception is "intervals," where the meter and rhyme scheme force a secondary stress on the third syllable.

5. Are significant sound patterns evident? Is there any repetition of whole lines, phrases, or words?

Alliteration is present in "<u>f</u>irelight" and "<u>f</u>our" in line three and "<u>w</u>an" and "<u>o</u>ne" in line eleven, and there are several instances of assonance ("W<u>i</u>ser for s<u>i</u>lence"; "end<u>ow</u>ed / And b<u>ow</u>ered") and consonance ("Se<u>ren</u>ely and pe<u>renn</u>ially <u>en</u>dowed"; the w<u>an</u> face of <u>one</u> somewhere al<u>one</u>"). However, these sound patterns do not call excessive attention to themselves and depart from the poem's relaxed, conversational sound. "Firelight" contains no prominent use of repetition, with the possible exception of the pronoun "they" and its variant forms "their" and "them" and the related use of the third person singular pronouns "he" and "she" in the last five lines of the poem. This pronoun usage, confusing at first glance, indirectly carries the poem's theme of the separateness of the lovers' thoughts. The only notable instance of parallel phrasing occurs in line seven with "No snake, no sword."

Content

1. To what genre (lyric, narrative, dramatic) does the poem belong? Does it contain elements of more than one genre?

"Firelight" is a narrative poem. Even though it has little plot in the conventional sense, it contains two characters in a specific setting who perform actions that give the reader insight into the true nature of their relationship. The sonnet form has traditionally been used for lyric poetry.

2. Who is the persona of the poem? Is there an auditor? If so, who? What is the relationship between persona and auditor? Does the poem have a specific setting? If so, where and when is it taking place? Is there any action that has taken place before the poem opens? What actions take place during the poem?

The persona here is a third-person omniscient narrator such as might be encountered in a short story; the narrator has the ability to read "Her thoughts a moment since" and directly comments that the couple is "Wiser for silence." The unnamed characters in the poem are a man and woman who have been married for ten years. The poem is set in their home, apparently in a comfortable room with a fireplace where they are spending a quiet evening together. Neither character speaks during the poem; the only action is their looking at "each other's eyes at intervals / Of gratefulness." Much of the poem's ironic meaning hinges on the couple's silence, "what neither says aloud."

3. Does the poem contain any difficulties with grammar or syntax? What individual words or phrases are striking because of their denotation or connotation?

The syntax of "Firelight" is straightforward and contains no inversions or ellipses. The poem's sentence structure is deceptively simple. The first four lines make up a single sentence with one main clause; the second four lines also make up a single sentence, this time with two main clauses; the final six lines also make up a single sentence, broken into two equal parts by the semicolon, and consisting of both main and dependent clauses. The poem's vocabulary is not unusual, though "obliteration" (literally an <u>erasure</u>) seems at first a curious choice to describe the effects of love. One should note the allusion implied by "bowered," "snake," and "sword" in the octave and the rather complicated use of the subjunctive "were" in lines nine, ten, and twelve. Again, this slight alteration in grammar bears indirectly on the theme of the poem. "Yet" in the first line provides an interesting touch since it injects a slight negative note into the picture of marital bliss.

4. Does the poem use any figures of speech? If so, how do they add to the overall meaning? Is the action of the poem to be taken literally, symbolically, or both ways?

"Firelight" uses several figures of speech. "Cloud" is a commonly employed metaphor for "foreboding." "Firelight" and "four walls" are a metonymy and synecdoche, respectively, for the couple's comfortable home. The allusion to the "snake" and "sword" direct the reader to the Garden of Eden story. "Wiser for silence" is a slight paradox. "The graven tale of lines / on the wan face" is an implied metaphor which compares the lines on a person's face to the written ("graven") story of her life. To say that a person "shines" instead of "excels" is another familiar metaphor. "Firelight" is to be understood primarily on the literal level. The characters are symbolic only in that the man and woman are perhaps representative of many married couples, who outwardly express happiness yet inwardly carry regrets and fantasies from past relationships.

5. Is the title of the poem appropriate? What are its subject, tone of voice, and theme? Is the theme stated or implied?

"Firelight" is a good title since it carries both the connotation of domestic tranquillity and a hint of danger. "To bring to the light" means to reveal the truth, and the narrator in this poem does

this. Robinson's attitude toward the couple is
ironic. On the surface they seem to be the picture of
ideal happiness, but he reveals that this happiness
has been purchased, in the man's case, at the expense
of an earlier lover and, in the woman's, by settling
for someone who has achieved less than another man
for whom she apparently had unrequited love.
Robinson's ironic view of marital stability is summed
up in the phrase "Wiser for silence." Several themes
are implied: the difference between surface appearance and deeper insight; the cynical idea that in
love ignorance of what one's partner is thinking may
be the key to bliss; the sense that individual happiness is not without its costs. All of these are possible ways to state Robinson's bittersweet theme.

Your instructor may ask you to employ specific strategies in your explication and may require a certain type of organization for the paper.
In writing the body of the explication, you will probably proceed
through the poem from beginning to end, summarizing and paraphrasing some lines and quoting others fully when you feel an explanation is
required. It should be stressed that there are many ways, in theory, to
approach a poem and that no two explications of the same poem will
agree in every detail. Some instructors may favor an explication that
links the poem to events in the author's life, to the sociohistorical con-
text in which it was written, or to some other critical approach.

An assignment in analysis, which looks closely at the way a single element—dramatic situation, meter, form, imagery, one or more figures of
speech, theme—functions in poetry, would probably require that you
write on two or more poems; in such cases a comparison-contrast or definition-illustration paper may be called for. An assignment of this type
might examine two related poems by the same poet, or it might inspect
the way that several poets have used a poetic device or theme.
Comparison-contrast essays look for both similarities and differences in
two poems. Definition-illustration papers usually begin with a general
discussion of the topic, say, a popular theme like the *carpe diem* motif,
and then go on to illustrate how this motif may be found in several different poems. Assignments in analysis often lead to longer papers which
may require the use of secondary sources. Appendix 1 lists some groups
of poems that have elements in common.

You may be required to use secondary sources from the library or Internet in writing your paper. A subject search through your library's books is a good starting place, especially for material on older poets who have attracted extensive critical attention. Reference books like *Twentieth Century Authors, Contemporary Authors, Critical Survey of Poetry*, and the *Dictionary of Literary Biography* provide compact overviews of poets' careers. *Contemporary Literary Criticism* and *Poetry Criticism* contain excerpts from critical pieces on poets' works, and the *MLA Index* will direct you to articles on poets and poems in scholarly journals. There are several popular indexes of book reviews; one of these, the annual *Book Review Digest*, reprints brief passages from the most representative reviews. A useful index to poetry explications published in periodicals and books is *Poetry Explication: A Checklist of Interpretations Since 1925 of British and American Poems Past and Present;* many of the articles listed there first appeared in the *Explicator,* a periodical whose indexes are also worth inspecting. In recent years, the Internet has facilitated the chores of research, and many online databases, reference works, and periodicals may be quickly located using search engines like Yahoo (www.yahoo.com) and Google (www.google.com). The Internet also holds a wealth of information in the form of individual websites devoted to authors, most of which are run by universities or organizations. Navigating the Internet can be a forbidding task, and a book like Lester Faigley's *The Longman Guide to the Web* is an invaluable traveler's companion. Students should be aware, however, that websites vary widely in quality. Some are legitimate academic sources displaying sound scholarship; others are little more than "fan pages" that may contain erroneous or misleading information.

Careful documentation of your sources is essential; if you use any material other than what is termed "common knowledge," you must cite it in your paper. Common knowledge includes biographical information, an author's publications, prizes and awards received, and other information that can be found in more than one reference book. Anything else—direct quotes or material you have put in your own words by paraphrasing—requires both a parenthetical citation in the body of your paper and an entry on your works cited pages. Doing less than this is to commit an act of plagiarism, for which the penalties are usually severe. Internet materials, which are so easily cut and pasted into a manuscript, provide an easy temptation but are immediately noticeable. Nothing is easier to spot in a paper than an uncited "lift" from a source; in most cases, the vocabulary and sentence structure will be radically different from the rest of the paper.

The fifth edition of the *MLA Handbook for Writers of Research Papers*, which can be found in the reference section of almost any library and which, if you plan to write papers for other English courses, is a good addition to your personal library, contains formats for bibliographies and manuscripts that most instructors consider standard; indeed, most of the handbooks of grammar and usage commonly used in college courses follow MLA style and may be sufficient for your needs. If you have doubts, ask your instructor about what format is preferred. The type of parenthetical citation used today to indicate the source of quotations is simple to learn and dispenses with such time-consuming and repetitive chores as footnotes and endnotes. In using parenthetical citations remember that your goal is to direct your reader from the quoted passage in the paper to its source in your bibliography, and from there, if necessary, to the book or periodical from which the quote is taken. A good parenthetical citation gives only the *minimal* information needed to accomplish this. Following are a few examples from student papers on Edwin Arlington Robinson's poetry.

> Robinson's insights into character are never sharper than in "Miniver Cheevy," a portrait of a town drunk who loves "the days of old / When swords were bright and steeds were prancing" and dreams incongruously "of Thebes and Camelot, / And Priam's neighbors" (347).

Here you should note a couple of conventions about writing about poetry. One is that the present tense is used in discussing the poem; in general, use the present tense throughout your critical writing except when you are giving biographical or historical information. Second, note how only parts of lines are quoted here to support the sentence and how the parts fit smoothly into the author's sentence structure. In general, brackets and ellipses [. . .] are not necessary at the beginning or end of these quotes because it is clear that they are quoted fragmentarily; they should, however, be used if something is omitted from the middle of a quote ("the days of old / When [. . .] steeds were prancing"). The virgule or slash (/) is used to indicate line breaks; a double slash (//) indicates stanza breaks. Quotes of up to three lines should be treated in this manner. If a quote is longer than three lines, it should be indented ten spaces (with no quotation marks) and printed as it appears in the original poem:

> Robinson opens one of his most effective and
> pitiless character sketches with an unsparing por-
> trait:
>> Miniver Cheevy, child of scorn,
>> Grew lean while he assailed the seasons;
>> He wept that he was ever born,
>> And he had reasons. (347)

The parenthetical citation here lists only a page number because only one work by Robinson appears in the bibliography (note that the *MLA Handbook* suggests that you also include line numbers, a practice that is probably unnecessary in discussing a short poem). If several works by the poet had been listed among the works cited, the parenthetical citation would clarify which one was being referred to by adding a shortened form of the book's title: (*Collected*, 347). The reader finds the following entry among the sources:

> Robinson, Edwin Arlington. <u>Collected Poems</u>. New York:
> MacMillan, 1934.

Similarly, quotes and paraphrases from secondary critical sources should follow the same rules of common sense.

> Louis O. Coxe observes that Robinson, even in
> using the most demanding forms, manages to avoid the
> artificial-sounding poetic diction of most son-
> neteers: "The best of Robinson's sonnets take an
> anti-rhetorical line though they often ride to elo-
> quence as they progress" (50-51).

In this case, the author of the quote is identified, so only the page numbers are included in the parenthetical citation. The reader knows where to look among the sources:

> Coxe, Louis O. <u>Edwin Arlington Robinson: The Life of
> Poetry</u>. New York: Pegasus, 1969.

To simplify the whole matter of parenthetical citation, it is recommended that quotes from secondary sources be introduced, wherever possible, in a manner that identifies the author so that only the page number of the quote is needed inside of the parentheses.

Of course, different types of sources—reference book entries, poems in anthologies, articles in periodicals, and book reviews—require different bibliographical information, so be sure to check the *MLA Handbook* if you have questions. Here are a few more examples of the most commonly used bibliographical formats:

A BOOK WITH AUTHOR AND EDITOR

```
Robinson, Edwin Arlington. Edwin Arlington Robinson's
     Letters to Edith Brower. Ed. Richard Cary.
     Cambridge: Harvard University Press, 1968.
```

A CASEBOOK OR COLLECTION OF CRITICAL ESSAYS

```
Barnard, Ellsworth, ed. Edwin Arlington Robinson:
     Centenary Essays. Athens: University of Georgia
     Press, 1969.
```

A POEM REPRINTED IN AN ANTHOLOGY OR TEXTBOOK

```
Robinson, Edwin Arlington. "Richard Cory."
     Literature: An Introduction to Poetry, Fiction,
     and Drama. 7th ed. Ed. X. J. Kennedy and Dana
     Gioia. New York: Longman, 1991. 793-94.
```

AN ARTICLE IN A REFERENCE BOOK

```
Seymour-Smith, Martin. "Robinson, Edwin Arlington."
     Who's Who in Twentieth Century Literature. New
     York: McGraw, 1976.
```

AN ARTICLE IN A SCHOLARLY JOURNAL

```
Read, Arthur M., II. "Robinson's 'The Man Against the
     Sky.'" Explicator 26 (Feb. 1968): 49.
```

A Book Review in a Periodical

Hutchison, Percy. "Robinson's Satire and Symbolism."
    Rev. of <u>King Jasper</u>, by Edwin Arlington
    Robinson. <u>New York Times Book Review</u> 10 Nov.
    1935: 8.

A Website

"A Page for Edwin." 5 Feb. 2001. <http://www.du.edu/
    ~dokonski/robin.html>.

An Online Reference Book

"Robinson, Edwin Arlington." <u>Encyclopedia Britannica
    Online</u>. 12 Dec. 2000. <http://www.britannica.com/
    bcom/eb/article/8/0,5716,65558+1+63916,00
    .html?query=edwin%20arlington%20robinson>.

Poetry

Some of the popular ballads and lyrics of England and Scotland, composed for the most part between 1300 and 1500, were first collected in their current forms by Thomas Percy, whose Reliques of Ancient English Poetry *(1765) helped to revive interest in folk poetry. Francis James Child (1825–1896), an American, gathered over a thousand variant versions of the three hundred-odd core of poems. The Romantic poets of the early nineteenth century showed their debt to the folk tradition by writing imitative "art ballads" (see Keats's "La Belle Dame sans Merci" or Burns's "John Barleycorn"), which incorporate many of their stylistic devices.*

Anonymous
Western Wind

Western wind, when will thou blow,
    The small rain down can rain?
Christ, if my love were in my arms
    And I in my bed again!

—1450?

Bonny Barbara Allan

It was in and about the Martinmas° time,
    When the green leaves were a falling,
That Sir John Græme, in the West Country,
    Fell in love with Barbara Allan.

He sent his men down through the town,   5
    To the place where she was dwelling.
"O haste and come to my master dear,
    Gin° ye be Barbara Allan."

O hooly,° hooly rose she up,
    To the place where he was lying,
And when she drew the curtain by: 10
    "Young man, I think you're dying."

1 Martinmas November 11   **8 Gin** if   **9 hooly** slowly

"O it's I'm sick, and very, very sick,
    And 'tis a'° for Barbara Allan."
"O the better for me ye s'° never be,   *15*
    Though your heart's blood were a-spilling.

"O dinna° ye mind, young man," said she,
    "When ye was in the tavern a drinking,
That ye made the healths gae° round and round,
    And slighted Barbara Allan?"   *20*

He turned his face unto the wall,
    And death was with him dealing:
"Adieu, adieu, my dear friends all,
    And be kind to Barbara Allan."

And slowly, slowly raise she up,   *25*
    And slowly, slowly left him,
And sighing said she could not stay,
    Since death of life had reft him.

She had not gane° a mile but twa,°
    When she heard the dead-bell ringing,   *30*
And every jow° that the dead-bell geid,°
    It cried, "Woe to Barbara Allan!"

"O mother, mother, make my bed!
    O make it saft° and narrow!
Since my love died for me to-day,   *35*
    I'll die for him to-morrow."

—1500?

Sir Patrick Spens

The king sits in Dumferling town,
    Drinking the blude-reid° wine:
"O whar will I get guid sailor,
    To sail this ship of mine?"

14 a' all   **15 s'** shall   **17 dinna** do not   **19 gae** go   **29 gane** gone   **twa** two   **31 jow** stroke   **geid**
gave   **34 saft** soft
2 blude-reid blood-red

Up and spak an eldern knicht,°   5
    Sat at the king's richt° knee:
"Sir Patrick Spens is the best sailor
    That sails upon the sea."

The king has written a braid° letter,
    And signed it wi' his hand,   10
And sent it to Sir Patrick Spens,
    Was walking on the sand.

The first line that Sir Patrick read,
    A loud lauch° lauched he;
The next line that Sir Patrick read,   15
    The tear blinded his ee.°

"O wha is this has done this deed,
    This ill deed done to me,
To send me out this time o' the year,
    To sail upon the sea?   20

"Mak haste, mak haste, my mirry men all,
    Our guid ship sails the morn."
"O say na sae,° my master dear,
    For I fear a deadly storm.

"Late, late yestre'en° I saw the new moon,   25
    Wi' the auld moon in hir arm,
And I fear, I fear, my dear master,
    That we will come to harm."

O our Scots nobles wer richt laith°
    To weet° their cork-heeled shoon,°   30
But lang or a'° the play were played,
    Their hats they swam aboon.°

O lang, lang may their ladies sit,
    Wi' their fans into their hand,
Or ere they see Sir Patrick Spens   35
    Come sailing to the land.

---

5 eldern knicht elderly knight   **6 richt** right   **9 braid** long   **14 lauch** laugh   **16 ee** eye   **23 na sae** not so   **25 yestre'en** last evening   **29 laith** loath   **30 weet** wet   **shoon** shoes   **31 lang or a'** long before   **32 Their hats they swam aboon** their hats swam above them

O lang, lang may the ladies stand,
 Wi' their gold kems° in their hair,
Waiting for their ain dear lords,
 For they'll see them na mair.   *40*

Half o'er, half o'er to Aberdour
 It's fifty fadom deep,
And there lies guid Sir Patrick Spens
 Wi' the Scots lords at his feet.

             —*1500?*

Sir Thomas Wyatt (1503?–1542) served Henry VIII as a diplomat in Italy. Wyatt read the love poetry of Petrarch (1304–1374) and is generally credited with having imported both the fashions of these lyrics—hyperbolic "conceits" or metaphorical descriptions of the woman's beauty and the lover's suffering—and their form, the sonnet, to England. "They Flee from Me," an example of one of his original lyrics, displays Wyatt's unique grasp of the rhythms of speech.

Sir Thomas Wyatt
They Flee from Me

They flee from me, that sometime did me seek,
With naked foot stalking in my chamber.
I have seen them gentle, tame and meek,
That now are wild, and do not remember
That sometime they put themself in danger   *5*
To take bread at my hand; and now they range,
Busily seeking with a continual change.

Thanked be Fortune it hath been otherwise,
Twenty times better; but once in special,
In thin array, after a pleasant guise,°   *10*
When her loose gown from her shoulders did fall,
And she me caught in her arms long and small,

---

38 kems combs
10 guise appearance

And therewith all sweetly did me kiss
And softly said, "Dear heart, how like you this?"

It was no dream, I lay broad waking.   15
But all is turned, thorough° my gentleness,
Into a strange fashion of forsaking;
And I have leave to go, of her goodness,
And she also to use newfangleness.
But since that I so kindely° am served,   20
I fain° would know what she hath deserved.

—1557

Queen Elizabeth I (1533–1603) was an amateur poet who drew praise from the members of her court, many of whom were also versifiers. A few of her lyrics survive, as do translations she made from the Roman writers Seneca and Horace. Her reign (1558–1603) established England as a world power and also nurtured the talents of Edmund Spenser, William Shakespeare, Christopher Marlowe, and Ben Jonson.

Queen Elizabeth I
When I Was Fair and Young

When I was fair and young, and favor gracèd me,
Of many was I sought, their mistress for to be;
But I did scorn them all, and answered them therefore,
    "Go, go, go seek some otherwhere!
                    Importune me no more!"   5

How many weeping eyes I made to pine with woe,
How many sighing hearts, I have no skill to show;
Yet I the prouder grew, and answered them therefore,
    "Go, go, go seek some otherwhere!
                    Importune me no more!"   10

---

16 thorough through   **20 kindely** in this manner   **21 fain** gladly

Then spake fair Venus' son,° that proud victorious boy,
And said, "Fine dame, since that you be so coy,
I will so pluck your plumes that you shall say no more,
   'Go, go, go seek some otherwhere!
                    Importune me no more!'"   15

When he had spake these words, such change grew in my breast
That neither night nor day since that, I could take any rest.
Then lo! I did repent that I had said before,
   "Go, go, go seek some otherwhere!
                    Importune me no more!"   20

—*1585*

Edmund Spenser *(1552–1599) was born in London, and spent most of his adult life in Ireland, where he held a variety of minor government posts.* The Faerie Queene, *a long allegorical romance about Elizabethan England, was uncompleted at his death. The eighty-odd sonnets that make up the sequence called* Amoretti *are generally thought to detail his courtship of his second wife, Elizabeth Boyle, whom he married in 1594.*

Edmund Spenser
Amoretti: Sonnet 75

One day I wrote her name upon the strand,
But came the waves and washèd it away:
Agayne I wrote it with a second hand,°
But came the tyde, and made my paynes his pray.
"Vayne man," sayd she, "that doest in vaine assay,°   5
A mortall thing so to immortalize,
For I my selve shall lyke° to this decay
And eek° my name bee wypèd out lykewize."
"Not so," quod° I, "let baser things devize
To dy in dust, but you shall live by fame: 10
My verse your vertues rare shall eternize,

---

11 Venus' son Eros or Cupid, god of love
3 second hand second time   **5 assay** attempt   **7 lyke** be similar to   **8 eek** also   **9 quod** said

And in the hevens wryte your glorious name.
Where whenas death shall all the world subdew
Our love shall live, and later life renew."

—*1595*

Sir Philip Sidney *(1554–1586) embodied many of the aspects of the ideal man of the Renaissance; he was a courtier, scholar, patron of the arts, and soldier who died of wounds received at the battle of Zutphen. His sonnet sequence* Astrophel and Stella *appeared in 1591, several years before Spenser's* Amoretti, *and helped to precipitate the fashion for sonnets that lasted in England well into the next century.*

Sir Philip Sidney
Astrophel and Stella: Sonnet 1

1

Loving in truth, and fain° in verse my love to show,
That she dear she might take some pleasure of my pain,
Pleasure might cause her read, reading might make her know,
Knowledge might pity win, and pity grace obtain,
I sought fit words to paint the blackest face of woe: 5
Studying inventions fine, her wits to entertain,
Oft turning others' leaves,° to see if thence would flow
Some fresh and fruitful showers upon my sunburned brain.
But words came halting forth, wanting Invention's stay;
Invention, Nature's child, fled stepdame Study's blows;   10
And others' feet° still seemed but strangers in my way.
Thus, great with child to speak, and helpless in my throes,
Biting my truant pen, beating myself for spite:
"Fool," said my Muse to me, "look in thy heart, and write."

—*1582*

---

1 fain glad   **7 leaves** pages   **11 feet** metrical feet in poetry

Robert Southwell (1561?–1595) *was a Roman Catholic priest in Elizabeth's Protestant England, who was executed for his religious beliefs. His devotional poems, most of them on the subject of spiritual love, were largely written during his three years in prison. Southwell was declared a saint in the Roman Catholic Church in 1970.*

Robert Southwell
The Burning Babe

As I in hoary winter's night stood shivering in the snow,
Surprised I was with sudden heat which made my heart to glow;
And lifting up a fearful eye to view what fire was near,
A pretty babe all burning bright did in the air appear;
Who, scorchèd with excessive heat, such floods of tears did shed   5
As though his floods should quench his flames which with his
    tears were fed.
"Alas," quoth he, "but newly born in fiery heats I fry,
Yet none approach to warm their hearts or feel my fire but I!
My faultless breast the furnace is, the fuel wounding thorns,
Love is the fire, and sighs the smoke, the ashes shame and
    scorns;   10
The fuel justice layeth on, and mercy blows the coals,
The metal in this furnace wrought are men's defilèd souls,
For which, as now on fire I am to work them to their good,
So will I melt into a bath to wash them in my blood."
With this he vanished out of sight and swiftly shrunk away,   15
And straight I callèd unto mind that it was Christmas day.

—1602

Michael Drayton (1563–1631), like his contemporary, Shakespeare, excelled in several literary genres. He collaborated on plays with Thomas Dekker and wrote long poems on English history, biography, and topography. Drayton labored almost three decades on the sixty-three sonnets in Idea, *publishing them in their present form in 1619.*

Michael Drayton
Idea: Sonnet 61

Since there's no help, come let us kiss and part;
Nay, I have done, you get no more of me,
And I am glad, yea glad with all my heart
That thus so cleanly I myself can free;
Shake hands forever, cancel all our vows,   5
And when we meet at any time again,
Be it not seen in either of our brows
That we one jot of former love retain.
Now at the last gasp of love's latest breath,
When, his pulse failing, passion speechless lies,   10
When faith is kneeling by his bed of death,
And innocence is closing up his eyes,
    Now if thou wouldst, when all have given him over,
    From death to life thou mightst him yet recover.

—*1619*

William Shakespeare (1564–1616) *first printed his sonnets in 1609, during the last years of his active career as a playwright, but they had circulated privately a dozen years before. Given the lack of concrete details about Shakespeare's life outside the theatre, critics have found the sonnets fertile ground for biographical speculation, and the sequence of 154 poems does contain distinct characters —a handsome youth to whom most of the first 126 sonnets are addressed, a "Dark Lady" who figures strongly in the remaining poems, and the poet himself, whose name is the source of many puns in the poems. There is probably no definitive "key" to the sonnets, but there is also little doubt that their place is secure among the monuments of English lyric verse. Shakespeare's other nondramatic poems include narratives, allegories, and songs, of which "When Daisies Pied," the companion pieces from his early comedy* Love's Labour's Lost, *are perhaps the best examples.*

William Shakespeare
Sonnet 18

Shall I compare thee to a summer's day?
Thou art more lovely and more temperate:
Rough winds do shake the darling buds of May,
And summer's lease hath all too short a date:
Sometimes too hot the eye of heaven shines,   5
And often is his gold complexion dimmed;
And every fair from fair° sometimes declines,
By chance or nature's changing course untrimmed;°
But thy eternal summer shall not fade,
Nor lose possession of that fair thou ow'st;°   10
Nor shall death brag thou wander'st in his shade,
When in eternal lines to time thou grow'st:
So long as men can breathe, or eyes can see,
So long lives this, and this gives life to thee.

—*1609*

---

7 fair from fair every fair thing from its fairness   **8 untrimmed** stripped   **10 ow'st** ownest

Sonnet 20

A woman's face, with nature's own hand painted,
Hast thou, the master mistress of my passion—
A woman's gentle heart, but not acquainted
With shifting change, as is false women's fashion;
An eye more bright than theirs, less false in rolling,°   *5*
Gilding the object whereupon it gazeth;
A man in hue all hues in his controlling,
Which steals men's eyes and women's souls amazeth.
And for a woman wert thou first created,
Till nature as she wrought thee fell a-doting,   *10*
And by addition me of thee defeated,
By adding one thing to my purpose nothing.
     But since she pricked thee out for women's pleasure,
     Mine be thy love and thy love's use their treasure.

         —1609

Sonnet 30

When to the sessions° of sweet silent thought
I summon up remembrance of things past,
I sigh the lack of many a thing I sought,
And with old woes new wail my dear time's waste:
Then can I drown an eye, unused to flow,   *5*
For precious friends hid in death's dateless° night,
And weep afresh love's long since canceled woe,
And moan the expense of many a vanished sight:
Then can I grieve at grievances foregone,
And heavily from woe to woe tell o'er   *10*
The sad account of fore-bemoanèd moan,
Which I new pay as if not paid before.
But if the while I think on thee, dear friend,
All losses are restored and sorrows end.

         —1609

5 rolling wandering
1 sessions as in sessions of a court of law   **6 dateless** endless

Sonnet 73

That time of year thou mayst in me behold
When yellow leaves, or none, or few, do hang
Upon those boughs which shake against the cold,
Bare ruined choirs, where late the sweet birds sang.
In me thou see'st the twilight of such day   5
As after sunset fadeth in the west;
Which by and by black night doth take away,
Death's second self, that seals up all in rest.
In me thou see'st the glowing of such fire,
That on the ashes of his youth doth lie,   10
As the deathbed whereon it must expire,
Consumed with that which it was nourished by.
This thou perceiv'st, which makes thy love more strong,
To love that well which thou must leave ere long.

—*1609*

Sonnet 116

Let me not to the marriage of true minds
Admit impediments. Love is not love
Which alters when it alteration finds,
Or bends with the remover to remove:
Oh, no! it is an ever-fixèd mark,   5
That looks on tempests and is never shaken:
It is the star to every wandering bark,
Whose worth's unknown, although his height be taken.°
Love's not Time's fool, though rosy lips and cheeks
Within his bending sickle's compass° come;   10
Love alters not with his brief hours and weeks,
But bears it out even to the edge of doom.
If this be error and upon me proved,
I never writ, nor no man ever loved.

—*1609*

8 **height be taken** elevation be measured   10 **compass** range

Sonnet 130

My mistress' eyes are nothing like the sun;
Coral is far more red than her lips' red;
If snow be white, why then her breasts are dun;
If hairs be wires, black wires grow on her head.
I have seen roses damasked,° red and white,   5
But no such roses see I in her cheeks;
And in some perfumes is there more delight
Than in the breath that from my mistress reeks.
I love to hear her speak, yet well I know
That music hath a far more pleasing sound;   10
I grant I never saw a goddess go;
My mistress, when she walks, treads on the ground.
And yet, by heaven, I think my love as rare
As any she belied° with false compare.°

—*1609*

When Daisies Pied°

SPRING

When daisies pied and violets blue
    And ladysmocks all silver-white
And cuckoobuds of yellow hue
    Do paint the meadows with delight,
The cuckoo then, on every tree,   5
Mocks married men;° for thus sings he,
                Cuckoo;
Cuckoo, cuckoo: Oh word of fear,
Unpleasing to a married ear!
When shepherds pipe on oaten straws,   10
    And merry larks are plowmen's clocks,

---

5 damasked multi-colored   **14 belied** lied about   **compare** comparisons
Pied multi-colored   **6 Mocks married men** The pun is on the similarity between "cuckoo" and "cuckold."

When turtles tread,° and rooks, and daws,
   And maidens bleach their summer smocks,
The cuckoo then, on every tree,
Mocks married men; for thus sings he,   15
           Cuckoo:
Cuckoo, cuckoo: Oh word of fear,
Unpleasing to a married ear!

WINTER

When icicles hang by the wall
And Dick the shepherd blows his nail°   20
And Tom bears logs into the hall,
   And milk comes frozen home in pail,
When blood is nipped and ways be foul,
Then nightly sings the staring owl,
          Tu-who;   25
Tu-whit, tu-who: a merry note,
While greasy Joan doth keel° the pot.

When all aloud the wind doth blow,
   And coughing drowns the parson's saw,°
And birds sit brooding in the snow,   30
   And Marian's nose looks red and raw,
When roasted crabs° hiss in the bowl,
Then nightly sings the staring owl,
         Tu-who;
Tu-whit, tu-who: a merry note   35
While greasy Joan doth keel the pot.

                     —*1598*

---

12 turtles tread turtledoves mate **20 nail** fingernails **27 keel** stir **29 saw** saying **32 crabs**
crabapples

Thomas Campion (1567–1620) was a poet and physician who wrote music and lyrics in a manner that was "chiefly aimed to couple my words and notes lovingly together." The imagery in "There Is a Garden in Her Face" represents a late flowering of the conceits of Petrarchan love poetry, so wittily mocked by Shakespeare in "Sonnet 130."

Thomas Campion

There Is a Garden in Her Face

There is a garden in her face,
Where roses and white lilies grow,
A heavenly paradise is that place,
Wherein all pleasant fruits do flow.
There cherries grow which none may buy   5
Till "Cherry-ripe!" themselves do cry.

Those cherries fairly do enclose
Of orient pearl a double row,
Which when her lovely laughter shows,
They look like rosebuds filled with snow.   10
Yet them nor peer nor prince can buy,
Till "Cherry-ripe!" themselves do cry.

Her eyes like angels watch them still;
Her brows like bended bows do stand,
Threatening with piercing frowns to kill   15
All that attempt with eye or hand
Those sacred cherries to come nigh,
Till "Cherry-ripe!" themselves do cry.

—1617

John Donne (1572–1631) was trained in the law for a career in government service, but Donne became the greatest preacher of his day, ending his life as dean of St. Paul's Cathedral in London. Only two of Donne's poems and a handful of his sermons were printed during his life, but both circulated widely in manuscript and his literary reputation among his contemporaries was considerable. His poetry falls into two distinct periods: the witty love poetry of his youth and the sober religious meditations of his maturity. In both, however, Donne shows remarkable originality in rhythm, diction, and the use of metaphor and conceit, which marks him as the chief poet of what has become commonly known as the metaphysical style.

John Donne
The Canonization

For God's sake hold your tongue, and let me love,
  Or chide my palsy, or my gout,
My five gray hairs, or ruined fortune, flout,
    With wealth your state, your mind with arts improve,
      Take you a course, get you a place,   5
      Observe His Honor, or His Grace,
Or the king's real,° or his stampèd face
  Contèmplate; what you will, approve,°
  So you will let me love.

Alas, alas, who's injured by my love?   10
  What merchant's ships have my sighs drowned?
Who says my tears have overflowed his ground?
  When did my colds a forward° spring remove?
    When did the heats which my veins fill
    Add one more to the plaguy bill?°   15
Soldiers find wars, and lawyers find out still
  Litigious men, which quarrels move,
  Though she and I do love.

Call us what you will, we're made such by love;
  Call her one, me another fly,   20

7 real coinage   **8 approve** attempt   **13 forward** early   **15 plaguy bill** list of dead by plague

We're tapers too, and at our own cost die,°
    And we in us find th' eagle and the dove.
        The phoenix° riddle hath more wit
        By us: we two being one, are it.
So, to one neutral thing both sexes fit,   25
    We die and rise the same, and prove
    Mysterious by this love.

We can die by it, if not live by love,
    And if unfit for tomb and hearse
Our legend be, it will be fit for verse;   30
    And if no piece of chronicle° we prove,
        We'll build in sonnets pretty rooms;
        As well a well-wrought urn becomes
The greatest ashes, as half-acre tombs;
    And by these hymns, all shall approve   35
    Us canonized for love:

And thus invoke us, "You whom reverend love
    Made one another's hermitage;
You, to whom love was peace, that now is rage;
    Who did the whole world's soul contract, and drove   40
        Into the glasses of your eyes
        (So made such mirrors, and such spies,°
That they did all to you epitomize)
    Countries, towns, courts: Beg from above
    A pattern of your love!"   45

—1633

The Flea

Mark but this flea, and mark in this,
How little that which thou deniest me is;
Me it sucked first, and now sucks thee,
And in this flea our two bloods mingled be;

21 die i.e., to have sexual intercourse   **23 phoenix** legendary bird which is reborn from its own ashes   **31 chronicle** history   **42 spies** telescopes

Thou know'st that this cannot be said   5
A sin, or shame, or loss of maidenhead,
    Yet this enjoys before it woo,
    And pampered swells with one blood made of two,
    And this, alas, is more than we would do.

Oh stay, three lives in one flea spare,   10
Where we almost, nay more than married are.
This flea is you and I, and this
Our marriage bed and marriage temple is;
Though parents grudge, and you, we are met,
And cloistered in these living walls of jet.°   15
    Though use° make you apt to kill me
    Let not to that, self-murder added be,
    And sacrilege, three sins in killing three.

Cruel and sudden, hast thou since
Purpled thy nail° in blood of innocence?   20
Wherein could this flea guilty be,
Except in that drop which it sucked from thee?
Yet thou triumph'st, and say'st that thou
Find'st not thy self nor me the weaker now;
    'Tis true; then learn how false fears be: 25
    Just so much honor, when thou yield'st to me,
    Will waste, as this flea's death took life from thee.

—*1633*

Holy Sonnet 10

Death, be not proud, though some have callèd thee
Mighty and dreadful, for thou art not so;
For those whom thou think'st thou dost overthrow
Die not, poor Death, nor yet canst thou kill me.
From rest and sleep, which but thy pictures be,   5
Much pleasure; then from thee much more must flow,

---

15 jet black   **16 use** familiarity, especially in the sexual sense   **20 Purpled thy nail** bloodied your fingernail

And soonest our best men with thee do go,
Rest of their bones, and soul's delivery.
Thou'art slave to fate, chance, kings, and desperate men,
And dost with poison, war, and sickness dwell,   10
And poppy° or charms can make us sleep as well
And better than thy stroke; why swell'st thou then?
One short sleep past, we wake eternally,
And death shall be no more; Death, thou shalt die.

—1633

Holy Sonnet 14

Batter my heart, three-personed God; for You
As yet but knock, breathe, shine, and seek to mend;
That I may rise, and stand, o'erthrow me, and bend
Your force to break, blow, burn, and make me new.
I, like an usurped town, to another due,   5
Labor to admit You, but O, to no end;
Reason, Your viceroy in me, me should defend,
But is captived, and proves weak or untrue.
Yet dearly I love You, and would be lovèd fain,°
But am betrothed unto Your enemy.   10
Divorce me, untie or break that knot again;
Take me to You, imprison me, for I,
Except You enthrall me, never shall be free,
Nor ever chaste, except You ravish me.

—1633

11 poppy opium
9 fain gladly

A Valediction:°
Forbidding Mourning

As virtuous men pass mildly away,
  And whisper to their souls to go,
Whilst some of their sad friends do say
  The breath goes now, and some say, No;

So let us melt, and make no noise,   5
  No tear-floods, nor sigh-tempests move,
'Twere profanation of our joys
  To tell the laity our love.

Moving of th' earth brings harms and fears,
  Men reckon what it did and meant;   10
But trepidation of the spheres,°
  Though greater far, is innocent.

Dull sublunary° lovers' love,
  (Whose soul is sense) cannot admit
Absence, because it doth remove   15
  Those things which elemented it.
But we by a love so much refined
  That our selves know not what it is,
Inter-assurèd of the mind,
  Care less, eyes, lips, and hands to miss.   20

Our two souls therefore, which are one,
  Though I must go, endure not yet
A breach, but an expansion,
  Like gold to airy thinness beat.

If they be two, they are two so   25
  As stiff twin compasses° are two;

Valediction farewell speech; Donne is addressing his wife before leaving on a diplomatic mission.
11 trepidation of the spheres natural trembling of the heavenly spheres, a concept of Ptolemaic astronomy   **13 sublunary** under the moon, hence, changeable (a Ptolemaic concept)   **26 stiff twin compasses** drafting compasses

Thy soul, the fixed foot, makes no show
    To move, but doth, if th' other do.

And though it in the center sit,
    Yet when the other far doth roam,
It leans and hearkens after it,   30
    And grows erect, as that comes home.

Such wilt thou be to me, who must
    Like th' other foot, obliquely run;
Thy firmness makes my circle just,°   35
    And makes me end where I begun.

—1633

Ben Jonson (1573–1637) was Shakespeare's chief rival on the stage, and their contentious friendship has been the subject of much speculation. Jonson became England's first unofficial poet laureate, receiving a royal stipend from James I, and was a great influence of a group of younger poets who became known as the "Tribe of Ben." His tragedies are little regarded today, and his comedies, while still performed occasionally, have nevertheless failed to hold the stage as brilliantly as Shakespeare's. Still, he was a poet of considerable talents, particularly in short forms. His elegy on Shakespeare contains a famous assessment: "He was not of an age, but for all time!"

Ben Jonson
On My First Son

Farewell, thou child of my right hand,° and joy;
My sin was too much hope of thee, loved boy:
Seven years thou'wert lent to me, and I thee pay,
Exacted by thy fate, on the just day.°
Oh, could I lose all father now! for why   5
Will man lament the state he should envy,
To have so soon 'scaped world's and flesh's rage,

---

35 just complete
1 child of my right hand Benjamin, the child's name, means this in Hebrew.   **4 the just day** Jonson's son died on his seventh birthday.

And, if no other misery, yet age?
Rest in soft peace, and asked, say, "Here doth lie
Ben Jonson his best piece of poetry."   *10*
For whose sake henceforth all his vows be such
As what he loves may never like too much.

                                                          —1616

Slow, Slow, Fresh Fount

From Cynthia's Revels°
Slow, slow, fresh fount, keep time with my salt tears;
Yet slower, yet, O faintly, gentle springs!
List to the heavy part the music bears,
Woe weeps out her division,° when she sings.
      Droop herbs and flowers;   *5*
      Fall grief in showers;
Our beauties are not ours. O, I could still,
Like melting snow upon some craggy hill,
      Drop, drop, drop, drop,
Since nature's pride is now a withered daffodil.   *10*

                                                          —1600

Slow, Slow, Fresh Fount: From Cynthia's Revels spoken in this masque by the nymph Echo to the dead Narcissus **4 division** part of a song

Mary Wroth (1587?–1651) *was the niece of Sir Philip Sidney and the cousin of Sir Walter Raleigh, both distinguished poets and courtiers. A friend of poet Ben Jonson, who dedicated* The Alchemist *to her, she was prominent in the court of King James I. Her prose romance,* Urania (1621), *stirred controversy because of its similarities to actual people and events. Wroth may have fallen into disfavor at court after the publication of* Urania, *and few facts are known about her later life.*

Mary Wroth

In This Strange Labyrinth How Shall I Turn

In this strange labyrinth how shall I turn,
Ways° are on all sides, while the way I miss:
If to the right hand, there in love I burn,
Let me go forward, therein danger is.

If to the left, suspicion hinders bliss: 5
Let me turn back, shame cries I ought return:
Nor faint, though crosses° with my fortunes kiss.
Stand still is harder, although sure to mourn.
Thus let me take the right, or left hand way,
Go forward, or stand still, or back retire: 10
I must these doubts endure without allay°
Or help, but travail find for my best hire
Yet that which most my troubled sense doth move,
Is to leave all and take the thread of Love°

---

2 ways paths   **7 crosses** troubles   **11 allay** alleviation   **14 Love** an allusion to the myth of Theseus, who, with the help of Ariddne, unrolled a thread behind him as he entered the labyrinth of Crete.

Robert Herrick (1591–1674) was the most distinguished member of the "Tribe of Ben." Herrick is grouped with the Cavalier poets, whose graceful lyrics are marked by wit and gentle irony. Surprisingly, Herrick was a minister; his Royalist sympathies during the English Civil War caused him hardship during the Puritan era, but his position in the church was returned to him by Charles II after the Restoration.

Robert Herrick

To the Virgins, to Make Much of Time

Gather ye rosebuds while ye may,
    Old time is still a-flying;
And this same flower that smiles today
    Tomorrow will be dying.

The glorious lamp of heaven, the sun,   5
    The higher he's a-getting,
The sooner will his race be run,
    And nearer he's to setting.

That age is best which is the first,
    When youth and blood are warmer;   10
But being spent, the worse, and worst
    Times still succeed the former.

Then be not coy, but use your time,
    And, while ye may, go marry;
For, having lost but once your prime,   15
    You may forever tarry.

—1648

George Herbert (1593–1633) was the great master of the English devotional lyric. Herbert was born into a distinguished family which included his mother, the formidable literary patroness Lady Magdalen Herbert, and his brother, the poet and statesman Edward, Lord Herbert of Cherbury. Like John Donne, with whom he shares the metaphysical label, Herbert early aimed at a political career but turned to the clergy, spending several happy years as rector of Bemerton before his death at age 40. The Temple, which contains most of his poems, was published posthumously in 1633.

George Herbert

Easter Wings

Lord, who createdst man in wealth and store,°
Though foolishly he lost the same,
Decaying more and more
Till he became
Most poor: 5
With Thee
O let me rise
As larks, harmoniously,
And sing this day Thy victories:
Then shall the fall further the flight in me.   10

My tender age in sorrow did begin;
And still with sicknesses and shame
Thou didst so punish sin,
That I became
Most thin.   15
With Thee
Let me combine,
And feel this day thy victory;
For, if I imp my wing on thine,°
Affliction shall advance the flight in me.   20

—*1633*

1 store abundance   **19 imp my wing on thine** to graft feathers from a strong wing onto a weak one, a term from falconry

Love (III)

Love bade me welcome: yet my soul drew back,
    Guilty of dust and sin.
But quick-eyed Love, observing me grow slack
    From my first entrance in,
Drew nearer to me, sweetly questioning   *5*
    If I lacked anything.

"A guest," I answered, "worthy to be here":
    Love said, "You shall be he."
"I, the unkind, ungrateful? Ah, my dear,
    I cannot look on thee."   *10*
Love took my hand, and smiling did reply,
    "Who made the eyes but I?"

"Truth, Lord, but I have marred them; let my shame
    Go where it doth deserve."
"And know you not," says Love, "who bore the blame?"   *15*
    "My dear, then I will serve."
"You must sit down," says Love, "and taste my meat."
    So I did sit and eat.

—1633

The Pulley

    When God at first made man,
Having a glass of blessings standing by,
    "Let us," said he, "pour on him all we can.
Let the world's riches, which dispersèd lie,
    Contract into a span."°   *5*

    So strength first made a way;
Then beauty flowed, then wisdom, honor, pleasure.
    When almost all was out, God made a stay,

5 span the distance between thumb tip and the tip of the little finger

Perceiving that, alone of all his treasure,
    Rest in the bottom lay.   *10*

    "For if I should," said he,
"Bestow this jewel also on my creature,
    He would adore my gifts instead of me,
And rest in Nature, not the God of Nature;
    So both should losers be.   *15*

    "Yet let him keep the rest,
But keep them with repining restlessness.
    Let him be rich and weary, that at least,
If goodness lead him not, yet weariness
    May toss him to my breast."   *20*

                                                        —1633

Redemption

Having been tenant long to a rich lord,
    Not thriving, I resolvèd to be bold,
    And make a suit° unto him, to afford°
A new small-rented lease, and cancel the old.
In heaven at his manor I him sought;   *5*
    They told me there that he was lately gone
    About some land, which he had dearly bought
Long since on earth, to take possession.

I straight returned, and knowing his great birth,
    Sought him accordingly in great resorts;   *10*
    In cities, theaters, gardens, parks, and courts;
At length I heard a ragged noise and mirth
    Of thieves and murderers; there I him espied,°
    Who straight, Your suit is granted, said, and died.

                                                        —1633

3 make a suit formally request   **afford** grant (me)   **13 him espied** saw him

Edmund Waller (1606–1687) was another Royalist sympathizer who suffered after the English Civil War, during Oliver Cromwell's protectorate. Waller is noted for having pioneered the use of the heroic couplet as a popular verse form. He has been often praised for the smoothness of his rhythms and sound patterns.

Edmund Waller

Song

Go, lovely rose!
Tell her that wastes her time and me
   That now she knows,
When I resemble° her to thee,
How sweet and fair she seems to be.   5

   Tell her that's young,
And shuns to have her graces spied,
   That hadst thou sprung
In deserts, where no men abide,
Thou must have uncommended died.   10

   Small is the worth
Of beauty from the light retired;
   Bid her come forth,
Suffer herself to be desired,
And not blush so to be admired.   15

   Then die! that she
The common fate of all things rare
   May read in thee;
How small a part of time they share
That are so wondrous sweet and fair!   20

—*1645*

4 resemble compare

John Milton (1608–1674) is best known as the author of Paradise Lost, *the greatest English epic poem. His life included service in the Puritan government of Cromwell, pamphleteering for liberal political causes, and brief imprisonment after the Restoration. Milton suffered from blindness in his later years. He excelled in the sonnet, a form to which he returned throughout his long literary life.*

John Milton

How Soon Hath Time

How soon hath Time, the subtle thief of youth,
    Stol'n on his wing my three and twentieth year!
    My hasting days fly on with full career,
    But my late spring no bud or blossom shew'th.°
Perhaps my semblance might deceive the truth,   *5*
    That I to manhood am arrived so near,
    And inward ripeness doth much less appear,
    That some more timely-happy spirits endu'th.°
Yet be it less or more, or soon or slow,
    It shall be still in strictest measure even°   *10*
    To that same lot, however mean or high,
Toward which Time leads me, and the will of Heaven;
    All is, if I have grace to use it so,
    As ever in my great Taskmaster's eye.

—*1645*

On the Late Massacre in Piedmont°

Avenge, O Lord, thy slaughtered saints, whose bones
    Lie scattered on the Alpine mountains cold,
    Even them who kept thy truth so pure of old
    When all our fathers worshiped stocks and stones,°

4 shew'th shows   **8 endu'th** endows   **10 even** equal
Massacre in Piedmont 1700 Protestants from this North Italian state were massacred by Papal forces on Easter Day, 1655.   **4 stocks and stones** idols

Forget not: in thy book record their groans   *5*
    Who were thy sheep and in their ancient fold
    Slain by the bloody Piedmontese that rolled
    Mother with infant down the rocks. Their moans
The vales redoubled to the hills, and they
    To Heaven. Their martyred blood and ashes sow   *10*
    O'er all th'Italian fields where still doth sway
The triple tyrant:° that from these may grow
    A hundredfold, who having learnt thy way
    Early may fly the Babylonian woe.°

                                  —*1655*

When I Consider How My Light Is Spent

When I consider how my light is spent
    Ere half my days, in this dark world and wide,
    And that one talent which is death to hide°
    Lodged with me useless, though my soul more bent
To serve therewith my Maker, and present   *5*
    My true account, lest he returning chide;
    "Doth God exact day-labor, light denied?"
    I fondly° ask; but Patience to prevent
That murmur, soon replies, "God doth not need
    Either man's work or his own gifts; who best   *10*
    Bear his mild yoke, they serve him best. His state
Is kingly. Thousands at his bidding speed
    And post o'er land and ocean without rest:
    They also serve who only stand and wait."

                                  —*1673*

---

12 triple tyrant the Pope   **14 Babylonian woe** Early Protestants often linked ancient Babylon to modern Rome as centers of vice.
3 talent which is death to hide See the Parable of the Talents, Matthew 25:14–30.   **8 fondly** foolishly

Anne Bradstreet (1612–1672) was an American Puritan who was one of the first settlers of the Massachusetts Bay Colony, along with her husband Simon, later governor of the colony. The Tenth Muse Lately Sprung Up in America, *published abroad by a relative without her knowledge, was the first American book of poetry published in England, and the circumstances of its appearance lie behind the witty tone of "The Author to Her Book."*

Anne Bradstreet
The Author to Her Book

Thou ill-formed offspring of my feeble brain,
Who after birth didst by my side remain,
Till snatched from thence by friends, less wise than true,
Who thee abroad, exposed to public view,
Made thee in rags, halting to th' press° to trudge,   5
Where errors were not lessened (all may judge).
At thy return my blushing was not small,
My rambling brat (in print) should mother call,
I cast thee by as one unfit for light,
Thy visage was so irksome in my sight;   10
Yet being mine own, at length affection would
Thy blemishes amend, if so I could:
I washed thy face, but more defects I saw,
And rubbing off a spot still made a flaw.
I stretched thy joints to make thee even feet,°   15
Yet still thou run'st more hobbling than is meet;
In better dress to trim thee was my mind,
But nought save homespun cloth i' th' house I find.
In this array 'mongst vulgars° may'st thou roam.
In critic's hands beware thou dost not come,   20
And take thy way where yet thou art not known;
If for thy father asked, say thou hadst none;
And for thy mother, she alas is poor,
Which caused her thus to send thee out of door.

—*1678*

5 press printing press; also a clothes closet or chest   **15 even feet** a pun on metrical feet
19 vulgars common people, i.e., average readers

Richard Lovelace (1618–1658) was another Cavalier lyricist who was a staunch supporter of Charles I, serving as a soldier in Scotland and France. He composed many of his poems in prison following the English Civil War.

Richard Lovelace
To Lucasta, Going to the Wars

Tell me not, sweet, I am unkind
That from the nunnery
Of thy chaste breast and quiet mind,
To war and arms I fly.

True, a new mistress now I chase,   5
The first foe in the field;
And with a stronger faith embrace
A sword, a horse, a shield.

Yet this inconstancy is such
As you too shall adore;   10
I could not love thee, dear, so much,
Loved I not honor more.

—1649

Andrew Marvell (1621–1678) was widely known for the playful sexual wit of this most famous example of the carpé diem *poem in English. Marvell was a learned Latin scholar who moved in high circles of government under both the Puritans and Charles II, serving as a member of parliament for two decades. Oddly, Marvell was almost completely forgotten as a lyric poet for almost two hundred years after his death, although today he is considered the last of the great exemplars of the metaphysical style.*

Andrew Marvell
To His Coy Mistress

Had we but world enough, and time,
This coyness,° lady, were no crime.
We would sit down, and think which way
To walk, and pass our long love's day.
Thou by the Indian Ganges' side   5
Shouldst rubies find; I by the tide
Of Humber° would complain. I would
Love you ten years before the flood,
And you should, if you please, refuse
Till the conversion of the Jews.°   10
My vegetable° love should grow
Vaster than empires, and more slow;
An hundred years should go to praise
Thine eyes, and on thy forehead gaze;
Two hundred to adore each breast,   15
But thirty thousand to the rest;
An age at least to every part,
And the last age should show your heart.
For, lady, you deserve this state,°
Nor would I love at lower rate.   20
   But at my back I always hear
Time's wingèd chariot hurrying near;
And yonder all before us lie

---

2 coyness here, artificial sexual reluctance   **7 Humber** an English river near Marvell's home
10 conversion of the Jews at the end of time   **11 vegetable** flourishing   **19 state** estate

Deserts of vast eternity.
Thy beauty shall no more be found; 25
Nor, in thy marble vault, shall sound
My echoing song; then worms shall try°
That long-preserved virginity,
And your quaint° honor turn to dust,
And into ashes all my lust: 30
The grave's a fine and private place,
But none, I think, do there embrace.
    Now therefore, while the youthful hue
Sits on thy skin like morning glow,
And while thy willing soul transpires 35
At every pore with instant fires,
Now let us sport us while we may,
And now, like amorous birds of prey,
Rather at once our time devour
Than languish in his slow-chapped° power. 40
Let us roll all our strength and all
Our sweetness up into one ball,
And tear our pleasures with rough strife
Thorough the iron gates of life:
Thus, though we cannot make our sun 45
Stand still, yet we will make him run.

—*1681*

27 **try** test 29 **quaint** too subtle 40 **chapped** jawed

John Dryden (1631–1700) excelled at long forms—verse dramas like All for Love, *his version of Shakespeare's* Antony and Cleopatra, *his translation of Virgil's* Aeneid, *political allegories like* Absalom and Achitophel, *and* MacFlecknoe, *the first great English literary satire. Dryden's balance and formal conservatism introduced the neoclassical style to English poetry, a manner that prevailed for a century after his death. He became poet laureate of England in 1668.*

John Dryden
To the Memory of Mr. Oldham°

Farewell, too little, and too lately known,
Whom I began to think and call my own:
For sure our souls were near allied, and thine
Cast in the same poetic mold with mine.
One common note on either lyre did strike,   5
And knaves and fools we both abhorred alike.
To the same goal did both our studies drive;
The last set out the soonest did arrive.
Thus Nisus° fell upon the slippery place,
While his young friend performed and won the race.   10
O early ripe! to thy abundant store
What could advancing age have added more?
It might (what nature never gives the young)
Have taught the numbers° of thy native tongue.
But satire needs not those, and wit will shine   15
Through the harsh cadence of a rugged line:
A noble error, and but seldom made,
When poets are by too much force betrayed.
Thy generous fruits, though gathered ere their prime,
Still showed a quickness, and maturing time   20
But mellows what we write to the dull sweets of rhyme.
Once more, hail and farewell; farewell, thou young,

John Oldham (1653–1683) was a poet and a satirist.   **9 Nisus** In Virgil's *Aeneid* he is defeated in a footrace by Euryalus, his friend.   **14 numbers** poetic meters

But ah too short, Marcellus° of our tongue;
Thy brows with ivy, and with laurels bound
But fate and gloomy night encompass thee around.   25

—*1684*

Epigram on Milton

Three poets, in three distant ages born,
Greece,° Italy,° and England did adorn.
The first in loftiness of thought surpassed,
The next in majesty, in both the last:
The force of Nature could no farther go;   5
To make a third, she joined the former two.

—*1688*

Edward Taylor (1642–1729) was a Calvinist minister in a village outside of Boston whose eccentric religious poems (obviously influenced by Donne and Herbert) remained in manuscript for over two centuries after his death, when they were discovered in the Yale University Library. Taylor was a true amateur, writing in isolation and apparently intending his poems as meditative exercises to assist him in his clerical duties. Taylor's poems were not published until the twentieth century.

Edward Taylor
Huswifery

Make me, O Lord, thy spinning wheel complete.
   Thy holy word my distaff° make for me.
Make mine affections thy swift flyers° neat,
   And make my soul thy holy spool° to be.
   My conversation make to be thy reel,°   5
   And reel the yarn thereon spun of thy wheel.

---

23 Marcellus Roman military leader who died at age twenty
2 Greece i.e., Homer   **Italy** i.e., Virgil
2 distaff part of a spinning wheel that holds raw material   **3 flyers** impart twist to yarn   **4 spool** collects spun yarn   **5 reel** receives finished thread

Make me thy loom then, knit therein this twine;
   And make thy holy spirit, Lord, wind quills.°
Then weave the web thyself. The yarn is fine.
   Thine ordinances make my fulling mills.°   *10*
   Then dye the same in heavenly colors choice,
   All pinked° with varnished° flowers of paradise.

Then clothe therewith mine understanding, will,
   Affections, judgment, conscience, memory,
My words, and actions, that their shine may fill   *15*
   My ways with glory and thee glorify.
   Then mine apparel shall display before ye
   That I am clothed in holy robes for glory.

—*1685?*

Jonathan Swift (1667–1745), the author of Gulliver's Travels, *stands unchallenged as the greatest English prose satirist, but his poetry too is remarkable in the unsparing realism of its best passages. Like many poets of the neoclassical era, Swift adds tension to his poetry by ironically emphasizing parallels between the heroic past and the familiar characters and scenes of contemporary London. A native of Dublin, Swift returned to Ireland in his maturity as dean of St. Patrick's Cathedral.*

Jonathan Swift

A Description of a City Shower

   Careful observers may foretell the hour
(By sure prognostics)° when to dread a shower:
While rain depends,° the pensive cat gives o'er
Her frolics, and pursues her tail no more.
Returning home at night, you'll find the sink°   *5*
Strike your offended sense with double stink.

8 quills spools   **10 fulling mills** where cloth is cleaned after weaving   **12 pinked** decorated
varnished shiny
2 prognostics forecasts   **3 depends** is imminent   **5 sink** sewer

If you be wise, then go not far to dine;
You'll spend in coach hire more than save in wine.
A coming shower your shooting corns presage,
Old achès throb, your hollow tooth will rage.   10
Sauntering in coffeehouse is Dulman° seen;
He damns the climate and complains of spleen.°

    Meanwhile the South, rising with dabbled wings,
A sable cloud athwart the welkin° flings,
That swilled more liquor than it could contain,   15
And, like a drunkard, gives it up again.
Brisk Susan whips her linen from the rope,
While the first drizzling shower is borne aslope:
Such is that sprinkling which some careless quean°
Flirts on you from her mop, but not so clean: 20
You fly, invoke the gods; then turning, stop
To rail; she singing, still whirls on her mop.
Not yet the dust had shunned the unequal strife,
But, aided by the wind, fought still for life,
And wafted with its foe by violent gust,   25
'Twas doubtful which was rain and which was dust.
Ah! where must needy poet seek for aid,
When dust and rain at once his coat invade?
Sole coat, where dust cemented by the rain
Erects the nap, and leaves a mingled stain.   30

    Now in contiguous drops the flood comes down,
Threatening with deluge this devoted° town.
To shops in crowds the daggled° females fly,
Pretend to cheapen° goods, but nothing buy.
The Templar° spruce, while every spout's abroach,°   35
Stays till 'tis fair, yet seems to call a coach.
The tucked-up sempstress walks with hasty strides,
While streams run down her oiled umbrella's sides.
Here various kinds, by various fortunes led,
Commence acquaintance underneath a shed.   40

---

11 **Dulman** i.e., dull man   12 **spleen** mental depression   14 **welkin** sky   19 **quean** ill-mannered
woman   32 **devoted** doomed   33 **daggled** spattered   34 **cheapen** inspect prices of   35 **Templar**
law student   **abroach** pouring

Triumphant Tories and desponding Whigs°
Forget their feuds, and join to save their wigs.
Boxed in a chair° the beau impatient sits,
While spouts run clattering o'er the roof by fits,
And ever and anon with frightful din   45
The leather sounds; he trembles from within.
So when Troy chairmen bore the wooden steed,
Pregnant with Greeks impatient to be freed
(Those bully Greeks, who, as the moderns do,
Instead of paying chairmen, run them through),   50
Laocoön° struck the outside with his spear,
And each imprisoned hero quaked for fear.
   Now from all parts the swelling kennels° flow,
And bear their trophies with them as they go:
Filth of all hues and odors seem to tell   55
What street they sailed from, by their sight and smell.
They, as each torrent drives with rapid force,
From Smithfield° or St. Pulchre's shape their course,
And in huge confluence joined at Snow Hill ridge,
Fall from the conduit prone to Holborn Bridge.   60
Sweepings from butchers' stalls, dung, guts, and blood,
Drowned puppies, stinking sprats,° all drenched in mud,
Dead cats, and turnip tops, come tumbling down the flood.

—*1710*

---

41 Tories . . . Whigs rival political factions   **43 chair** sedan chair   **51 Laocoön** For his attempt to warn the Trojans, he was crushed by sea serpents sent by Poseidon.   **53 kennels** storm drains   **58 Smithfield** site of London cattle exchange   **62 sprats** small fish

Alexander Pope (1688–1744) was a tiny man who was afflicted in childhood by a crippling disease. Pope was the dominant poet of eighteenth-century England, particularly excelling as a master of mock-epic satire in "The Rape of the Lock" and "The Dunciad." His translations of the Iliad *and the* Odyssey *made him famous and financially independent and remained the standard versions of Homer for almost two hundred years. "An Essay on Criticism," a long didactic poem modeled on Horace's* Ars Poetica, *remains the most complete statement of the neoclassical aesthetic.*

Alexander Pope
from An Essay on Criticism

But most by numbers judge a poet's song,
And smooth or rough with them is right or wrong.
In the bright Muse though thousand charms conspire,
Her voice is all these tuneful fools admire,
Who haunt Parnassus° but to please their ear,   5
Not mend their minds; as some to church repair,
Not for the doctrine, but the music there.
These equal syllables alone require,
Though oft the ear the open vowels tire,
While expletives° their feeble aid do join,   10
And ten low words oft creep in one dull line:
While they ring round the same unvaried chimes,
With sure returns of still expected rhymes;
Where'er you find "the cooling western breeze,"
In the next line, it "whispers through the trees";   15
If crystal streams "with pleasing murmurs creep,"
The reader's threatened (not in vain) with "sleep";
Then, at the last and only couplet fraught
With some unmeaning thing they call a thought,
A needless Alexandrine° ends the song   20
That, like a wounded snake, drags its slow length along.
Leave such to tune their own dull rhymes, and know
What's roundly smooth or languishingly slow;

5 Parnassus mountain of the Muses   **10 expletives** unnecessary filler words   **20 Alexandrine** line
of six iambic feet (as in the next line)

And praise the easy vigor of a line
Where Denham's strength and Waller's° sweetness join.   25
True ease in writing comes from art, not chance,
As those move easiest who have learned to dance.
'Tis not enough no harshness gives offense,
The sound must seem an echo to the sense.
Soft is the strain when Zephyr° gently blows,   30
And the smooth stream in smoother numbers flows;
But when loud surges lash the sounding shore,
The hoarse, rough verse should like the torrent roar.
When Ajax° strives some rock's vast weight to throw,
The line too labors, and the words move slow;   35
Not so when swift Camilla° scours the plain,
Flies o'er the unbending corn, and skims along the main.
Hear how Timotheus'° varied lays surprise,
And bid alternate passions fall and rise!
While at each change the son of Libyan Jove°   40
Now burns with glory, and then melts with love;
Now his fierce eyes with sparkling fury glow,
Now sighs steal out, and tears begin to flow:
Persians and Greeks like turns of nature found
And the world's victor stood subdued by sound!   45
The power of music all our hearts allow,
And what Timotheus was is Dryden now.
    Avoid extremes; and shun the fault of such
Who still are pleased too little or too much.
At every trifle scorn to take offense: 50
That always shows great pride, or little sense.
Those heads, as stomachs, are not sure the best,
Which nauseate all, and nothing can digest.
Yet let not each gay turn thy rapture move;
For fools admire, but men of sense approve: 55
As things seem large which we through mists descry,
Dullness is ever apt to magnify.

—1711

25 **Denham's . . . Waller's** earlier English poets praised by Pope   30 **Zephyr** the west wind
34 **Ajax** legendary strong man of the *Iliad*   36 **Camilla** messenger of the goddess Diana
38 **Timotheus** a legendary musician   40 **son of Libyan Jove** Alexander the Great

Ode on Solitude

Happy the man whose wish and care
    A few paternal acres bound,
Content to breathe his native air,
       In his own ground.

Whose herds with milk, whose fields with bread,   5
    Whose flocks supply him with attire,
Whose trees in summer yield him shade,
       In winter fire.

Blest, who can unconcernedly find
    Hours, days, and years slide soft away,   10
In health of body, peace of mind,
       Quiet by day,

Sound sleep by night; study and ease,
    Together mixed; sweet recreation;
And innocence, which most does please   15
       With meditation.

Thus let me live, unseen, unknown;
    Thus unlamented let me die;
Steal from the world, and not a stone
       Tell where I lie.   20

—*1736*

Thomas Gray (1716–1771) possesses a contemporary reputation that rests primarily on a single poem, but it remains one of the most often quoted in the whole English canon, and the quatrain stanza is often called "elegiac" in its honor. Gray lived almost all of his adult life at Cambridge University, where he was a professor of history and languages. He declined the poet laureateship of England in 1757.

Thomas Gray
Elegy Written in a Country Churchyard

The curfew tolls the knell of parting day,
    The lowing herd wind slowly o'er the lea,
The plowman homeward plods his weary way,
    And leaves the world to darkness and to me.

Now fades the glimmering landscape on the sight,   5
    And all the air a solemn stillness holds,
Save where the beetle wheels his droning flight,
    And drowsy tinklings lull the distant folds;

Save that from yonder ivy-mantled tower
    The moping owl does to the moon complain   10
Of such, as wandering near her secret bower,
    Molest her ancient solitary reign.

Beneath those rugged elms, that yew tree's shade,
    Where heaves the turf in many a moldering heap,
Each in his narrow cell forever laid,   15
    The rude° forefathers of the hamlet sleep.

The breezy call of incense-breathing morn,
    The swallow twittering from the straw-built shed,
The cock's shrill clarion, or the echoing horn,
    No more shall rouse them from their lowly bed.   20

For them no more the blazing hearth shall burn,
    Or busy housewife ply her evening care;

16 rude unlearned

No children run to lisp their sire's return,
    Or climb his knees the envied kiss to share.

Oft did the harvest to their sickle yield,   25
    Their furrow oft the stubborn glebe° has broke;
How jocund did they drive their team afield!
    How bowed the woods beneath their sturdy stroke!

Let not Ambition mock their useful toil,
    Their homely joys, and destiny obscure;   30
Nor Grandeur hear with a disdainful smile
    The short and simple annals of the poor.

The boast of heraldry, the pomp of power,
    And all that beauty, all that wealth e'er gave,
Awaits alike the inevitable hour.   35
    The paths of glory lead but to the grave.

Nor you, ye proud, impute to these the fault,
    If Memory o'er their tomb no trophies raise,
Where through the long-drawn aisle and fretted° vault
    The pealing anthem swells the note of praise.   40

Can storied urn or animated bust
    Back to its mansion call the fleeting breath?
Can Honor's voice provoke the silent dust,
    Or Flattery soothe the dull cold ear of Death?

Perhaps in this neglected spot is laid   45
    Some heart once pregnant with celestial fire;
Hands that the rod of empire might have swayed,
    Or waked to ecstasy the living lyre.

But Knowledge to their eyes her ample page
    Rich with the spoils of time did ne'er unroll;   50
Chill Penury repressed their noble rage,
    And froze the genial current of the soul.

Full many a gem of purest ray serene,
    The dark unfathomed caves of ocean bear:

26 glebe plot of farmland   **39 fretted** carved

Full many a flower is born to blush unseen,   55
  And waste its sweetness on the desert air.

Some village Hampden,° that with dauntless breast
  The little tyrant of his field withstood;
Some mute inglorious Milton here may rest,
  Some Cromwell° guiltless of his country's blood.   60

The applause of listening senates to command,
  The threats of pain and ruin to despise,
To scatter plenty o'er a smiling land,
  And read their history in a nation's eyes,

Their lot forbade: nor circumscribed alone   65
  Their growing virtues, but their crimes confined;
Forbade to wade through slaughter to a throne,
  And shut the gates of mercy on mankind,

The struggling pangs of conscious truth to hide,
  To quench the blushes of ingenuous shame,   70
Or heap the shrine of Luxury and Pride
  With incense kindled at the Muse's flame.

Far from the madding° crowd's ignoble strife,
  Their sober wishes never learned to stray;
Along the cool sequestered vale of life   75
  They kept the noiseless tenor of their way.

Yet even these bones from insult to protect
  Some frail memorial still erected nigh,
With uncouth rhymes and shapeless sculpture decked,
  Implores the passing tribute of a sigh.   80

Their name, their years, spelt by the unlettered Muse,
  The place of fame and elegy supply:
And many a holy text around she strews,
  That teach the rustic moralist to die.

---

57 Hampden hero of the English Civil War **60 Cromwell** Lord Protector of England from 1653 to 1658 **73 madding** frenzied

For who to dumb Forgetfulness a prey,   *85*
    This pleasing anxious being e'er resigned,
Left the warm precincts of the cheerful day,
    Nor cast one longing lingering look behind?

On some fond breast the parting soul relies,
    Some pious drops the closing eye requires;   *90*
Even from the tomb the voice of Nature cries,
    Even in our ashes live their wonted fires.

For thee, who mindful of the unhonored dead
    Dost in these lines their artless tale relate;
If chance, by lonely contemplation led,   *95*
    Some kindred spirit shall inquire thy fate,

Haply some hoary°-headed swain° may say,
    "Oft have we seen him at the peep of dawn
Brushing with hasty steps the dews away
    To meet the sun upon the upland lawn.   *100*

"There at the foot of yonder nodding beech
    That wreathes its old fantastic roots so high,
His listless length at noontide would he stretch,
    And pore upon the brook that babbles by.

"Hard by yon wood, now smiling as in scorn,   *105*
    Muttering his wayward fancies he would rove,
Now drooping, woeful wan, like one forlorn,
    Or crazed with care, or crossed in hopeless love.

"One morn I missed him on the customed hill,
    Along the heath and near his favorite tree;   *110*
Another came; nor yet beside the rill,
    Nor up the lawn, nor at the wood was he;

"The next with dirges due in sad array
    Slow through the churchway path we saw him borne.
Approach and read (for thou canst read) the lay,   *115*
    Graved on the stone beneath yon aged thorn."

97 hoary frosty, white   **swain** peasant

The Epitaph

Here rests his head upon the lap of Earth
    A youth to Fortune and to Fame unknown.
Fair Science frowned not on his humble birth,
    And Melancholy marked him for her own.   120

Large was his bounty, and his soul sincere,
    Heaven did a recompense as largely send:
He gave to Misery all he had, a tear,
    He gained from Heaven ('twas all he wished) a friend.

No farther seek his merits to disclose,   125
    Or draw his frailties from their dread abode
(There they alike in trembling hope repose),
    The bosom of his Father and his God.

—1751

Christopher Smart (1722–1771) was educated, like Thomas Gray, at Cambridge, but fell victim to religious mania and insanity yet continued to write throughout his life. Jubilate Agno ("Rejoice in the Lamb") is a long meditation on the immanence of God, even in such insignificant forms as Gray's cat Jeoffry. The poem is one of the earliest examples of free verse in English.

Christopher Smart
from Jubilate Agno

For I will consider my Cat Jeoffry.
For he is the servant of the Living God, duly and daily serving him.
For at the first glance of the glory of God in the East he worships in
    his way.
For is this done by wreathing his body seven times round with
    elegant quickness.
For then he leaps up to catch the musk,° which is the blessing of
    God upon his prayer.   5
For he rolls upon prank to work it in.

5 musk scented object or toy

For having done duty and received blessing he begins to
    consider himself.

For this he performs in ten degrees.

For first he looks upon his forepaws to see if they are clean.

For secondly he kicks up behind to clear away there.   *10*

For thirdly he works it upon stretch with the forepaws
    extended.

For fourthly he sharpens his paws by wood.

For fifthly he washes himself.

For sixthly he rolls upon wash.

For seventhly he fleas himself, that he may not be
    interrupted upon the beat.°   *15*

For eighthly he rubs himself against a post.

For ninthly he looks up for his instructions.

For tenthly he goes in quest of food.

For having considered God and himself he will consider his
    neighbor.

For if he meets another cat he will kiss her in kindness.   *20*

For when he takes his prey he plays with it to give it a chance.

For one mouse in seven escapes by his dallying.

For when his day's work is done his business more properly
    begins.

For he keeps the Lord's watch in the night against the
    adversary.°

For he counteracts the powers of darkness by his electrical
    skin and glaring eyes.   *25*

For he counteracts the Devil, who is death, by brisking about
    the life.

For in his morning orisons he loves the sun and the sun loves
    him.

For he is of the tribe of Tiger.

For the Cherub Cat is a term° of the Angel Tiger.

For he has the subtlety and hissing of a serpent, which in
    goodness he suppresses.   *30*

For he will not do destruction if he is well-fed, neither will he
    spit without provocation.

---

15 beat accustomed path   **24 adversary** i.e., Satan   **29 term** immature version

For he purrs in thankfulness when God tells him he's a good Cat.

For he is an instrument for the children to learn benevolence upon.

For every house is incomplete without him, and a blessing is lacking in the spirit.

For the Lord commanded Moses concerning the cats at the departure of the Children of Israel from Egypt.   35

For every family had one cat at least in the bag.

For the English Cats are the best in Europe.

For he is the cleanest in the use of his forepaws of any quadruped.

For the dexterity of his defense is an instance of the love of God to him exceedingly.

For he is the quickest to his mark of any creature.   40

For he is tenacious of his point.

For he is a mixture of gravity and waggery.

For he knows that God is his Saviour.

For there is nothing sweeter than his peace when at rest.

For there is nothing brisker than his life when in motion.   45

For he is of the Lord's poor, and so indeed is he called by benevolence perpetually—Poor Jeoffry! poor Jeoffry! the rat has bit thy throat.

For I bless the name of the Lord Jesus that Jeoffry is better.

For the divine spirit comes about his body to sustain it in complete cat.

For his tongue is exceeding pure so that it has in purity what it wants in music.

For he is docile and can learn certain things.   50

For he can sit up with gravity, which is patience upon approbation.

For he can fetch and carry, which is patience in employment.

For he can jump over a stick, which is patience upon proof positive.

For he can spraggle upon waggle at the word of command.

For he can jump from an eminence into his master's bosom.   55

For he can catch the cork and toss it again.

For he is hated by the hypocrite and miser.

For the former is afraid of detection.

For the latter refuses the charge.

For he camels his back to bear the first notion of business.   60
For he is good to think on, if a man would express himself
    neatly.
For he made a great figure in Egypt for his signal services.
For he killed the Icneumon° rat, very pernicious by land.
For his ears are so acute that they sting again.
For from this proceeds the passing quickness of his attention.   65
For by stroking of him I have found out electricity.
For I perceived God's light about him both wax and fire.
For the electrical fire is the spiritual substance which God
    sends from heaven to sustain the bodies both of man and
    beast.
For God has blessed him in the variety of his movements.
For, though he cannot fly, he is an excellent clamberer.   70
For his motions upon the face of the earth are more than
    any other quadruped.
For he can tread to all the measures upon the music.
For he can swim for life.
For he can creep.

—ca. 1760

Philip Freneau (1752–1832) was a friend and political ally of Thomas Jefferson. Freneau was a popular journalist and writer whose patriotic verse earned him the moniker "Poet of the Revolution." This reputation has unfortunately overshadowed his considerable talents as a lyric poet whose fine eye for nature prefigures the next generation of American romantics.

Philip Freneau
The Wild Honey Suckle

Fair flower, that dost so comely grow,
Hid in this silent, dull retreat,
Untouched thy honied blossoms blow,
Unseen thy little branches greet:

63 Icneumon resembling the mongoose *(Herpestes ichneumon)*

No roving foot shall crush thee here,   5
No busy hand provoke a tear.°

By Nature's self in white arrayed,
She bade thee shun the vulgar° eye,
And planted here the guardian shade,
And sent soft waters murmuring by;   10
    Thus quietly thy summer goes,
    Thy days declining to repose.

Smit with those charms, that must decay,
I grieve to see your future doom;
They died—nor were those flowers more gay,   15
The flowers that did in Eden bloom;
    Unpitying frosts, and Autumn's power
    Shall leave no vestige of this flower.

From morning suns and evening dews
At first thy little being came: 20
If nothing once, you nothing lose,
For when you die you are the same;
    The space between, is but an hour,
    The frail duration of a flower.

—1788

---

6 provoke a tear i.e., the nectar of the flower   **8 vulgar** common

William Blake (1757–1827) was a poet, painter, engraver, and visionary. Blake does not fit easily into any single category, although his political sympathies link him to the later romantic poets. His first book, Poetical Sketches, *attracted little attention, but his mature works, starting with* Songs of Innocence *and* Songs of Experience, *combine poetry with his own remarkable illustrations and are unique in English literature. Thought mad by many in his own day, Blake anticipated many future directions of both literature and modern psychology.*

William Blake
The Chimney Sweeper

When my mother died I was very young,
And my father sold me while yet my tongue
Could scarcely cry "'weep! 'weep! 'weep! 'weep!"
So your chimneys I sweep & in soot I sleep.

There's little Tom Dacre, who cried when his head   5
That curl'd like a lamb's back, was shav'd, so I said,
"Hush, Tom! never mind it, for when your head's bare,
You know that the soot cannot spoil your white hair."

And so he was quiet, & that very night,
As Tom was a-sleeping, he had such a sight!   10
That thousands of sweepers, Dick, Joe, Ned, & Jack,
Were all of them lock'd up in coffins of black;

And by came an Angel who had a bright key,
And he open'd the coffins & set them all free;
Then down a green plain, leaping, laughing, they run,   15
And wash in a river and shine in the Sun.

Then naked & white, all their bags left behind,
They rise upon clouds, and sport in the wind.
And the Angel told Tom, if he'd be a good boy,
He'd have God for his father, & never want joy.   20

And so Tom awoke; and we rose in the dark,
And got with our bags & our brushes to work.
Tho' the morning was cold, Tom was happy & warm;
So if all do their duty, they need not fear harm.

—*1789*

The Little Black° Boy

My mother bore me in the southern wild,
And I am black, but O! my soul is white;
White as an angel is the English child:
But I am black as if bereav'd of light.

My mother taught me underneath a tree,   5
And sitting down before the heat of day,
She took me on her lap and kissèd me,
And pointing to the east, began to say:

"Look on the rising sun: there God does live,
And gives his light, and gives his heat away;   10
And flowers and trees and beasts and men receive
Comfort in morning, joy in the noon day.

"And we are put on earth a little space,
That we may learn to bear the beams of love,
And these black bodies and this sun-burnt face   15
Is but a cloud, and like a shady grove.

"For when our souls have learn'd the heat to bear,
The cloud will vanish; we shall hear his voice,
Saying: 'Come out from the grove, my love & care,
And round my golden tent like lambs rejoice.'"   20

Thus did my mother say, and kissèd me;
And thus I say to little English boy:
When I from black and he from white cloud free,
And round the tent of God like lambs we joy,

I'll shade him from the heat till he can bear   25
To lean in joy upon our father's knee:
And then I'll stand and stroke his silver hair,
And be like him, and he will then love me.

—*1789*

Black probably Indian rather than African

A Poison Tree

I was angry with my friend:
I told my wrath, my wrath did end.
I was angry with my foe:
I told it not, my wrath did grow.

And I water'd it in fears,   5
Night & morning with my tears;
And I sunnèd it with smiles,
And with soft deceitful wiles.

And it grew both day and night,
Till it bore an apple bright;   10
And my foe beheld it shine,
And he knew that it was mine,

And into my garden stole
When the night had veil'd the pole;
In the morning glad I see   15
My foe outstretch'd beneath the tree.

—1794

The Tyger

Tyger! Tyger! burning bright
In the forests of the night,
What immortal hand or eye
Could frame thy fearful symmetry?

In what distant deeps or skies   5
Burnt the fire of thine eyes?
On what wings dare he aspire?
What the hand, dare seize the fire?

And what shoulder, & what art,
Could twist the sinews of thy heart?   10
And when thy heart began to beat,
What dread hand? & what dread feet?

What the hammer? what the chain?
In what furnace was thy brain?
What the anvil? what dread grasp   15
Dare its deadly terrors clasp?

When the stars threw down their spears,
And water'd heaven with their tears,
Did he smile his work to see?
Did he who made the Lamb make thee?   20

Tyger! Tyger! burning bright
In the forests of the night,
What immortal hand or eye,
Dare frame thy fearful symmetry?

—*1794*

Robert Burns (1759–1796) was a Scot known in his day as the "Ploughman Poet" and was one of the first English poets to put dialect to serious literary purpose. Chiefly known for his realistic depictions of peasant life, he was also an important lyric poet who prefigured many of the later concerns of the romantic era.

Robert Burns
A Red, Red Rose

O my luve's like a red, red rose,
    That's newly sprung in June;
O my luve's like the melodie
    That's sweetly played in tune.

As fair art thou, my bonnie lass,
    So deep in luve am I;   5
And I will luve thee still, my dear,
    Till a' the seas gang° dry.

Till a' the seas gang dry, my dear,
    And the rocks melt wi' the sun;   10

8 gang go

O I will luve thee still, my dear,
    While the sands o' life shall run.

And fare thee weel, my only luve,
    And fare thee weel awhile!
And I will come again, my luve   15
    Though it were ten thousand mile.

                    —*1791*

John Barleycorn

There were three kings into the east,
Three kings both great and high;
And they has sworn a solemn oath
John Barleycorn should die.

They took a plough and plough'd him down,   5
Put clods upon his head;
And they hae sworn a solemn oath
John Barleycorn was dead.

But the cheerful spring came kindly on,
And showers began to fall;   10
John Barleycorn got up again,
And sore surprised them all.

The sultry suns of summer came,
And he grew thick and strong;
His head well armed wi' point'd spears,   15
That no one should him wrong.

The sober autumn enter'd mild,
When he grew wan and pale;
His bending joints and drooping head
Show'd he began to fail.   20

His colour sicken'd more and more
He faded into age;

And then his enemies began
To show their deadly rage.

They've ta'en a weapon long and sharp,   25
And cut him by the knee;
Then tied him fast upon a cart,
Like a rogue for forgery.

They laid him down upon his back,
And cudgell'd him full sore;   30
They hung him up before the storm,
And turn'd him o'er and o'er.

They fill'd up a darksome pit
With water to the brim;
They heaved in John Barleycorn,   35
There let him sink or swim.

They laid him out upon the floor,
To work him further woe;
And still as signs of life appear'd,
They toss'd him to and fro.   40

They wasted o'er a scorching flame
The marrow of his bones;
But a miller used him worst of all
He crushed him 'tween two stones.

And they has ta'en his very heart's blood,   45
And drank it round and round,
And still the more and more they drank,
Their joy did more abound.

John Barleycorn was a hero bold,
Of noble enterprise;   50
For if you do but taste his blood,
'Twill make your courage rise.

'Twill make a man forget his woe;
'Twill heighten all his joy;

'Twill make the widow's heart to sing,   55
Though the tear were in her eye.

Then let us toast John Barleycorn,
Each man a glass in hand;
And may his great posterity
Ne'er fail in old Scotland!   60

—*1786*

William Wordsworth (1770–1850) is generally considered the first of the English romantics. Lyrical Ballads, *the 1798 volume that introduced both his poetry and Samuel Taylor Coleridge's to a wide readership, remains one of the most influential collections of poetry ever published. Wordsworth's preface to the revised edition of 1800 contains the famous Romantic formulation of poetry as the "spontaneous overflow of powerful feelings," a theory exemplified in short lyrics like "I Wandered Lonely as a Cloud" and in longer meditative pieces like "Tintern Abbey" (the title by which "Lines" is commonly known). Wordsworth served as poet laureate from 1843 to his death.*

William Wordsworth
I Wandered Lonely as a Cloud

I wandered lonely as a cloud
That floats on high o'er vales and hills,
When all at once I saw a crowd,
A host, of golden daffodils;
Beside the lake, beneath the trees,   5
Fluttering and dancing in the breeze.

Continuous as the stars that shine
And twinkle on the milky way,
They stretched in never-ending line
Along the margin of a bay: 10
Ten thousand saw I at a glance,
Tossing their heads in sprightly dance.

The waves beside them danced, but they
Outdid the sparkling waves in glee;
A poet could not but be gay,   15
In such a jocund company;
I gazed—and gazed—but little thought
What wealth the show to me had brought:

For oft, when on my couch I lie
In vacant or in pensive mood,   20
They flash upon that inward eye
Which is the bliss of solitude;
And then my heart with pleasure fills,
And dances with the daffodils.

—*1807*

It Is a Beauteous Evening

It is a beauteous evening, calm and free,
The holy time is quiet as a Nun
Breathless with adoration; the broad sun
Is sinking down in its tranquillity;
The gentleness of heaven broods o'er the Sea: 5
Listen! the mighty Being is awake,
And doth with his eternal motion make
A sound like thunder—everlastingly.
Dear Child! dear Girl!° that walkest with me here,
If thou appear untouched by solemn thought,   10
Thy nature is not therefore less divine:
Thou liest in Abraham's bosom° all the year,
And worship'st at the Temple's inner shrine,
God being with thee when we know it not.

—*1807*

---

9 Dear Child! dear Girl! the poet's daughter   **12 Abraham's bosom** where souls rest in Heaven

Lines

Composed a Few Miles Above Tintern Abbey on Revisiting the Banks of the Wye During a Tour. July 13, 1798

Five years have passed; five summers, with the length
Of five long winters! and again I hear
These waters, rolling from their mountain-springs
With a sweet inland murmur.—Once again
Do I behold these steep and lofty cliffs,   5
That on a wild secluded scene impress
Thoughts of more deep seclusion; and connect
The landscape with the quiet of the sky.
The day is come when I again repose
Here, under this dark sycamore, and view   10
These plots of cottage ground, these orchard tufts,
Which at this season, with their unripe fruits,
Are clad in one green hue, and lose themselves
'Mid groves and copses. Once again I see
These hedgerows, hardly hedgerows, little lines   15
Of sportive wood run wild; these pastoral farms,
Green to the very door; and wreaths of smoke
Sent up, in silence, from among the trees!
With some uncertain notice, as might seem
Of vagrant dwellers in the houseless woods,   20
Or of some Hermit's cave, where by his fire
The Hermit sits alone.

                        These beauteous forms,
Through a long absence, have not been to me
As is a landscape to a blind man's eye;
But oft, in lonely rooms, and 'mid the din   25
Of towns and cities, I have owed to them,
In hours of weariness, sensations sweet,
Felt in the blood, and felt along the heart;
And passing even into my purer mind,
With tranquil restoration:—feelings too   30
Of unremembered pleasure; such, perhaps,
As have no slight or trivial influence

On that best portion of a good man's life,
His little, nameless, unremembered, acts
Of kindness and of love. Nor less, I trust,   35
To them I may have owed another gift,
Of aspect more sublime; that blessed mood,
In which the burthen° of the mystery,
In which the heavy and the weary weight
Of all this unintelligible world,   40
Is lightened—that serene and blessed mood,
In which the affections gently lead us on—
Until, the breath of this corporeal frame
And even the motion of our human blood
Almost suspended, we are laid asleep   45
In body, and become a living soul;
While with an eye made quiet by the power
Of harmony, and the deep power of joy,
We see into the life of things.

                                        If this
Be but a vain belief, yet, oh! how oft—   50
In darkness and amid the many shapes
Of joyless daylight; when the fretful stir
Unprofitable, and the fever of the world,
Have hung upon the beatings of my heart—
How oft, in spirit, have I turned to thee,   55
O sylvan Wye! Thou wanderer through the woods,
How often has my spirit turned to thee!

    And now, with gleams of half-extinguished thought,
With many recognitions dim and faint,
And somewhat of a sad perplexity,   60
The picture of the mind revives again:
While here I stand, not only with the sense
Of present pleasure, but with pleasing thoughts
That in this moment there is life and food
For future years. And so I dare to hope,   65
Though changed, no doubt, from what I was when first

38 burthen burden

I came among these hills; when like a roe
I bounded o'er the mountains, by the sides
Of the deep rivers, and the lonely streams,
Wherever nature led—more like a man   70
Flying from something that he dreads than one
Who sought the thing he loved. For nature then
(The coarser pleasures of my boyish days,
And their glad animal movements all gone by)
To me was all in all.—I cannot paint   75
What then I was. The sounding cataract
Haunted me like a passion: the tall rock,
The mountain, and the deep and gloomy wood,
Their colours and their forms, were then to me
An appetite: a feeling and a love,   80
That had no need of a remoter charm,
By thought supplied, or any interest
Unborrowed from the eye.—That time is past,
And all its aching joys are now no more,
And all its dizzy raptures. Not for this   85
Faint I, nor mourn nor murmur: other gifts
Have followed; for such loss, I would believe,
Abundant recompense. For I have learned
To look on nature, not as in the hour
Of thoughtless youth; but hearing oftentimes   90
The still, sad music of humanity,
Nor harsh nor grating, though of ample power
To chasten and subdue. And I have felt
A presence that disturbs me with the joy
Of elevated thoughts; a sense sublime   95
Of something far more deeply interfused,
Whose dwelling is the light of setting suns,
And the round ocean and the living air,
And the blue sky, and in the mind of man:
A motion and a spirit, that impels   100
All thinking things, all objects of all thought,
And rolls through all things. Therefore am I still
A lover of the meadows and the woods,
And mountains; and of all that we behold

From this green earth; of all the mighty world   *105*
Of eye, and ear—both what they half create,
And what perceive; well pleased to recognize
In nature and the language of the sense
The anchor of my purest thoughts, the nurse,
The guide, the guardian of my heart, and soul   *110*
Of all my moral being.

                                        Nor, perchance,
If I were not thus taught, should I the more
Suffer my genial spirits° to decay:
For thou art with me, here, upon the banks
Of this fair river; thou, my dearest Friend,°   *115*
My dear, dear Friend; and in thy voice I catch
The language of my former heart, and read
My former pleasures in the shooting lights
Of thy wild eyes. Oh! yet a little while
May I behold in thee what I was once,   *120*
My dear, dear Sister! And this prayer I make,
Knowing that Nature never did betray
The heart that loved her; 'tis her privilege,
Through all the years of this our life, to lead
From joy to joy: for she can so inform   *125*
The mind that is within us, so impress
With quietness and beauty, and so feed
With lofty thoughts, that neither evil tongues,
Rash judgments, nor the sneers of selfish men,
Nor greetings where no kindness is, nor all   *130*
The dreary intercourse of daily life,
Shall e'er prevail against us, or disturb
Our cheerful faith, that all which we behold
Is full of blessings. Therefore let the moon
Shine on thee in thy solitary walk;   *135*
And let the misty mountain winds be free
To blow against thee: and, in after years,
When these wild ecstasies shall be matured

113 genial spirits natural abilities   **115 Friend** the poet's sister Dorothy (1771–1855)

Into a sober pleasure; when thy mind 140
Shall be a mansion for all lovely forms,
Thy memory be as a dwelling place
For all sweet sounds and harmonies; oh! then,
If solitude, or fear, or pain, or grief,
Should be thy portion, with what healing thoughts 145
Of tender joy wilt thou remember me,
And these my exhortations! Nor, perchance—
If I should be, where I no more can hear
Thy voice, nor catch from thy wild eyes these gleams
Of past existence—wilt thou then forget 150
That on the banks of this delightful stream
We stood together; and that I, so long
A worshipper of Nature, hither came,
Unwearied in that service: rather say
With warmer love,—oh! with far deeper zeal 155
Of holier love. Nor wilt thou then forget,
That after many wanderings, many years
Of absence, these steep woods and lofty cliffs,
And this green pastoral landscape, were to me
More dear, both for themselves and for thy sake!

—*1798*

Nuns Fret Not at Their Convent's Narrow Room

Nuns fret not at their convent's narrow room;
And hermits are contented with their cells;
And students with their pensive citadels;
Maids at the wheel, the weaver at his loom,
Sit blithe and happy; bees that soar for bloom, 5
High as the highest Peak of Furness-fells,°
Will murmur by the hour in foxglove bells:
In truth the prison, into which we doom
Ourselves, no prison is: and hence for me,

6 **Furness-fells** mountains located in the English Lake District

In sundry moods, 'twas pastime to be bound   *10*
Within the Sonnet's scanty plot of ground;
Pleased if some Souls (for such there needs must be)
Who have felt the weight of too much liberty,
Should find brief solace there, as I have found.

—1807

Ode

Intimations of Immortality
from Recollections of Early Childhood

The Child is Father of the Man;
And I could wish my days to be
Bound each to each by natural piety.°

1

There was a time when meadow, grove, and stream,
The earth, and every common sight,
    To me did seem
    Appareled in celestial light,
The glory and the freshness of a dream.
It is not now as it hath been of yore;—   *5*
    Turn wheresoe'er I may,
    By night or day,
The things which I have seen I now can see no more.

2

    The Rainbow comes and goes,   *10*
    And lovely is the Rose,
    The Moon doth with delight
Look round her when the heavens are bare,
    Waters on a starry night
    Are beautiful and fair;   *15*
    The sunshine is a glorious birth;
    But yet I know, where'er I go,
That there hath past away a glory from the earth.

The Child . . . natural piety last three lines of the poet's "My Heart Leaps Up"

3

Now, while the birds thus sing a joyous song,
    And while the young lambs bound 20
      As to the tabor's° sound,
To me alone there came a thought of grief:
A timely utterance gave that thought relief,
      And I again am strong:
The cataracts blow their trumpets from the steep; 25
No more shall grief of mine the season wrong;
I hear the Echoes through the mountains throng,
The Winds come to me from the fields of sleep,
      And all the earth is gay;
        Land and sea 30
      Give themselves up to jollity,
      And with the heart of May
      Doth every Beast keep holiday;—
        Thou Child of Joy,
Shout round me, let me hear thy shouts, thou happy
    Shepherd-boy! 35

4

Ye blessèd Creatures, I have heard the call
    Ye to each other make; I see
The heavens laugh with you in your jubilee;
    My heart is at your festival, 40
    My head hath its coronal,°
The fulness of your bliss, I feel—I feel it all.
      Oh evil day! if I were sullen
      While Earth herself is adorning,
        This sweet May-morning, 45
      And the Children are culling
        On every side,
      In a thousand valleys far and wide,
      Fresh flowers; while the sun shines warm,
And the Babe leaps up on his Mother's arm:— 50

---

21 tabor's small drum's   **41 coronal** floral crown

I hear, I hear, with joy I hear!
 —But there's a Tree, of many, one,
A single Field which I have looked upon,
Both of them speak of something that is gone:
  The Pansy at my feet
  Doth the same tale repeat:
Whither is fled the visionary gleam?
Where is it now, the glory and the dream?

  5

Our birth is but a sleep and a forgetting:
The Soul that rises with us, our life's Star,
  Hath had elsewhere its setting,
   And cometh from afar:
  Not in entire forgetfulness,
  And not in utter nakedness,
But trailing clouds of glory do we come
  From God, who is our home:
Heaven lies about us in our infancy!
Shades of the prison-house begin to close
  Upon the growing Boy,
But he beholds the light, and whence it flows,
  He sees it in his joy;
The Youth, who daily farther from the east
  Must travel, still is Nature's Priest,
  And by the vision splendid
  Is on his way attended;
At length the Man perceives it die away,
And fade into the light of common day.

  6

Earth fills her lap with pleasures of her own;
Yearnings she hath in her own natural kind,
And, even with something of a Mother's mind,
  And no unworthy aim,
  The homely Nurse doth all she can
To make her Foster-child, her Inmate Man,
  Forget the glories he hath known,

55

60

65

70

75

80

7

Behold the Child among his new-born blisses,
A six years' Darling of a pigmy size!
See where 'mid work of his own hand he lies,
Fretted° by sallies of his mother's kisses,
With light upon him from his father's eyes!   90
See, at his feet, some little plan or chart,
Some fragment from his dream of human life,
Shaped by himself with newly-learnèd art;
  A wedding or a festival,
  A mourning or a funeral;   95
   And this hath now his heart,
  And unto this he frames his song:
  Then will he fit his tongue
To dialogues of business, love, or strife;
  But it will not be long   100
  Ere this be thrown aside,
  And with new joy and pride
The little Actor cons another part;
Filling from time to time his "humorous stage"°
With all the Persons, down to palsied Age,   105
That Life brings with her in her equipage;
  As if his whole vocation
  Were endless imitation.

8

Thou whose exterior semblance doth belie
  Thy Soul's immensity;   110
Thou best Philosopher, who yet dost keep
Thy heritage, thou Eye among the blind,
That, deaf and silent, read'st the eternal deep,
Haunted for ever by the eternal mind,—
  Mighty Prophet! Seer blest!   115
  On whom those truths do rest,
Which we are toiling all our lives to find,
In darkness lost, the darkness of the grave;

---

89 fretted annoyed or marked **104 "humorous stage"** phrase from poet Samuel Daniel
(1563–1619)

Thou, over whom thy Immortality
Broods like the Day, a Master o'er a Slave,   *120*
A Presence which is not to be put by;
Thou little Child, yet glorious in the might
Of heaven-born freedom on thy being's height,
Why with such earnest pains dost thou provoke
The years to bring the inevitable yoke,   *125*
Thus blindly with thy blessedness at strife?
Full soon thy Soul shall have her earthly freight,
And custom lie upon thee with a weight,
Heavy as frost, and deep almost as life!

9

   O joy! that in our embers   *130*
   Is something that doth live,
   That nature yet remembers
   What was so fugitive!
The thought of our past years in me doth breed
Perpetual benediction: not indeed   *135*
For that which is most worthy to be blest;
Delight and liberty, the simple creed
Of Childhood, whether busy or at rest,
With new-fledged hope still fluttering in his breast:—
     Not for these I raise
     The song of thanks and praise;   *140*
   But for those obstinate questionings
   Of sense and outward things,
   Fallings from us, vanishings;
   Blank misgivings of a Creature   *145*
Moving about in worlds not realized,
High instincts before which our mortal Nature
Did tremble like a guilty Thing surprised:
     But for those first affections,
     Those shadowy recollections,   *150*
   Which, be they what they may,
Are yet the fountain light of all our day,
Are yet a master light of all our seeing;
   Uphold us, cherish, and have power to make
Our noisy years seem moments in the being   *155*

Of the eternal Silence: truths that wake,
      To perish never;
Which neither listlessness, nor mad endeavour,
      Nor Man nor Boy,
Nor all that is at enmity with joy,   160
Can utterly abolish or destroy!
   Hence in a season of calm weather
      Though inland far we be,
Our Souls have sight of that immortal sea
      Which brought us hither,   165
   Can in a moment travel thither,
And see the Children sport upon the shore,
And hear the mighty waters rolling evermore.

    10

Then sing, ye Birds, sing, sing a joyous song!
       And let the young Lambs bound   170
       As to the tabor's sound!
We in thought will join your throng,
      Ye that pipe and ye that play,
      Ye that through your hearts to-day
      Feel the gladness of the May!   175
What though the radiance which was once so bright
Be now for ever taken from my sight,
      Though nothing can bring back the hour
Of splendour in the grass, of glory in the flower;
      We will grieve not, rather find   180
      Strength in what remains behind;
      In the primal sympathy
      Which having been must ever be;
      In the soothing thoughts that spring
      Out of human suffering;   185
      In the faith that looks through death,
In years that bring the philosophic mind.

    11

And O, ye Fountains, Meadows, Hills, and Groves,
Forbode not any severing of our loves!

Yet in my heart of hearts I feel your might; 190
I only have relinquished one delight
To live beneath your more habitual sway.
I love the Brooks which down their channels fret,
Even more than when I tripped lightly as they;
The innocent brightness of a new-born Day 195
    Is lovely yet;
The Clouds that gather round the setting sun
Do take a sober colouring from an eye
That hath kept watch o'er man's mortality;
Another race hath been, and other palms are won. 200
Thanks to the human heart by which we live,
Thanks to its tenderness, its joys, and fears,
To me the meanest° flower that blows can give
Thoughts that do often lie too deep for tears.

—*1807*

Samuel Taylor Coleridge (1772–1834), *inspired but erratic, did his best work, like Wordsworth, during the great first decade of their friendship, the period that produced* Lyrical Ballads. *Coleridge's later life is a tragic tale of financial and marital problems, unfinished projects, and a ruinous addiction to opium. A brilliant critic, Coleridge lectured on Shakespeare and other writers and wrote the* Biographia Literaria, *perhaps the greatest literary autobiography ever written.*

Samuel Taylor Coleridge
Frost at Midnight

The Frost performs its secret ministry,
Unhelped by any wind. The owlet's cry
Came loud—and hark, again! loud as before.
The inmates of my cottage, all at rest,
Have left me to that solitude, which suits 5
Abstruser musings: save that at my side
My cradled infant° slumbers peacefully.

203 meanest least significant
7 My cradled infant the poet's son Hartley (1796–1849)

'Tis calm indeed! so calm, that it disturbs
And vexes meditation, with its strange
And extreme silentness. Sea, hill, and wood,   10
This populous village! Sea, and hill, and wood,
With all the numberless goings-on of life,
Inaudible as dreams! the thin blue flame
Lies on my low-burnt fire, and quivers not;
Only that film,° which fluttered on the grate,   15
Still flutters there, the sole unquiet thing.
Methinks its motion in this hush of nature
Gives it dim sympathies with me who live,
Making it a companionable form,
Whose puny flaps and freaks the idling Spirit   20
By its own moods interprets, everywhere
Echo or mirror seeking of itself,
And makes a toy of Thought.

                But O! how oft,
How oft, at school, with most believing mind,
Presageful,° have I gazed upon the bars,   25
To watch that fluttering *stranger!* and as oft
With unclosed lids, already had I dreamt
Of my sweet birthplace, and the old church tower,
Whose bells, the poor man's only music, rang
From morn to evening, all the hot Fair-day,   30
So sweetly, that they stirred and haunted me
With a wild pleasure, falling on mine ear
Most like articulate sounds of things to come!
So gazed I, till the soothing things, I dreamt,
Lulled me to sleep, and sleep prolonged my dreams!   35
And so I brooded all the following morn,
Awed by the stern preceptor's° face, mine eye
Fixed with mock study on my swimming book:
Save if the door half opened, and I snatched
A hasty glance, and still my heart leaped up,   40
For still I hoped to see the *stranger's* face,

---

15 film a piece of ash   **25 Presageful** with hints of the future   **37 preceptor** teacher

Townsman, or aunt, or sister more beloved,
My playmate when we both were clothed alike!

    Dear Babe, that sleepest cradled by my side,
Whose gentle breathings, heard in this deep calm,   45
Fill up the interspersèd vacancies
And momentary pauses of the thought!
My babe so beautiful! it thrills my heart
With tender gladness, thus to look at thee,
And think that thou shalt learn far other lore,   50
And in far other scenes! For I was reared
In the great city, pent 'mid cloisters dim,
And saw nought lovely but the sky and stars.
But *thou*, my babe! shalt wander like a breeze
By lakes and sandy shores, beneath the crags   55
Of ancient mountain, and beneath the clouds,
Which image in their bulk both lakes and shores
And mountain crags: so shalt thou see and hear
The lovely shapes and sounds intelligible
Of that eternal language, which thy God   60
Utters, who from eternity doth teach
Himself in all, and all things in himself.
Great universal Teacher! he shall mold
Thy spirit, and by giving make it ask.

    Therefore all seasons shall be sweet to thee,   65
Whether the summer clothe the general earth
With greenness, or the redbreast sit and sing
Betwixt the tufts of snow on the bare branch
Of mossy apple tree, while the nigh thatch
Smokes in the sun-thaw; whether the eave-drops fall   70
Heard only in the trances of the blast,
Or if the secret ministry of frost
Shall hang them up in silent icicles,
Quietly shining to the quiet Moon.

                                                —1798

Kubla Khan°

OR A VISION IN A DREAM,° A FRAGMENT

In Xanadu did Kubla Khan
A stately pleasure-dome decree:
Where Alph, the sacred river, ran
Through caverns measureless to man
    Down to a sunless sea.   5
So twice five miles of fertile ground
With walls and towers were girdled round:
And there were gardens bright with sinuous rills,
Where blossomed many an incense-bearing tree;
And here were forests ancient as the hills,   10
Enfolding sunny spots of greenery.

But oh! that deep romantic chasm which slanted
Down the green hill athwart a cedarn cover!
A savage place! as holy and enchanted
As e'er beneath a waning moon was haunted   15
By woman wailing for her demon lover!
And from this chasm, with ceaseless turmoil seething,
As if this earth in fast thick pants were breathing,
A mighty fountain momently was forced:
Amid whose swift half-intermitted burst   20
Huge fragments vaulted like rebounding hail,
Or chaffy grain beneath the thresher's flail:
And 'mid these dancing rocks at once and ever
It flung up momently the sacred river.
Five miles meandering with a mazy motion   25
Through wood and dale the sacred river ran,
Then reached the caverns measureless to man,

Kubla Khan ruler of China (1216–1294) **vision in a dream** Coleridge's own account tells how he took opium for an illness and slept for three hours, during which time he envisioned a complete poem of some 300 lines. When he awoke, he began to write down the details of his dream. "At this moment he was unfortunately called out by a person on business from Porlock, and detained by him above an hour, and on his return to the room found, to his no small surprise and mortification, that though he still retained some vague and dim recollection of the general purport of the vision, yet, with the exception of some eight or ten scattered lines and images on the surface of a stream into which a stone has been cast . . ." [Coleridge's note]

And sank in tumult to a lifeless ocean:
And 'mid this tumult Kubla heard from far
Ancestral voices prophesying war!

30

    The shadow of the dome of pleasure
    Floated midway on the waves;
    Where was heard the mingled measure
    From the fountain and the caves.
It was a miracle of rare device,

35

A sunny pleasure-dome with caves of ice!

    A damsel with a dulcimer
    In a vision once I saw:
    It was an Abyssinian maid,
    And on her dulcimer she played,

40

    Singing of Mount Abora.
    Could I revive within me
    Her symphony and song,
    To such a deep delight 'twould win me,
That with music loud and long,

45

I would build that dome in air,
That sunny dome! those caves of ice!
And all who heard should see them there,
And all should cry, Beware! Beware!
His flashing eyes, his floating hair!

50

Weave a circle round him thrice,
And close your eyes with holy dread,
For he on honey-dew hath fed,
And drunk the milk of Paradise.

—1797–98

Work Without Hope

Lines Composed 21st February 1825

All Nature seems at work. Slugs leave their lair—
The bees are stirring—birds are on the wing—
And Winter slumbering in the open air

Wears on his smiling face a dream of Spring!
And I the while, the sole unbusy thing,   5
Nor honey make, nor pair, nor build, nor sing.

Yet well I ken° the banks where amaranths° blow,
Have traced the fount whence streams of nectar flow.
Bloom, O ye amaranths! bloom for whom ye may,
For me ye bloom not! Glide, rich streams, away!   10
With lips unbrightened, wreathless brow, I stroll:
And would you learn the spells that drowse my soul?
Work without Hope draws° nectar in a sieve,
And Hope without an object cannot live.

—*1828*

George Gordon, Lord Byron (1788–1824) attained flamboyant celebrity status, leading an unconventional lifestyle that contributed to his notoriety. Byron was the most widely read of all the English romantic poets, but his verse romances and mock-epic poems like Don Juan *have not proved as popular in this century. An English aristocrat who was committed to revolutionary ideals, Byron died while lending military assistance to the cause of Greek freedom.*

George Gordon, Lord Byron
Stanzas

When A Man Hath No Freedom To Fight For At Home

When a man hath no freedom to fight for at home,
    Let him combat for that of his neighbors;
Let him think of the glories of Greece and of Rome,
    And get knocked on his head for his labors.

To do good to mankind is the chivalrous plan,   5
    And is always as nobly requited:
Then battle for freedom wherever you can,
    And, if not shot or hanged, you'll get knighted.

—*1824*

---

7 ken know   **amaranths** legendary flowers that never fade   **13 draws** dips

When We Two Parted

When we two parted
   In silence and tears,
Half broken-hearted
   To sever for years,
Pale grew thy cheek and cold,   *5*
   Colder thy kiss;
Truly that hour foretold
   Sorrow to this.

The dew of the morning
   Sunk chill on my brow—
It felt like the warning   *10*
   Of what I feel now.
Thy vows are all broken,
   And light is thy fame;
I hear thy name spoken,
   And share in its shame.   *15*

They name thee before me,
   A knell to mine ear;
A shudder comes o'er me—
   Why wert thou so dear?
They know not I knew thee,   *20*
   Who knew thee too well:—
Long, long shall I rue thee,
   Too deeply to tell.

In secret we met—
   In silence I grieve   *25*
That thy heart could forget,
   Thy spirit deceive.
If I should meet thee
   After long years,
How should I greet thee?—   *30*
   With silence and tears.

—1813

Percy Bysshe Shelley (1792–1822), like his friend Byron, has not found as much favor in recent eras as the other English romantics, although his political liberalism anticipates many currents of our own day. Perhaps his unbridled emotionalism is sometimes too intense for modern readers. His wife, Mary Wollstonecraft Shelley, will be remembered as the author of the classic horror novel Frankenstein.

Percy Bysshe Shelley
Ode to the West Wind

1

O wild West Wind, thou breath of Autumn's being,
Thou, from whose unseen presence the leaves dead
Are driven, like ghosts from an enchanter fleeing,

Yellow, and black, and pale, and hectic red,
Pestilence-stricken multitudes: O thou,   5
Who chariotest to their dark wintry bed

The wingèd seeds, where they lie cold and low,
Each like a corpse within its grave, until
Thine azure sister of the Spring° shall blow

Her clarion o'er the dreaming earth, and fill   10
(Driving sweet buds like flocks to feed in air)
With living hues and odors plain and hill:

Wild Spirit, which art moving everywhere;
Destroyer and preserver; hear, oh, hear!

2

Thou on whose stream, mid the steep sky's commotion,   15
Loose clouds like earth's decaying leaves are shed,
Shook from the tangled boughs of Heaven and Ocean,

Angels of rain and lightning: there are spread
On the blue surface of thine aëry surge,
Like the bright hair uplifted from the head   20

9 azure sister of the Spring i.e., the South Wind

Of some fierce Mænad,° even from the dim verge
Of the horizon to the zenith's height,
The locks of the approaching storm. Thou dirge

Of the dying year, to which this closing night
Will be the dome of a vast sepulcher,   25
Vaulted with all thy congregated might

Of vapors, from whose solid atmosphere
Black rain, and fire, and hail will burst: oh, hear!

3

Thou who didst waken from his summer dreams
The blue Mediterranean, where he lay,   30
Lulled by the coil of his crystàlline streams,

Beside a pumice isle in Baiae's bay,°
And saw in sleep old palaces and towers
Quivering within the wave's intenser day,

All overgrown with azure moss and flowers   35
So sweet, the sense faints picturing them! Thou
For whose path the Atlantic's level powers

Cleave themselves into chasms, while far below
The sea-blooms and the oozy woods which wear
The sapless foliage of the ocean, know   40

Thy voice, and suddenly grow gray with fear,
And tremble and despoil themselves: oh, hear!

4

If I were a dead leaf thou mightest bear;
If I were a swift cloud to fly with thee;
A wave to pant beneath thy power, and share   45

The impulse of thy strength, only less free
Than thou, O uncontrollable! If even
I were as in my boyhood, and could be

---

21 Mænad female worshipper of Bacchus, god of wine   **32 Baiae's bay** near Naples

The comrade of thy wanderings over Heaven,
As then, when to outstrip thy skyey speed   50
Scarce seemed a vision; I would ne'er have striven

As thus with thee in prayer in my sore need.
Oh, lift me as a wave, a leaf, a cloud!
I fall upon the thorns of life! I bleed!

A heavy weight of hours has chained and bowed   55
One too like thee: tameless, and swift, and proud.

    5

Make me thy lyre, even as the forest is:
What if my leaves are falling like its own!
The tumult of thy mighty harmonies

Will take from both a deep, autumnal tone,   60
Sweet though in sadness. Be thou, Spirit fierce,
My spirit! Be thou me, impetuous one!

Drive my dead thoughts over the universe
Like withered leaves to quicken a new birth!
And, by the incantation of this verse,   65

Scatter, as from an unextinguished hearth
Ashes and sparks, my words among mankind!
Be through my lips to unawakened earth

The trumpet of a prophecy! O Wind,
If Winter comes, can Spring be far behind?   70
                                                      —*1820*

Ozymandias°

I met a traveler from an antique land
Who said: Two vast and trunkless legs of stone
Stand in the desert. . . . Near them, on the sand,
Half sunk, a shattered visage lies, whose frown,

Ozymandias Ramses II of Egypt (c. 1250 B.C.)

And wrinkled lip, and sneer of cold command, 5
Tell that its sculptor well those passions read
Which yet survive, stamped on these lifeless things,
The hand that mocked them, and the heart that fed:
And on the pedestal these words appear:
"My name is Ozymandias, king of kings: 10
Look on my works, ye Mighty, and despair!"
Nothing beside remains. Round the decay
Of that colossal wreck, boundless and bare
The lone and level sands stretch far away.

—*1818*

William Cullen Bryant (1794–1878) was often called "the American Wordsworth" for his adaptation of the techniques of English romanticism to the American landscape. Bryant's observations of nature have rarely been equaled.

William Cullen Bryant
To the Fringed Gentian

Thou blossom bright with autumn dew,
And colored with the heaven's own blue,
That openest when the quiet light
Succeeds the keen and frosty night—

Thou comest not when violets lean 5
O'er wandering brooks and springs unseen,
Or columbines, in purple dressed,
Nod o'er the ground-bird's hidden nest.

Thou waitest late and com'st alone,
When woods are bare and birds are flown, 10
And frosts and shortening days portend
The aged year is near his end.

Then doth thy sweet and quiet eye
Look through its fringes to the sky,
Blue—blue—as if that sky let fall 15
A flower from its cerulean wall.

I would that thus, when I shall see
The hour of death draw near to me,
Hope, blossoming within my heart,
May look to heaven as I depart.   20

—*1829*

John Keats (1795–1821) is now perhaps the most admired of all the major romantics. Certainly his tragic death from tuberculosis in his twenties gives poignancy to thoughts of the doomed young poet writing feverishly in a futile race against time; "Here lies one whose name was writ in water" are the words he chose for his own epitaph. Many of Keats's poems are concerned with glimpses of the eternal, whether a translation of an ancient epic poem or a pristine artifact of a vanished civilization.

John Keats
La Belle Dame sans Merci°

O what can ail thee, Knight at arms,
    Alone and palely loitering?
The sedge has withered from the Lake
    And no birds sing!

O what can ail thee, Knight at arms,   5
    So haggard, and so woebegone?
The squirrel's granary is full
    And the harvest's done.

I see a lily on thy brow
    With anguish moist and fever dew,   10
And on thy cheeks a fading rose
    Fast withereth too.

"I met a Lady in the Meads,
    Full beautiful, a faery's child,
Her hair was long, her foot was light,   15
    And her eyes were wild.

La Belle Dame sans Merci "the beautiful lady without pity"

"I made a Garland for her head,
    And bracelets too, and fragrant Zone;°
She looked at me as she did love
    And made sweet moan.   *20*

"I set her on my pacing steed
    And nothing else saw all day long,
For sidelong would she bend and sing
    A faery's song.

"She found me roots of relish sweet,   *25*
    And honey wild, and manna dew,
And sure in language strange she said
    'I love thee true.'

"She took me to her elfin grot°
    And there she wept and sighed full sore,   *30*
And there I shut her wild wild eyes
    With kisses four.

"And there she lullèd me asleep,
    And there I dreamed, Ah Woe betide!
The latest dream I ever dreamt   *35*
    On the cold hill side.

"I saw pale Kings, and Princes too,
    Pale warriors, death-pale were they all;
They cried, 'La belle Dame sans merci
    Hath thee in thrall!'   *40*

"I saw their starved lips in the gloam
    With horrid warning gapèd wide,
And I awoke, and found me here
    On the cold hill's side.

"And this is why I sojourn here   *45*
    Alone and palely loitering;
Though the sedge is withered from the Lake,
    And no birds sing."

—*1819*

18 **Zone** belt   29 **grot** cave

Ode on a Grecian Urn

1

Thou still unravished bride of quietness,
    Thou foster-child of silence and slow time,
Sylvan historian, who canst thus express
    A flowery tale more sweetly than our rhyme:
What leaf-fringed legend haunts about thy shape   *5*
      Of deities or mortals, or of both,
          In Tempe or the dales of Arcady?°
      What men or gods are these? What maidens loath?°
What mad pursuit? What struggle to escape?
          What pipes and timbrels?° What wild ecstasy?   *10*

2

Heard melodies are sweet, but those unheard
    Are sweeter; therefore, ye soft pipes, play on;
Not to the sensual ear, but, more endeared,
    Pipe to the spirit ditties of no tone:
Fair youth, beneath the trees, thou canst not leave   *15*
      Thy song, nor ever can those trees be bare;
          Bold Lover, never, never canst thou kiss,
Though winning near the goal—yet, do not grieve;
          She cannot fade, though thou hast not thy bliss,
      Forever wilt thou love, and she be fair!   *20*

3

Ah, happy, happy boughs! that cannot shed
    Your leaves, nor ever bid the Spring adieu;
And, happy melodist, unwearièd,
    Forever piping songs forever new;
More happy love! more happy, happy love!   *25*
      Forever warm and still to be enjoyed,
          Forever panting, and forever young;
All breathing human passion far above,

---

7 Tempe or the dales of Arcady idealized Greek settings   **8 loath** reluctant   **10 timbrels** tambourines

That leaves a heart high-sorrowful and cloyed,
　　A burning forehead, and a parching tongue. 　　　　*30*

4

Who are these coming to the sacrifice?
　　To what green altar, O mysterious priest,
Lead'st thou that heifer lowing at the skies,
　　And all her silken flanks with garlands dressed?
What little town by river or sea shore, 　　　　　　*35*
　　Or mountain-built with peaceful citadel,
　　　Is emptied of this folk, this pious morn?
And, little town, thy streets forevermore
　　Will silent be; and not a soul to tell
　　　Why thou art desolate, can e'er return. 　　　*40*

5

O Attic° shape! Fair attitude! with brede°
　　Of marble men and maidens overwrought,
With forest branches and the trodden weed;
　　Thou, silent form, dost tease us out of thought
As doth eternity: Cold Pastoral! 　　　　　　　*45*
　　When old age shall this generation waste,
　　　Thou shalt remain, in midst of other woe
　　Than ours, a friend to man, to whom thou say'st,
"Beauty is truth, truth beauty,"—that is all
　　Ye know on earth, and all ye need to know. 　*50*

　　　　　　　　　　　　　　　　　　—1819

Ode to a Nightingale

1

My heart aches, and a drowsy numbness pains
　　My sense, as though of hemlock° I had drunk,
Or emptied some dull opiate to the drains

---

41 Attic Greek　**brede** ornamental pattern
2 hemlock a deadly poison

One minute past, and Lethe-wards° had sunk.
'Tis not through envy of thy happy lot,   5
 But being too happy in thine happiness—
  That thou, light-wingèd Dryad° of the trees,
   In some melodious plot
 Of beechen green, and shadows numberless,
  Singest of summer in full-throated ease.   10

  2

O, for a draught of vintage! that hath been
 Cooled a long age in the deep-delvèd earth,
Tasting of Flora° and the country green,
 Dance, and Provençal° song, and sunburnt mirth!
O for a beaker full of the warm South,   15
 Full of the true, the blushful Hippocrene,°
  With beaded bubbles winking at the brim,
   And purple-stainèd mouth;
 That I might drink, and leave the world unseen,
  And with thee fade away into the forest dim: 20

  3

Fade far away, dissolve, and quite forget
 What thou among the leaves hast never known,
The weariness, the fever, and the fret
 Here, where men sit and hear each other groan;
Where palsy shakes a few, sad, last gray hairs,   25
 Where youth grows pale, and specter-thin, and dies;
  Where but to think is to be full of sorrow
   And leaden-eyed despairs,
 Where Beauty cannot keep her lustrous eyes,
  Or new Love pine at them beyond tomorrow.   30

  4

Away! away! for I will fly to thee,
 Not charioted by Bacchus° and his pards,°

---

4 **Lethe-wards** toward the waters of forgetfulness 7 **Dryad** tree nymph 13 **Flora** Roman goddess
of spring 14 **Provençal** of Provence, in South of France 16 **Hippocrene** fountain of the Muses
32 **Bacchus** Roman god of wine **pards** leopards

But on the viewless wings of Poesy,°
    Though the dull brain perplexes and retards:
Already with thee! tender is the night,   *35*
    And haply the Queen-Moon is on her throne,
        Clustered around by all her starry Fays;°
           But here there is no light,
    Save what from heaven is with the breezes blown
        Through verdurous glooms and winding mossy ways.   *40*

    5

I cannot see what flowers are at my feet,
    Nor what soft incense hangs upon the boughs,
But, in embalmèd darkness, guess each sweet
    Wherewith the seasonable month endows
The grass, the thicket, and the fruit-tree wild;   *45*
    White hawthorn, and the pastoral eglantine;
        Fast fading violets covered up in leaves;
           And mid-May's eldest child,
    The coming musk-rose, full of dewy wine,
        The murmurous haunt of flies on summer eves.   *50*

    6

Darkling° I listen; and for many a time
    I have been half in love with easeful Death,
Called him soft names in many a musèd rhyme,
    To take into the air my quiet breath;
Now more than ever seems it rich to die,   *55*
    To cease upon the midnight with no pain,
        While thou art pouring forth thy soul abroad
           In such an ecstasy!
    Still wouldst thou sing, and I have ears in vain—
        To thy high requiem become a sod.   *60*

    7

Thou wast not born for death, immortal Bird!
    No hungry generations tread thee down;

33 Poesy poetry   **37 Fays** fairies   **51 Darkling** in the dark

The voice I hear this passing night was heard
   In ancient days by emperor and clown;
Perhaps the selfsame song that found a path   65
    Through the sad heart of Ruth, when, sick for home,
      She stood in tears amid the alien corn;°
        The same that ofttimes hath
   Charmed magic casements, opening on the foam
     Of perilous seas, in faery lands forlorn.   70

    8

Forlorn! the very word is like a bell
   To toll me back from thee to my sole self!
Adieu! the fancy cannot cheat so well
   As she is famed to do, deceiving elf.
Adieu! adieu! thy plaintive anthem fades   75
    Past the near meadows, over the still stream,
     Up the hill side; and now 'tis buried deep
      In the next valley-glades:
Was it a vision, or a waking dream?
    Fled is that music:—Do I wake or sleep?   80
                          —*1819*

On First Looking into Chapman's Homer°

Much have I traveled in the realms of gold,
   And many goodly states and kingdoms seen;
   Round many western islands have I been
Which bards in fealty to Apollo° hold.
Oft of one wide expanse had I been told   5
    That deep-browed Homer ruled as his demesne;
    Yet did I never breathe its pure serene

66-67 Ruth . . . alien corn in the Old Testament she is a stranger working in the grain fields of Judah
Chapman's Homer translation of the *Iliad* and *Odyssey* by George Chapman (1559–1634)
4 Apollo here, the god of poetry

Till I heard Chapman speak out loud and bold:
Then felt I like some watcher of the skies
    When a new planet swims into his ken;   10
Or like stout Cortez° when with eagle eyes
    He stared at the Pacific—and all his men
Looked at each other with a wild surmise—
    Silent, upon a peak in Darien.°

—1816

When I Have Fears

When I have fears that I may cease to be
    Before my pen has gleaned my teeming brain,
Before high-pilèd books, in charact'ry,°
    Hold like rich garners the full-ripened grain;
When I behold, upon the night's starred face,   5
    Huge cloudy symbols of a high romance,
And think that I may never live to trace
    Their shadows, with the magic hand of chance;
And when I feel, fair creature of an hour,
    That I shall never look upon thee more,   10
Never have relish in the faery power
    Of unreflecting love!—then on the shore
Of the wide world I stand alone, and think
Till Love and Fame to nothingness do sink.

—1818

11 Cortez Balboa was actually the first European to see the Pacific   **14 Darien** in modern-day Panama
3 charact'ry writing

Elizabeth Barrett Browning (1806–1861) was already a famous poet when she met her husband-to-be, Robert Browning, who had been corresponding with her on literary matters. She originally published her famous sonnet sequence, written in the first years of her marriage, in the guise of a translation of Portuguese poems, perhaps to mask their personal revelations.

Elizabeth Barrett Browning
Sonnets from the Portuguese, 43

How do I love thee? Let me count the ways.
I love thee to the depth and breadth and height
My soul can reach, when feeling out of sight
For the ends of Being and ideal Grace.
I love thee to the level of everyday's   5
Most quiet need, by sun and candle-light.
I love thee freely, as men strive for Right;
I love thee purely, as they turn from Praise.
I love thee with the passion put to use
In my old griefs, and with my childhood's faith.   10
I love thee with a love I seemed to lose
With my lost saints—I love thee with the breath,
Smiles, tears, of all my life!—and, if God choose,
I shall but love thee better after death.

—1845–46

Henry Wadsworth Longfellow (1807–1882) was by far the most prominent nineteenth-century American poet, and his international fame led to his bust being placed in Westminster Abbey after his death. The long epic poems like Evangeline *and* Hiawatha *that were immensely popular among contemporary readers are seldom read today, but his shorter poems reveal a level of craftsmanship that few poets have equaled.*

Henry Wadsworth Longfellow
The Arsenal at Springfield

This is the Arsenal. From floor to ceiling,
    Like a huge organ, rise the burnished arms;
But from their silent pipes no anthem pealing
    Startles the villages with strange alarms.

Ah! what a sound will rise, how wild and dreary,   5
    When the death-angel touches those swift keys!
What loud lament and dismal Miserere°
    Will mingle with their awful symphonies!

I hear even now the infinite fierce chorus,
    The cries of agony, the endless groan,   10
Which, through the ages that have gone before us,
    In long reverberations reach our own.

On helm and harness rings the Saxon hammer,
    Through Cimbric° forest roars the Norseman's song,
And loud, amid the universal clamor,   15
    O'er distant deserts sounds the Tartar gong.

I hear the Florentine, who from his palace
    Wheels out his battle-bell with dreadful din,
And Aztec priests upon their teocallis°
    Beat the wild war-drums made of serpent's skin;   20

7 Miserere Latin hymn from Psalm 1: "Have mercy on me, Lord."   **14 Cimbric** in Denmark
19 teocallis temples atop pyramids

The tumult of each sacked and burning village;
    The shout that every prayer for mercy drowns;
The soldiers' revels in the midst of pillage;
    The wail of famine in beleaguered towns;

The bursting shell, the gateway wrenched asunder,   25
    The rattling musketry, the clashing blade;
And ever and anon, in tones of thunder
    The diapason° of the cannonade.

Is it, O man, with such discordant noises,
    With such accursed instruments as these,   30
Thou drownest Nature's sweet and kindly voices,
    And jarrest the celestial harmonies?

Were half the power, that fills the world with terror,
    Were half the wealth bestowed on camps and courts,
Given to redeem the human mind from error,   35
    There were no need of arsenals or forts:

The warrior's name would be a name abhorred!
    And every nation, that should lift again
Its hand against a brother, on its forehead
    Would wear forevermore the curse of Cain!   40

Down the dark future, through long generations,
    The echoing sounds grow fainter and then cease;
And like a bell, with solemn, sweet vibrations,
    I hear once more the voice of Christ say, "Peace!"

Peace! and no longer from its brazen portals   45
    The blast of War's great organ shakes the skies!
But beautiful as songs of the immortals,
    The holy melodies of love arise.

                                                              —1846

---

28 diapason full range of pipe organ

The Cross of Snow

In the long, sleepless watches of the night,
    A gentle face—the face of one long dead—
    Looks at me from the wall, where round its head
    The night-lamp casts a halo of pale light.
Here in this room she died; and soul more white   5
    Never through martyrdom of fire° was led
    To its repose; nor can in books be read
    The legend of a life more benedight.°
There is a mountain in the distant West
    That, sun-defying, in its deep ravines   10
    Displays a cross of snow upon its side.
Such is the cross I wear upon my breast
    These eighteen years, through all the changing scenes
    And seasons, changeless since the day she died.

—1886

Edgar Allan Poe (1809–1849) has survived his own myth as a deranged, drug-crazed genius, despite the wealth of evidence to the contrary that can be gleaned from his brilliant, though erratic, career as a poet, short-story writer, critic, and editor. Poe's brand of romanticism seems at odds with that of other American poets of his day, and is perhaps more in keeping with the spirit of Coleridge than that of Wordsworth. "The Raven" has been parodied perhaps more than any other American poem, yet it still retains a powerful hold on its audience.

Edgar Allan Poe
The Haunted Palace

In the greenest of our valleys,
    By good angels tenanted,
Once a fair and stately palace—
    Radiant palace—reared its head.

---

6 martyrdom of fire Longfellow's second wife, Frances, died as the result of a household fire in 1861.   **8 benedight** blessed

In the monarch Thought's dominion—   5
    It stood there!
Never seraph spread a pinion
    Over fabric half so fair!

Banners yellow, glorious, golden,
    On its roof did float and flow,   10
(This—all this—was in the olden
    Time long ago,)
And every gentle air that dallied,
    In that sweet day,
Along the ramparts plumed and pallid,   15
    A wingéd odor went away.

Wanderers in that happy valley,
    Through two luminous windows, saw
Spirits moving musically
    To a lute's well-tunéd law,   20
Round about a throne where, sitting,
    Porphyrogene!°
In state his glory well befitting,
    The ruler of the realm was seen.

And all with pearl and ruby glowing   25
    Was the fair palace door,
Through which came flowing, flowing, flowing,
    And sparkling evermore,
A troop of Echoes, whose sweet duty
    Was but to sing,   30
In voices of surpassing beauty,
    The wit and wisdom of their king.

But evil things, in robes of sorrow,
    Assailed the monarch's high estate.
(Ah, let us mourn!—for never morrow   35
    Shall dawn upon him, desolate!)
And round about his home the glory
    That blushed and bloomed,

---

22 Porphyrogene born to the purple, i.e., royal

Is but a dim-remembered story
    Of the old time entombed.

                    40

and travellers, now, within that valley,
    Through the red-litten windows see
Vast forms that move fantastically
    To a discordant melody,
While, like a ghastly rapid river,
                    45
    Through the pale door
A hideous throng rush out forever,
    And laugh—but smile no more.

—*1845*

The Raven

Once upon a midnight dreary, while I pondered, weak and weary,
Over many a quaint and curious volume of forgotten lore—
While I nodded, nearly napping, suddenly there came a tapping,
As of some one gently rapping, rapping at my chamber door.
"'Tis some visitor," I muttered, "tapping at my chamber door—   5
                Only this and nothing more."

Ah, distinctly I remember it was in the bleak December;
And each separate dying ember wrought its ghost upon the floor.
Eagerly I wished the morrow;—vainly I had sought to borrow
From my books surcease of sorrow—sorrow for the lost Lenore—   10
For the rare and radiant maiden whom the angels name Lenore—
                Nameless *here* for evermore.

And the silken, sad, uncertain rustling of each purple curtain
Thrilled me—filled me with fantastic terrors never felt before;
So that now, to still the beating of my heart, I stood repeating   15
"'Tis some visitor entreating entrance at my chamber door;—
Some late visitor entreating entrance at my chamber door;—
                This it is and nothing more."

Presently my soul grew stronger; hesitating then no longer,
"Sir," said I, "or Madam, truly your forgiveness I implore;   20
But the fact is I was napping, and so gently you came rapping,

And so faintly you came tapping, tapping at my chamber door,
That I scarce was sure I heard you"—here I opened wide the door;—
    Darkness there and nothing more.

Deep into that darkness peering, long I stood there wondering,
 fearing,   25
Doubting, dreaming dreams no mortal ever dared to dream before;
But the silence was unbroken, and the stillness gave no token,
And the only word there spoken was the whispered word, "Lenore?"
This I whispered, and an echo murmured back the word, "Lenore!"
    Merely this and nothing more. 30

Back into the chamber turning, all my soul within me burning,
Soon again I heard a tapping somewhat louder than before.
"Surely," said I, "surely that is something at my window lattice;
Let me see, then, what thereat is, and this mystery explore—
Let my heart be still a moment and this mystery explore;— 35
    'Tis the wind and nothing more!"

Open here I flung the shutter, when, with many a flirt and flutter,
In there stepped a stately Raven of the saintly days of yore;
Not the least obeisance made he; not a minute stopped or stayed he;
But, with mien of lord or lady, perched above my chamber door— 40
Perched upon a bust of Pallas° just above my chamber door—
    Perched, and sat, and nothing more.

Then this ebony bird beguiling my sad fancy into smiling,
By the grave and stern decorum of the countenance it wore,
"Though thy crest be shorn and shaven, thou," I said, "art sure no
 craven,   45
Ghastly grim and ancient Raven wandering from the Nightly shore—
Tell me what thy lordly name is on the Night's Plutonian° shore!"
    Quoth the Raven, "Nevermore."

Much I marvelled this ungainly fowl to hear discourse so plainly,
Though its answer little meaning—little relevancy bore; 50
For we cannot help agreeing that no living human being

---

41 Pallas Athena, goddess of wisdom **47 Plutonian** after Pluto, Roman god of the underworld

Ever yet was blessed with seeing bird above his chamber door—
Bird or beast upon the sculptured bust above his chamber door,
           With such name as "Nevermore."

But the Raven, sitting lonely on the placid bust, spoke only   55
That one word, as if his soul in that one word he did outpour.
Nothing farther then he uttered—not a feather then he fluttered—
Till I scarcely more than muttered, "Other friends have flown
    before—
On the morrow *he* will leave me, as my Hopes have flown before."
           Then the bird said, "Nevermore."   60

Startled at the stillness broken by reply so aptly spoken,
"Doubtless," said I, "what it utters is its only stock and store
Caught from some unhappy master whom unmerciful Disaster
Followed fast and followed faster till his songs one burden bore—
Till the dirges of his Hope that melancholy burden bore   65
           Of 'Never—nevermore.' "

But the Raven still beguiling all my sad fancy into smiling,
Straight I wheeled a cushioned seat in front of bird and bust and
    door;
Then, upon the velvet sinking, I betook myself to linking
Fancy unto fancy, thinking what this ominous bird of yore—   70
What this grim, ungainly, ghastly, gaunt, and ominous bird of yore
           Meant in croaking "Nevermore."

This I sat engaged in guessing, but no syllable expressing
To the fowl whose fiery eyes now burned into my bosom's core;
This and more I sat divining, with my head at ease reclining   75
On the cushion's velvet lining that the lamp-light gloated o'er,
But whose velvet-violet lining with the lamp-light gloating o'er,
           She shall press, ah, nevermore!

Then, methought, the air grew denser, perfumed from an unseen
    censer
Swung by seraphim whose foot-falls tinkled on the tufted floor.   80
"Wretch," I cried, "thy God hath lent thee—by these angels he
    hath sent thee.

Respite—respite and nepenthe° from thy memories of Lenore;
Quaff, oh quaff this kind nepenthe and forget this lost Lenore!"
Quoth the Raven, "Nevermore."

"Prophet!" said I, "thing of evil!—prophet still, if bird or devil!—   *85*
Whether Tempter sent, or whether tempest tossed thee here ashore,
Desolate yet all undaunted, on this desert land enchanted—
On this home by Horror haunted—tell me truly, I implore—
Is there—*is* there balm in Gilead?—tell me—tell me, I implore!"
Quoth the Raven, "Nevermore."   *90*

"Prophet!" said I, "thing of evil!—prophet still, if bird or devil!
By that Heaven that bends above us—by that God we both adore—
Tell this soul with sorrow laden if, within the distant Aidenn,°
It shall clasp a sainted maiden whom the angels name Lenore—
Clasp a rare and radiant maiden whom the angels name Lenore."   *95*
Quoth the Raven, "Nevermore."

"Be that word our sign of parting, bird or fiend!" I shrieked,
    upstarting—
"Get thee back into the tempest and the Night's Plutonian shore!
Leave no black plume as a token of that lie thy soul hath spoken!
Leave my loneliness unbroken!—quit the bust above my door!   *100*
Take thy beak from out my heart, and take thy form from off my
    door!"
Quoth the Raven, "Nevermore."

And the Raven, never flitting, still is sitting, *still* is sitting
On the pallid bust of Pallas just above my chamber door;
And his eyes have all the seeming of a demon's that is dreaming,   *105*
And the lamp-light o'er him streaming throws his shadow on the floor;
And my soul from out that shadow that lies floating on the floor
Shall be lifted—nevermore!

—*1845*

82 nepenthe drug causing forgetfulness **93 Aidenn** Eden

To Helen

Helen, thy beauty is to me
    Like those Nicean° barks of yore,
That gently, o'er a perfumed sea
    The weary, way-worn wanderer bore
    To his own native shore.   *5*

On desperate seas long wont to roam,
    Thy hyacinth° hair, thy classic face
Thy Naiad° airs have brought me home
    To the glory that was Greece
And the grandeur that was Rome.   *10*

Lo! in yon brilliant window-niche
    How statue-like I see thee stand!
    The agate lamp within thy hand,
Ah! Psyche,° from the regions which
    Are Holy Land!   *15*

                                      —1831

2 Nicean possibly of Nice (in the South of France); or Phoenician   **7 hyacinth** reddish, like the flower of Greek myth   **8 Naiad** water nymph   **14 Psyche** the soul

Alfred, Lord Tennyson (1809–1892) became the most famous English poet with the 1850 publication of In Memoriam, a sequence of poems on the death of his friend A. H. Hallam. In the same year he became poet laureate. Modern critical opinion has focused more favorably on Tennyson's lyrical gifts than on his talents for narrative or drama. T. S. Eliot and W. H. Auden, among other critics, praised Tennyson's rhythms and sound patterns but had reservations about his depth of intellect, especially when he took on the role of official apologist for Victorian England.

Alfred, Lord Tennyson

The Eagle

FRAGMENT

He clasps the crag with crooked hands;
Close to the sun in lonely lands,
Ringed with the azure world, he stands.

The wrinkled sea beneath him crawls;   5
He watches from his mountain walls,
And like a thunderbolt he falls.

—*1851*

In Memoriam A. H. H.,° 54

O, yet we trust that somehow good
    Will be the final goal of ill,
    To pangs of nature, sins of will,
Defects of doubt, and taints of blood;

That nothing walks with aimless feet;   5
    That not one life shall be destroyed,
    Or cast as rubbish to the void,
When God hath made the pile complete;

A. H. H. the poet's college friend Arthur Henry Hallam (1811–1833)

That not a worm is cloven in vain;
    That not a moth with vain desire   *10*
    Is shriveled in a fruitless fire,
Or but subserves another's gain.

Behold, we know not anything;
    I can but trust that good shall fall
    At last—far off—at last, to all,   *15*
And every winter change to spring.

So runs my dreams; but what am I?
    An infant crying in the night;
    An infant crying for the light,
And with no language but a cry.   *20*

                                        —1833

Tears, Idle Tears

FROM *THE PRINCESS*

    Tears, idle tears, I know not what they mean,
Tears from the depth of some divine despair
Rise in the heart, and gather to the eyes,
In looking on the happy autumn-fields,
And thinking of the days that are no more.   *5*

    Fresh as the first beam glittering on a sail,
That brings our friends up from the underworld,
Sad as the last which reddens over one
That sinks with all we love below the verge;
So sad, so fresh, the days that are no more.   *10*

    Ah, sad and strange as in dark summer dawns
The earliest pipe of half-awakened birds
To dying ears, when unto dying eyes
The casement slowly grows a glimmering square;
So sad, so strange, the days that are no more.   *15*

Dear as remembered kisses after death,
And sweet as those by hopeless fancy feigned
On lips that are for others; deep as love,
Deep as first love, and wild with all regret;
O Death in Life, the days that are no more!

20

—*1847*

Ulysses°

It little profits that an idle king,
By this still hearth, among these barren crags,
Matched with an aged wife, I mete and dole
Unequal laws unto a savage race,
That hoard, and sleep, and feed, and know not me.

5

I cannot rest from travel; I will drink
Life to the lees. All times I have enjoyed
Greatly, have suffered greatly, both with those
That loved me, and alone; on shore, and when
Through scudding drifts the rainy Hyades°

10

Vexed the dim sea. I am become a name;
For always roaming with a hungry heart
Much have I seen and known—cities of men
And manners, climates, councils, governments,
Myself not least, but honored of them all—

15

And drunk delight of battle with my peers,
Far on the ringing plains of windy Troy.
I am a part of all that I have met;
Yet all experience is an arch wherethrough
Gleams that untraveled world whose margin fades

20

For ever and for ever when I move.
How dull it is to pause, to make an end,
To rust unburnished, not to shine in use!
As though to breathe were life! Life piled on life

Ulysses Homer's *Odyssey* ends with the return of Odysseus (Ulysses) to his island kingdom, Ithaca. Tennyson's poem takes place some years later.   **10 Hyades** a constellation thought to predict rain

Were all too little, and of one to me   25
Little remains; but every hour is saved
From that eternal silence, something more,
A bringer of new things; and vile it were
For some three suns to store and hoard myself,
And this gray spirit yearning in desire   30
To follow knowledge like a sinking star,
Beyond the utmost bound of human thought.
    This is my son, mine own Telemachus,
To whom I leave the scepter and the isle,
Well-loved of me, discerning to fulfill   35
This labor, by slow prudence to make mild
A rugged people, and through soft degrees
Subdue them to the useful and the good.
Most blameless is he, centered in the sphere
Of common duties, decent not to fail   40
In offices of tenderness, and pay
Meet adoration to my household gods,
When I am gone. He works his work, I mine.
    There lies the port; the vessel puffs her sail;
There gloom the dark, broad seas. My mariners,   45
Souls that have toiled, and wrought, and thought with me,
That ever with a frolic welcome took
The thunder and the sunshine, and opposed
Free hearts, free foreheads—you and I are old;
Old age hath yet his honor and his toil.   50
Death closes all; but something ere the end,
Some work of noble note, may yet be done,
Not unbecoming men that strove with gods.
The lights begin to twinkle from the rocks;
The long day wanes; the low moon climbs; the deep   55
Moans round with many voices. Come, my friends,
'Tis not too late to seek a newer world.
Push off, and sitting well in order smite
The sounding furrows; for my purpose holds
To sail beyond the sunset, and the baths   60
Of all the western stars, until I die.
It may be that the gulfs will wash us down;

It may be we shall touch the Happy Isles,°
And see the great Achilles, whom we knew.
Though much is taken, much abides; and though   65
We are not now that strength which in old days
Moved earth and heaven, that which we are, we are,
One equal temper of heroic hearts,
Made weak by time and fate, but strong in will
To strive, to seek, to find, and not to yield.   70

—*1833*

Robert Browning (1812–1889) wrote many successful dramatic monologues that are his lasting legacy, for he brings the genre to a level of achievement rarely equaled. Less regarded during his lifetime than his contemporary Tennyson, he has consistently risen in the esteem of modern readers. Often overlooked in his gallery of often grotesque characters are his considerable metrical skills and ability to simulate speech while working in demanding poetic forms.

Robert Browning
My Last Duchess

FERRARA°

That's my last duchess painted on the wall,
Looking as if she were alive. I call
That piece a wonder, now: Frà Pandolf's° hands
Worked busily a day, and there she stands.
Will't please you sit and look at her? I said   5
"Frà Pandolf" by design, for never read
Strangers like you that pictured countenance,
The depth and passion of its earnest glance,
But to myself they turned (since none puts by

---

63 Happy Isles Elysium, the resting place of dead heroes
Ferrara The speaker is probably Alfonso II d'Este, Duke of Ferrara (1533–158?)   **3 Frà Pandolf** an
imaginary painter

The curtain I have drawn for you, but I) 10
And seemed as they would ask me, if they durst,
How such a glance came there; so, not the first
Are you to turn and ask thus. Sir, 'twas not
Her husband's presence only, called that spot
Of joy into the Duchess' cheek: perhaps 15
Frà Pandolf chanced to say "Her mantle laps
Over my lady's wrist too much," or "Paint
Must never hope to reproduce the faint
Half-flush that dies along her throat": such stuff
Was courtesy, she thought, and cause enough 20
For calling up that spot of joy. She had
A heart—how shall I say?—too soon made glad,
Too easily impressed; she liked whate'er
She looked on, and her looks went everywhere.
Sir, 'twas all one! My favor at her breast, 25
The dropping of the daylight in the West,
The bough of cherries some officious fool
Broke in the orchard for her, the white mule
She rode with round the terrace—all and each
Would draw from her alike the approving speech, 30
Or blush, at least. She thanked men—good! but thanked
Somehow—I know not how—as if she ranked
My gift of a nine-hundred-years-old name
With anybody's gift. Who'd stoop to blame
This sort of trifling? Even had you skill 35
In speech—which I have not—to make your will
Quite clear to such an one, and say, "Just this
Or that in you disgusts me; here you miss,
Or there exceed the mark"—and if she let
Herself be lessoned so, nor plainly set 40
Her wits to yours, forsooth, and made excuse,
—E'en then would be some stooping; and I choose
Never to stoop. Oh sir, she smiled, no doubt,
Whene'er I passed her; but who passed without
Much the same smile? This grew; I gave commands; 45

Then all smiles stopped together. There she stands
As if alive. Will't please you rise? We'll meet
The company below, then. I repeat,
The Count your master's° known munificence
Is ample warrant that no just pretense   50
Of mine for dowry will be disallowed;
Though his fair daughter's self, as I avowed
At starting, is my object. Nay, we'll go
Together down, sir. Notice Neptune, though,
Taming a sea horse, thought a rarity,   55
Which Claus of Innsbruck cast in bronze for me!

          —1842

Porphyria's° Lover

The rain set early in tonight,
    The sullen wind was soon awake,
It tore the elm-tops down for spite,
    And did its worst to vex the lake:
    I listened with heart fit to break.   5
When glided in Porphyria; straight
    She shut the cold out and the storm,
And kneeled and made the cheerless grate
    Blaze up, and all the cottage warm;
    Which done, she rose, and from her form   10
Withdrew the dripping cloak and shawl,
    And laid her soiled gloves by, untied
Her hat and let the damp hair fall,
    And, last, she sat down by my side
    And called me. When no voice replied,   15
She put my arm about her waist,
    And made her smooth white shoulder bare,

---

49 Count your master's The auditor is apparently an envoy sent to arrange a marriage between the Duke of Ferrara and a count's daughter
Porphyria name suggesting purple, the color of nobility and royalty

And all her yellow hair displaced,
        And, stooping, made my cheek lie there,
        And spread, o'er all, her yellow hair,   20
Murmuring how she loved me—she
        Too weak, for all her heart's endeavor,
To set its struggling passion free
        From pride, and vainer ties dissever,
        And give herself to me forever.   25
But passion sometimes would prevail,
        Nor could tonight's gay feast restrain
A sudden thought of one so pale
        For love of her, and all in vain:
        So, she was come through wind and rain.   30
Be sure I looked up at her eyes
        Happy and proud; at last I knew
Porphyria worshipped me; surprise
        Made my heart swell, and still it grew
        While I debated what to do.   35
That moment she was mine, mine, fair,
        Perfectly pure and good: I found
A thing to do, and all her hair
        In one long yellow string I wound
        Three times her little throat around,   40
And strangled her. No pain felt she;
        I am quite sure she felt no pain.
As a shut bud that holds a bee,
        I warily oped her lids: again
        Laughed the blue eyes without a stain.   45
And I untightened next the tress
        About her neck; her cheek once more
Blushed bright beneath my burning kiss:
        I propped her head up as before,
        Only, this time my shoulder bore   50
Her head, which droops upon it still:
        The smiling rosy little head
So glad it has its utmost will,
        That all it scorned at once is fled,
        And I, its love, am gained instead!   55

Porphyria's love: she guessed not how
    Her darling one wish would be heard.
And thus we sit together now,
    And all night long we have not stirred,
    And yet God has not said a word!   60

                                                                    —*1842*

---

*Walt Whitman (1819–1892) pioneered the use of free verse, which established
him as one of the forebears of modern poetry, but his subject matter, often dealing
with sexual topics, and his unsparing realism were equally controversial in his day.
An admirer of Emerson, he adapted many of the ideas of transcendentalism in* Song
of Myself, *his first major sequence, and also incorporated many of Emerson's calls
for poets to use American subjects and patterns of speech.* Leaves of Grass, *which
he revised from 1855 until his death, expanded to include virtually all of his poems,
including the graphic poems he wrote while serving as a volunteer in Civil War army
hospitals.*

Walt Whitman
A Sight in Camp in the Daybreak Gray and Dim

A sight in camp in the daybreak gray and dim,
As from my tent I emerge so early sleepless,
As slow I walk in the cool fresh air the path near by the hospital
    tent,
Three forms I see on stretchers lying, brought out there untended
    lying,
Over each the blanket spread, ample brownish woolen blanket,   5
Gray and heavy blanket, folding, covering all.

Curious I halt and silent stand,
Then with light fingers I from the face of the nearest the first just
    lift the blanket;
Who are you elderly man so gaunt and grim, with well-gray'd
    hair, and flesh all sunken about the eyes?
Who are you my dear comrade?   10

Then to the second I step—and who are you my child and darling?
Who are you sweet boy with cheeks yet blooming?

Then to the third—a face nor child nor old, very calm, as of
    beautiful yellow-white ivory;
Young man I think I know you—I think this face is the face of
    the Christ himself,
Dead and divine and brother of all, and here again he lies.   *15*

             —1867

Crossing Brooklyn Ferry

1

Flood-tide below me! I see you face to face!
Clouds of the west—sun there half an hour high—I see you also
    face to face.

Crowds of men and women attired in the usual costumes, how
    curious you are to me!
On the ferry-boats the hundreds and hundreds that cross,
    returning home, are more curious to me than you suppose,
And you that shall cross from shore to shore years hence are
    more to me, and more in my meditations, than you might
    suppose.   *5*

2

The impalpable sustenance of me from all things at all hours of
    the day,
The simple, compact, well-join'd scheme, myself disintegrated,
    every one disintegrated yet part of the scheme,
The similitudes of the past and those of the future,
The glories strung like beads on my smallest sights and hearings,
    on the walk in the street and the passage over the river,
The current rushing so swiftly and swimming with me
    far away,   *10*
The others that are to follow me, the ties between me and them,
The certainty of others, the life, love, sight, hearing of others.

Others will enter the gates of the ferry and cross from shore to shore,
Others will watch the run of the flood-tide,
Others will see the shipping of Manhattan north and west, and
    the heights of Brooklyn to the south and east,   15
Others will see the islands large and small;
Fifty years hence, others will see them as they cross, the sun
    half an hour high,
A hundred years hence, or ever so many hundred years hence,
    others will see them,
Will enjoy the sunset, the pouring-in of the flood-tide, the
    falling-back to the sea of the ebb-tide.

3

It avails not, time nor place—distance avails not,   20
I am with you, you men and women of a generation, or ever so
    many generations hence,
Just as you feel when you look on the river and sky, so I felt,
Just as any of you is one of a living crowd, I was one of a crowd,
Just as you are refresh'd by the gladness of the river and the
    bright flow, I was refresh'd,
Just as you stand and lean on the rail, yet hurry with the swift
    current, I stood yet was hurried,   25
Just as you look on the numberless masts of ships and the
    thick-stemm'd pipes of steamboats, I look'd.

I too many and many a time cross'd the river of old,
Watched the Twelfth-month° sea-gulls, saw them high in the
    air floating with motionless wings, oscillating their bodies,
Saw how the glistening yellow lit up parts of their bodies and
    left the rest in strong shadow,
Saw the slow-wheeling circles and the gradual edging toward
    the south,   30
Saw the reflection of the summer sky in the water,
Had my eyes dazzled by the shimmering track of beams,
Look'd at the fine centrifugal spokes of light round the shape
    of my head in the sunlit water,

---

28 **Twelfth-month** Whitman's mother was a Quaker, hence this phrase for December.

Look'd on the haze on the hills southward and south-westward,
Look'd on the vapor as it flew in fleeces tinged with violet,   35
Look'd toward the lower bay to notice the vessels arriving,
Saw their approach, saw aboard those that were near me,
Saw the white sails of schooners and sloops, saw the ships at
    anchor,
The sailors at work in the rigging or out astride the spars,
The round masts, the swinging motion of the hulls, the slender
    serpentine pennants,   40
The large and small steamers in motion, the pilots in their
    pilothouses,
The white wake left by the passage, the quick tremulous whirl
    of the wheels,
The flags of all nations, the falling of them at sunset,
The scallop-edged waves in the twilight, the ladled cups, the
    frolicsome crests and glistening,
The stretch afar growing dimmer and dimmer, the gray walls
    of the granite storehouses by the docks,   45
On the river the shadowy group, the big steam-tug closely
    flank'd on each side by the barges, the hay-boat, the belated
    lighter,
On the neighboring shore the fires from the foundry chimneys
    burning high and glaringly into the night,
Casting their flicker of black contrasted with wild red and yellow
    light over the tops of houses, and down into the clefts of streets.

4

These and all else were to me the same as they are to you,
I loved well those cities, loved well the stately and rapid river,   50
The men and women I saw were all near to me,
Others the same—others who look back on me because I look'd
    forward to them,
(The time will come, though I stop here to-day and to-night.)

5

What is it then between us?
What is the count of the scores or hundreds of years between us?   55

Whatever it is, it avails not—distance avails not, and place avails not,
I too lived, Brooklyn of ample hills was mine,
I too walk'd the streets of Manhattan island, and bathed in the
    waters around it,
I too felt the curious abrupt questionings stir within me,
In the day among crowds of people sometimes they came
    upon me,   *60*
In my walks home late at night or as I lay in my bed they came
    upon me,
I too had been struck from the float forever held in solution,
I too had receiv'd identity by my body,
That I was I knew was of my body, and what I should be I
    knew I should be of my body.

6

It is not upon you alone the dark patches fall,   *65*
The dark threw its patches down upon me also,
The best I had done seem'd to me blank and suspicious,
My great thoughts as I supposed them, were they not in reality
    meagre?
Nor is it you alone who know what it is to be evil,
I am he who knew what it was to be evil,   *70*
I too knitted the old knot of contrariety,
Blabb'd, blush'd, resented, lied, stole, grudg'd,
Had guile, anger, lust, hot wishes I dared not speak,
Was wayward, vain, greedy, shallow, sly, cowardly, malignant,
The wolf, the snake, the hog, not wanting in me,   *75*
The cheating look, the frivolous word, the adulterous wish,
    not wanting,
Refusals, hates, postponements, meanness, laziness, none of
    these wanting,
Was one with the rest, the days and haps of the rest,
Was call'd by my nighest name by clear loud voices of young
    men as they saw me approaching or passing,
Felt their arms on my neck as I stood, or the negligent leaning
    of their flesh against me as I sat,   *80*
Saw many I loved in the street or ferry-boat or public
    assembly, yet never told them a word,

Lived the same life with the rest, the same old laughing, gnawing,
    sleeping,
Play'd the part that still looks back on the actor or actress,
The same old role, the role that is what we make it, as great as
    we like,
Or as small as we like, or both great and small.   *85*

7

Closer yet I approach you,
What thought you have of me now, I had as much of you—I laid
    in my stores in advance,
I consider'd long and seriously of you before you were born.

Who was to know what should come home to me?
Who knows but I am enjoying this?   *90*
Who knows, for all the distance, but I am as good as looking
    at you now, for all you cannot see me?

8

Ah, what can ever be more stately and admirable to me than
    mast-hemm'd Manhattan?
River and sunset and scallop-edg'd waves of flood-tide?
The sea-gulls oscillating their bodies, the hay-boat in the twilight,
    and the belated lighter?
What gods can exceed these that clasp me by the hand, and
    with voices I love call me promptly and loudly by my
    nighest name as I approach?   *95*
What is more subtle than this which ties me to the woman or
    man that looks in my face?
Which fuses me into you now, and pours my meaning into you?

We understand then do we not?
What I promis'd without mentioning it, have you not accepted?
What the study could not teach—what the preaching could not
    accomplish'd is accomplish'd, is it not?   *100*

9

Flow on, river! flow with the flood-tide, and ebb with the ebbtide!
Frolic on, crested and scallop-edg'd waves!

Gorgeous clouds of the sunset! drench with your splendor me, or
    the men and women generations after me!
Cross from shore to shore, countless crowds of passengers!
Stand up, tall masts of Mannahatta! stand up, beautiful hills
    of Brooklyn!   *105*
Throb, baffled and curious brain! throw out questions and
    answers!
Suspend here and everywhere, eternal float of solution!
Gaze, loving and thirsting eyes, in the house or street or public
    assembly!
Sound out, voices of young men! loudly and musically call me
    by my nighest name!
Live, old life! play the part that looks back on the actor or
    actress!   *110*
Play the old role, the role that is great or small according as one
    makes it!
Consider, you who peruse me, whether I may not in unknown
    ways be looking upon you;
Be firm, rail over the river, to support those who lean idly, yet
    haste with the hasting current;
Fly on, sea-birds! fly sideways, or wheel in large circles high in
    the air;
Receive the summer sky, you water, and faithfully hold it till
    all downcast eyes have time to take it from you!   *115*
Diverge, fine spokes of light, from the shape of my head, or
    any one's head, in the sunlit water!
Come on, ships from the lower bay! pass up or down, white-sail'd
    schooners, sloops, lighters!
Flaunt away, flags of all nations! be duly lower'd at sunset!
Burn high your fires, foundry chimneys! cast black shadows at
    nightfall! cast red and yellow light over the tops of the
    houses!
Appearances, now or henceforth, indicate what you are,   *120*
You necessary film, continue to envelop the soul,
About my body for me, and your body for you, be hung our
    divinest aromas,
Thrive, cities—bring your freight, bring your shows, ample and
    sufficient rivers,

Expand, being than which none else is perhaps more
    spiritual,
Keep your places, objects than which none else is more l
    asting.   125

You have waited, you always wait, you dumb, beautiful
    ministers,
We receive you with free sense at last, and are insatiate hence-
    forward,
Not you any more shall be able to foil us, or withhold yourselves
    from us,
We use you, and do not cast you aside—we plant you
    permanently within us,
We fathom you not—we love you—there is perfection in you
    also,   130
You furnish your parts toward eternity,
Great or small, you furnish your parts toward the soul.

             —*1881–82*

A Noiseless Patient Spider

A noiseless patient spider,
I mark'd where on a little promontory it stood isolated,
Mark'd how to explore the vacant vast surrounding,
It launch'd forth filament, filament, filament, out of itself,
Ever unreeling them, ever tirelessly speeding them.   5

And you O my soul where you stand,
Surrounded, detached, in measureless oceans of space,
Ceaselessly musing, venturing, throwing, seeking the spheres to
    connect them,
Till the bridge you will need be form'd, till the ductile anchor
    hold,
Till the gossamer thread you fling catch somewhere, O my
    soul.

             10
             —*1876*

Out of the Cradle Endlessly Rocking

Out of the cradle endlessly rocking,
Out of the mocking-bird's throat, the musical shuttle,
Out of the Ninth-month° midnight,
Over the sterile sands and the fields beyond, where the child
    leaving his bed wander'd alone, bareheaded, barefoot,
Down from the shower'd halo,   5
Up from the mystic play of shadows twining and twisting as if
    they were alive,
Out from the patches of briers and blackberries,
From the memories of the bird that chanted to me,
From your memories sad brother, from the fitful risings and
    fallings I heard,
From under that yellow half-moon late-risen and swollen as if
    with tears,   10
From those beginning notes of yearning and love there in the
    mist,
From the thousand responses of my heart never to cease,
From the myriad thence-arous'd words,
From the word stronger and more delicious than any,
From such as now they start the scene revisiting,   15
As a flock, twittering, rising, or overhead passing,
Borne hither, ere all eludes me, hurriedly,
A man, yet by these tears a little boy again,
Throwing myself on the sand, confronting the waves,
I, chanter of pains and joys, uniter of here and hereafter,   20
Taking all hints to use them, but swiftly leaping beyond them,
A reminiscence sing.

Once Paumanok,°
When the lilac-scent was in the air and Fifth-month° grass was
    growing,

---

3 Ninth-month Quaker term for September   **23 Paumanok** Indian name for Long Island
24 Fifth-month May (Quaker)

Up this seashore in some briers,   25
Two feather'd guests from Alabama, two together,
And their nest, and four light-green eggs spotted with brown,
And every day the he-bird to and fro near at hand,
And every day the she-bird crouch'd on her nest, silent, with
    bright eyes,
And every day I, a curious boy, never too close, never
    disturbing them,   30
Cautiously peering, absorbing, translating.

Shine! shine! shine!
Pour down your warmth, great sun!
While we bask, we two together.

Two together!   35
Winds blow south, or winds blow north,
Day come white, or night come black,
Home, or rivers and mountains from home,
Singing all time, minding no time,
While we two keep together.   40

Till of a sudden,
May-be kill'd, unknown to her mate,
One forenoon the she-bird crouch'd not on the nest,
Nor return'd that afternoon, nor the next,
Nor ever appear'd again.   45

And thenceforward all summer in the sound of the sea,
And at night under the full of the moon in calmer weather,
Over the hoarse surging of the sea,
Or flitting from brier to brier by day,
I saw, I heard at intervals the remaining one, the he-bird,   50
The solitary guest from Alabama.

Blow! blow! blow!
Blow up sea-winds along Paumanok's shore;
I wait and I wait till you blow my mate to me.

Yes, when the stars glisten'd,   55
All night long on the prong of a moss-scallop'd stake,
Down almost amid the slapping waves,
Sat the lone singer wonderful causing tears.

He call'd on his mate,
He pour'd forth the meaning which I of all men know.   60
Yes my brother I know,
The rest might not, but I have treasur'd every note,
For more than once dimly down to the beach gliding,
Silent, avoiding the moonbeams, blending myself with the
    shadows,
Recalling now the obscure shapes, the echoes, the sounds and
    sights after their sorts,   65
The white arms out in the breakers tirelessly tossing,
I, with bare feet, a child, the wind wafting my hair,
Listen'd long and long.

Listen'd to keep, to sing, now translating the notes,
Following you my brother.   70

Soothe! soothe! soothe!
Close on its wave soothes the wave behind,
And again another behind embracing and lapping, every one
    close,
But my love soothes not me, not me.

Low hangs the moon, it rose late,   75
It is lagging—O I think it is heavy with love, with love.

O madly the sea pushes upon the land,
With love, with love.

O night! do I not see my love fluttering out among the breakers?
What is that little black thing I see there in the white?   80

Loud! loud! loud!
Loud I call to you, my love!

High and clear I shoot my voice over the waves,
Surely you must know who is here, is here,
You must know who I am, my love.   85

Low-hanging moon!
What is that dusky spot in your brown yellow?
O it is the shape, the shape of my mate!
O moon do not keep her from me any longer.

Land! land! O land!   90
Whichever way I turn, O I think you could give me my mate
    back again if you only would,
For I am almost sure I see her dimly whichever way I look.

O rising stars!
Perhaps the one I want so much will rise, will rise with some
    of you.

O throat! O trembling throat!   95
Sound clearer through the atmosphere!
Pierce the woods, the earth,
Somewhere listening to catch you must be the one I want.

Shake out carols!
Solitary here, the night's carols!   100
Carols of lonesome love! death's carols!
Carols under that lagging, yellow, waning moon!
O under that moon where she droops almost down into the sea!
O reckless despairing carols.

But soft! sink low!   105
Soft! let me just murmur,
And do you wait a moment you husky-nois'd sea,
For somewhere I believe I heard my mate responding to me,
So faint, I must be still, be still to listen,
But not altogether still, for then she might not come
    immediately to me.   110

Hither my love!
Here I am! here!
With this just-sustain'd note I announce myself to you,
This gentle call is for you my love, for you.

Do not be decoy'd elsewhere,   115
That is the whistle of the wind, it is not my voice,
That is the fluttering, the fluttering of the spray,
Those are the shadows of leaves.

O darkness! O in vain!
O I am very sick and sorrowful.   120

O brown halo in the sky near the moon, drooping upon the sea!
O troubled reflection in the sea!
O throat! O throbbing heart!
And I singing uselessly, uselessly all the night.

O past! O happy life! O songs of joy! 125
In the air, in the woods, over fields,
Loved! loved! loved! loved! loved!
But my mate no more, no more with me!
We two together no more.

The aria sinking, 130
All else continuing, the stars shining,
The winds blowing, the notes of the bird continuous echoing,
With angry moans the fierce old mother incessantly moaning,
On the sands of Paumanok's shore gray and rustling,
The yellow half-moon enlarged, sagging down, drooping, the
    face of the sea almost touching, 135
The boy ecstatic, with his bare feet the waves, with his hair
    the atmosphere dallying,
The love in the heart long pent, now loose, now at last
    tumultuously bursting,
The aria's meaning, the ears, the soul, swiftly depositing,
The strange tears down the cheeks coursing,
The colloquy there, the trio, each uttering, 140
The undertone, the savage old mother incessantly crying,
To the boy's soul's questions sullenly timing, some drown'd
    secret hissing,
To the outsetting bard.

Demon or bird! (said the boy's soul,)
Is it indeed toward your mate you sing? or is it really to me? 145
For I, that was a child, my tongue's use sleeping, now I have
    heard you,
Now in a moment I know what I am for, I awake,
And already a thousand singers, a thousand songs, clearer,
    louder and more sorrowful than yours,
A thousand warbling echoes have started to life within me,
    never to die.

O you singer solitary, singing by yourself, projecting me,   *150*
O solitary me listening, never more shall I cease perpetuating
    you,
Never more shall I escape, never more the reverberations,
Never more the cries of unsatisfied love be absent from me,
Never again leave me to be the peaceful child I was before what
    there in the night,
By the sea under the yellow and sagging moon,   *155*
The messenger there arous'd, the fire, the sweet hell within,
The unknown want, the destiny of me.

O give me the clew!° (it lurks in the night here somewhere,)
O if I am to have so much, let me have more!

A word then, (for I will conquer it,)   *160*
The word final, superior to all,
Subtle, sent up—what is it?—I listen;
Are you whispering it, and have been all the time, you sea waves?
Is that it from your liquid rims and wet sands?

Whereto answering, the sea,   *165*
Delaying not, hurrying not,
Whisper'd me through the night, and very plainly before
    daybreak,
Lisp'd to me the low and delicious word death,
And again death, death, death, death,
Hissing melodious, neither like the bird nor like my arous'd
    child's heart,   *170*
But edging near as privately for me rustling at my feet,
Creeping thence steadily up to my ears and laving me softly
    all over,
Death, death, death, death, death.

Which I do not forget,
But fuse the song of my dusky demon and brother,   *175*
That he sang to me in the moonlight on Paumanok's gray
    beach,

158 clew clue

With the thousand responsive songs at random,
My own songs awaked from that hour,
And with them the key, the word up from the waves,
The word of the sweetest song and all songs,   *180*
That strong and delicious word which, creeping to my feet,
(Or like some old crone rocking the cradle, swathed in sweet
　　garments, bending aside,)
The sea whisper'd me.

　　　　　　　　　　　　　　　　　　　　　　—*1881–82*

Song of Myself, 6

A child said *What is the grass?* fetching it to me with full hands;
How could I answer the child? I do not know what it is any more
　　than he.

I guess it must be the flag of my disposition, out of hopeful green
　　stuff woven.

Or I guess it is the handkerchief of the Lord,
A scented gift and remembrancer designedly dropped,   *5*
Bearing the owner's name someway in the corners, that we may
　　see and remark, and say *Whose?*

Or I guess the grass is itself a child, the produced babe of the
　　vegetation.

Or I guess it is a uniform hieroglyphic,
And it means, Sprouting alike in broad zones and narrow
　　zones,
Growing among black folks as among white,   *10*
Kanuck,° Tuckahoe,° Congressman, Cuff,° I give them the
　　same, I receive them the same.

And now it seems to me the beautiful uncut hair of graves.

Tenderly will I use you curling grass,
It may be you transpire from the breasts of young men,

---

11 Kanuck French-Canadian　　**Tuckahoe** coastal Virginian　　**Cuff** a black slave

It may be if I had known them I would have loved them, 15
It may be you are from old people, or from offspring taken
    soon out of their mothers' laps,
And here you are the mothers' laps.

This grass is very dark to be from the white heads of old mothers.
Darker than the colorless beards of old men.
Dark to come from under the faint red roofs of mouths. 20

O I perceive after all so many uttering tongues,
And I perceive they do not come from the roofs of mouths for
    nothing.

I wish I could translate the hints about the dead young men
    and women,
And the hints about old men and mothers, and the offspring
    taken soon out of their laps.

What do you think has become of the young and old men? 25
And what do you think has become of the women and
    children?

They are alive and well somewhere,
The smallest sprout shows there is really no death,
And if ever there was it led forward life, and does not wait at
    the end to arrest it.
And ceased the moment life appeared. 30

All goes onward and outward, nothing collapses.
And to die is different from what anyone supposed, and luckier.

—1855

When I Heard the Learn'd Astronomer

When I heard the learn'd astronomer,
When the proofs, the figures, were ranged in columns before me,
When I was shown the charts and diagrams, to add, divide, and
    measure them,

When I sitting heard the astronomer where he lectured with much
    applause in the lecture-room,
How soon unaccountable I became tired and sick,   5
Till rising and gliding out I wander'd off by myself,
In the mystical moist night-air, and from time to time,
Look'd up in perfect silence at the stars.

—*1865*

Matthew Arnold (1822–1888) was the son of the headmaster of Rugby School and himself served as an inspector of schools during much of his adult life. An influential essayist as well as a poet, Arnold was unsparing in his criticism of middle-class "Philistinism." At least part of "Dover Beach" is thought to date from his honeymoon in 1851.

Matthew Arnold
Dover Beach

The sea is calm tonight.
The tide is full, the moon lies fair
Upon the straits; on the French coast the light
Gleams and is gone; the cliffs of England stand,
Glimmering and vast, out in the tranquil bay.   5
Come to the window, sweet is the night-air!
Only, from the long line of spray
Where the sea meets the moon-blanched land,
Listen! you hear the grating roar
Of pebbles which the waves draw back, and fling,   10
At their return, up the high strand,
Begin, and cease, and then again begin,
With tremulous cadence slow, and bring
The eternal note of sadness in.

Sophocles° long ago   15
Heard it on the Aegean, and it brought

15 Sophocles Athenian tragic poet (496–406 B.C.)

Into his mind the turbid ebb and flow
Of human misery; we
Find also in the sound a thought,
Hearing it by this distant northern sea.   20

The Sea of Faith
Was once, too, at the full, and round earth's shore
Lay like the folds of a bright girdle° furled.
But now I only hear
Its melancholy, long, withdrawing roar,   25
Retreating, to the breath
Of the night-wind, down the vast edges drear
And naked shingles° of the world.

Ah, love, let us be true
To one another! for the world, which seems   30
To lie before us like a land of dreams,
So various, so beautiful, so new,
Hath really neither joy, nor love, nor light,
Nor certitude, nor peace, nor help for pain;
And we are here as on a darkling plain   35
Swept with confused alarms of struggle and flight,
Where ignorant armies clash by night.

—*1867*

23 girdle sash   **28 shingles** beach pebbles

Emily Dickinson (1830–1886) has been reinvented with each generation, and readers' views of her have ranged between two extremes —one perceiving her as the abnormally shy "Belle of Amherst" making poetry out of her own neuroses and another seeing her as a proto-feminist carving out a world of her own in self-willed isolation. What remains is her brilliant poetry —unique, original, and marked with the stamp of individual talent. Dickinson published only seven poems during her lifetime, but left behind hundreds of poems in manuscript at her death. Published by her relatives, they were immediately popular, but it was not until the edition of Thomas Johnson in 1955 that they were read with Dickinson's eccentric punctuation and capitalization intact.

Emily Dickinson
Because I Could Not Stop for Death

Because I could not stop for Death—
He kindly stopped for me—
The Carriage held but just Ourselves—
And Immortality.

We slowly drove—He knew no haste   5
And I had put away
My labor and my leisure too,
For His Civility—

We passed the School, where Children strove
At Recess—in the Ring—   10
We passed the Fields of Gazing Grain—
We passed the Setting Sun—

Or rather—He passed Us—
The Dews drew quivering and chill—
For only Gossamer, my Gown—   15
My Tippet°—only Tulle°—

We paused before a House that seemed
A Swelling of the Ground—

16 Tippet shawl   **Tulle** net-like fabric

The Roof was scarcely visible—
The Cornice—in the Ground—

Since then—'tis Centuries—and yet
Feels shorter than the Day
I first surmised the Horses' Heads
Were toward Eternity—

—*1890*

I Died for Beauty—But Was Scarce

I died for Beauty—but was scarce
Adjusted in the Tomb
When One who died for Truth, was lain
In an adjoining Room—

He questioned softly "Why I failed?"
"For Beauty," I replied—
"And I—for Truth—Themself are One—
We Brethren, are," He said—

5

And so, as Kinsmen, met a Night—
We talked between the Rooms—
Until the Moss had reached our lips—
And covered up—our names—

10

—*1890*

I Heard a Fly Buzz— When I Died—

I heard a Fly buzz—when I died—
The Stillness in the Room
Was like the Stillness in the Air—
Between the Heaves of Storm—

The Eyes around—had wrung them dry—   5
And Breaths were gathering firm
For that last Onset—when the King
Be witnessed—in the Room—

I willed my Keepsakes—Signed away
What portion of me be   10
Assignable—and then it was
There interposed a Fly—

With Blue—uncertain stumbling Buzz—
Between the light—and me—
And then the Windows failed—and then   15
I could not see to see—

—*1896*

My Life Closed Twice Before Its Close

My life closed twice before its close;
It yet remains to see
If Immortality unveil
A third event to me

So huge, so hopeless to conceive   5
As these that twice befell.
Parting is all we know of heaven,
And all we need of hell.

—*1896*

A Narrow Fellow in the Grass

A narrow Fellow in the Grass
Occasionally rides—
You may have met Him—did you not
His notice sudden is—

The Grass divides as with a Comb—   5
A spotted shaft is seen—
And then it closes at your feet
And opens further on—

He likes a Boggy Acre
A Floor to cool for Corn—   10
Yet when a Boy, and Barefoot—
I more than once at Noon
Have passed, I thought, a Whip lash
Unbraiding in the Sun
When stooping to secure it   15
It wrinkled, and was gone—

Several of Nature's People
I know, and they know me—
I feel for them a transport
Of cordiality—   20

But never met this Fellow
Attended, or alone
Without a tighter breathing
And Zero at the Bone—

                                                          —1866

The Soul Selects Her Own Society—

The Soul selects her own Society—
Then—shuts the Door—
To her divine Majority—
Present no more—

Unmoved—she notes the Chariots—pausing—   5
At her low Gate—
Unmoved—an Emperor be kneeling
Upon her Mat—

I've known her—from an ample nation—
Choose One—   *10*
Then—close the Valves° of her attention—
Like Stone—

—1890

Christina Rossetti (1830–1894) *was the younger sister of Dante Gabriel and William, also distinguished writers, and was the author of numerous devotional poems and prose works. Her collected poems, edited by her brother William, appeared posthumously in 1904.*

Christina Rossetti
Up-Hill

Does the road wind up-hill all the way?
    Yes, to the very end.
Will the day's journey take the whole long day?
    From morn to night, my friend.

But is there for the night a resting-place?   *5*
    A roof for when the slow dark hours begin.
May not the darkness hide it from my face?
    You cannot miss that inn.

Shall I meet other wayfarers at night?
    Those who have gone before.   *10*
Then must I knock, or call when just in sight?
    They will not keep you waiting at that door.

Shall I find comfort, travel-sore and weak?
    Of labor you shall find the sum.
Will there be beds for me and all who seek?   *15*
    Yea, beds for all who come.

—1858

11 Valves sliding doors

Thomas Hardy (1840–1928), *after the disappointing response to his novel* Jude the Obscure *in 1895, returned to his first love, writing poetry for the last thirty years of his long life. The language and life of Hardy's native Wessex inform both his novels and poems. His subject matter is very much of the nineteenth century, but his ironic, disillusioned point of view marks him as one of the chief predecessors of modernism.*

Thomas Hardy
Ah, Are You Digging on My Grave?

"Ah, are you digging on my grave
      My loved one?—planting rue?"°
—"No: yesterday he went to wed
One of the brightest wealth has bred.
'It cannot hurt her now,' he said,   5
      'That I should not be true.'"

"Then who is digging on my grave?
      My nearest dearest kin?"
—"Ah, no; they sit and think, 'What use!
What good will planting flowers produce?   10
No tendance of her mound can loose
      Her spirit from Death's gin.'"

"But some one digs upon my grave?
      My enemy?—prodding sly?"
—"Nay: when she heard you had passed the Gate   15
That shuts on all flesh soon or late.
She thought you no more worth her hate,
      And cares not where you lie."

"Then who is digging on my grave?
Say—since I have not guessed!"   20
—"O it is I, my mistress dear,
Your little dog, who still lives near,
And much I hope my movements here
      Have not disturbed your rest?"

2 rue yellow flower traditionally associated with sadness

"Ah, yes! *You* dig upon my grave . . .   *25*
     Why flashed it not on me
That one true heart was left behind!
What feeling do we ever find
To equal among human kind
     A dog's fidelity!"   *30*

"Mistress, I dug upon your grave
     To bury a bone, in case
I should be hungry near this spot
When passing on my daily trot.
I am sorry, but I quite forgot   *35*
     It was your resting-place."

                                                  —1914

The Convergence of the Twain

Lines on the Loss of the Titanic

1

    In a solitude of the sea
    Deep from human vanity,
And the Pride of Life that planned her, stilly couches she.

2

    Steel chambers, late the pyres
    Of her salamadrine fires,°   5
Cold currents thrid,° and turn to rhythmic tidal lyres.

3

    Over the mirrors meant
    To glass the opulent
The sea-worm crawls—grotesque, slimed, dumb, indifferent.

5 salamandrine fires The salamander, according to legend, could live in fire **6 thrid** thread

4

> Jewels in joy designed   *10*
> To ravish the sensuous mind
> Lie lightless, all their sparkles bleared and black and blind.

5

> Dim moon-eyed fishes near
> Gaze at the gilded gear
> And query: "What does this vaingloriousness down here?"   *15*

6

> Well: while was fashioning
> This creature of cleaving wing,
> The Immanent Will° that stirs and urges everything

7

> Prepared a sinister mate
> For her—so gaily great—   *20*
> A Shape of Ice, for the time far and dissociate.

8

> And as the smart ship grew
> In stature, grace, and hue,
> In shadowy silent distance grew the Iceberg too.

9

> Alien they seemed to be: *25*
> No mortal eye could see
> The intimate welding of their later history,

10

> Or sign that they were bent
> By paths coincident
> On being anon twin halves of one august event,   *30*

18 **Immanent Will** Term used by Hardy for fate

11

Till the Spinner of the Years
Said "Now!" And each one hears,
And consummation comes, and jars two hemispheres.

—*1912*

Neutral Tones

We stood by a pond that winter day,
And the sun was white, as though chidden of God,
And a few leaves lay on the starving sod;
    —They had fallen from an ash, and were gray.

Your eyes on me were as eyes that rove   5
Over tedious riddles of years ago;
And some words played between us to and fro
    On which lost the more by our love.

The smile on your mouth was the deadest thing
Alive enough to have strength to die;   10
And a grin of bitterness swept thereby
    Like an ominous bird a-wing . . .

Since then, keen lessons that love deceives,
And wrings with wrong, have shaped to me
Your face, and the God-curst sun, and a tree,   15
    And a pond edged with grayish leaves.

—*1898*

The Ruined Maid

"O 'Melia, my dear, this does everything crown!
Who could have supposed I should meet you in Town?
And whence such fair garments, such prosperi-ty?"
"O didn't you know I'd been ruined?" said she.

"You left us in tatters, without shoes or socks,   5
Tired of digging potatoes, and spudding up docks;°
And now you've gay bracelets and bright feathers three!"
"Yes: that's how we dress when we're ruined," said she.

"At home in the barton° you said 'thee' and 'thou,'
And 'thik oon,' and 'theäs oon,'° and 't'other'; but now   10
Your talking quite fits 'ee for high compa-ny!"
"Some polish is gained with one's ruin," said she.

"Your hands were like paws then, your face blue and bleak
But now I'm bewitched by your delicate cheek,
And your little gloves fit as on any la-dy!"   15
"We never do work when we're ruined," said she.

"You used to call home-life a hag-ridden dream,
And you'd sigh, and you'd sock; but at present you seem
To know not of megrims° or melancho-ly!"
"True. One's pretty lively when ruined," said she.   20

"I wish I had feathers, a fine sweeping gown,
And a delicate face, and could strut about Town!"
"My dear—a raw country girl, such as you be,
Cannot quite expect that. You ain't ruined," said she.

—1866

---

6 docks weeds   **9 barton** barnyard   **10 thik oon and theäs oon** dialect: "that one and this one"
19 megrims migraines

Gerard Manley Hopkins (1844–1889) was an English Jesuit priest who developed elaborate theories of poetic meter (what he called "sprung rhythm") and language to express his own spiritual ardor. Most of his work was posthumously printed through the efforts of his Oxford friend and later correspondent Robert Bridges, who was poet laureate.

Gerard Manley Hopkins
God's Grandeur

The world is charged with the grandeur of God.
    It will flame out, like shining from shook foil;°
    It gathers to a greatness, like the ooze of oil
Crushed.° Why do men then now not reck his rod?
Generations have trod, have trod, have trod;   *5*
    And all is seared with trade; bleared, smeared with toil;
    And wears man's smudge and shares man's smell: the soil
Is bare now, nor can foot feel, being shod.

And for all this, nature is never spent;
    There lives the dearest freshness deep down things;   *10*
And though the last lights off the black West went
    Oh, morning, at the brown brink eastward, springs—
Because the Holy Ghost over the bent
    World broods with warm breast and with ah! bright wings.

—1877

Pied Beauty

Glory be to God for dappled things—
    For skies of couple-color as a brinded° cow;
        For rose-moles all in stipple upon trout that swim;
Fresh-firecoal chestnut-falls;° finches' wings;
    Landscape plotted and pieced—fold, fallow, and plough;   *5*
        And all trades, their gear and tackle and trim.

---

2 foil gold leaf   **4 Crushed** Hopkins is referring to olive oil
2 brinded streaked   **4 Fresh-firecoal chestnut-falls** according to the poet, chestnuts have a red color

All things counter, original, spare, strange;
   Whatever is fickle, freckled (who knows how?)
      With swift, slow; sweet, sour; adazzle, dim;
He fathers-forth whose beauty is past change: *10*
        Praise him.

                          —1877

A. E. Housman (1859–1936) was educated in the classics at Oxford and was almost forty before he began to write verse seriously. His ballad-like poems of Shropshire (an area in which he never actually lived) have proved some of the most popular lyrics in English, despite their pervasive mood of bittersweet pessimism.

A. E. Housman
Eight O'Clock

He stood, and heard the steeple
   Sprinkle the quarters° on the morning town.
One, two, three, four, to market-place and people
   It tossed them down.

Strapped, noosed, nighing his hour,   *5*
   He stood and counted them and cursed his luck;
And then the clock collected in the tower
   Its strength, and struck.

                          —1922

Loveliest of Trees, the Cherry Now

Loveliest of trees, the cherry now
Is hung with bloom along the bough,
And stands about the woodland ride
Wearing white for Eastertide.

2 quarters quarter hours

Now, of my threescore years and ten,   5
Twenty will not come again,
And take from seventy springs a score,
It only leaves me fifty more.

And since to look at things in bloom
Fifty springs are little room,   10
About the woodlands I will go
To see the cherry hung with snow.

—1896

Stars, I Have Seen Them Fall

Stars, I have seen them fall,
    But when they drop and die
No star is lost at all
    From all the star-sown sky.
The toil of all that be   5
    Helps not the primal fault;
It rains into the sea
    And still the sea is salt.

—1936

"Terence, This Is Stupid Stuff . . ."

"Terence, this is stupid stuff:
You eat your victuals fast enough;
There can't be much amiss, 'tis clear,
To see the rate you drink your beer.
But oh, good Lord, the verse you make,   5
It gives a chap the belly-ache.
The cow, the old cow, she is dead;
It sleeps well, the hornèd head:

We poor lads, 'tis our turn now
To hear such tunes as killed the cow.   10
Pretty friendship 'tis to rhyme
Your friends to death before their time
Moping melancholy mad:
Come, pipe a tune to dance to, lad."

    Why, if 'tis dancing you would be,   15
There's brisker pipes than poetry.
Say, for what were hop-yards meant,
Or why was Burton built on Trent?°
Oh many a peer of England brews
Livelier liquor than the Muse,   20
And malt does more than Milton can
To justify God's ways to man.
Ale, man, ale's the stuff to drink
For fellows whom it hurts to think:
Look into the pewter pot   25
To see the world as the world's not.
And faith, 'tis pleasant till 'tis past:
The mischief is that 'twill not last.
Oh I have been to Ludlow fair
And left my necktie God knows where,   30
And carried halfway home, or near,
Pints and quarts of Ludlow beer:
Then the world seemed none so bad,
And I myself a sterling lad;
And down in lovely muck I've lain,   35
Happy till I woke again.
Then I saw the morning sky:
Heigho, the tale was all a lie;
The world, it was the old world yet,
I was I, my things were wet,   40
And nothing now remained to do
But begin the game anew.

18 **Burton built on Trent** site of breweries

Therefore, since the world has still
Much good, but much less good than ill,
And while the sun and moon endure   45
Luck's a chance, but trouble's sure,
I'd face it as a wise man would,
And train for ill and not for good.
'Tis true, the stuff I bring for sale
Is not so brisk a brew as ale: 50
Out of a stem that scored the hand
I wrung it in a weary land.
But take it: if the smack is sour,
The better for the embittered hour;
It should do good to heart and head   50
When your soul is in my soul's stead;
And I will friend you, if I may,
In the dark and cloudy day.

There was a king reigned in the East:
There, when kings will sit to feast,   60
They get their fill before they think
With poisoned meat and poisoned drink.
He gathered all that springs to birth
From the many-venomed earth;
First a little, thence to more,   65
He sampled all her killing store;
And easy, smiling, seasoned sound,
Sate the king when healths went round.
They put arsenic in his meat
And stared aghast to watch him eat;   70
They poured strychnine in his cup
And shook to see him drink it up:
They shook, they stared as white's their shirt:
Them it was their poison hurt.
—I tell the tale that I heard told.   75
Mithridates,° he died old.

—1896

76 Mithridates legendary King of Pontus, he protected himself from poisons by taking small doses
regularly

To an Athlete Dying Young

The time you won your town the race
We chaired you through the market-place;
Man and boy stood cheering by,
And home we brought you shoulder-high.

Today, the road all runners come,   5
Shoulder-high we bring you home,
And set you at your threshold down,
Townsman of a stiller town.

Smart lad, to slip betimes° away
From fields where glory does not stay   10
And early though the laurel grows
It withers quicker than the rose.

Eyes the shady night has shut
Cannot see the record cut,
And silence sounds no worse than cheers   15
After earth has stopped the ears:

Now you will not swell the rout
Of lads that wore their honours out,
Runners whom renown outran
And the name died before the man.   20

So set, before its echoes fade,
The fleet foot on the sill of shade,
And hold to the low lintel up
The still-defended challenge-cup.

And round that early-laurelled head   25
Will flock to gaze the strengthless dead,
And find unwithered on its curls
The garland briefer than a girl's.

—1896

9 betimes early

William Butler Yeats (1865–1939) is considered the greatest Irish poet and provides an important link between the late romantic era and early modernism. His early poetry, focusing on Irish legend and landscape, is regional in the best sense of the term, but his later work, with its prophetic tone and symbolist texture, moves on a larger stage. Yeats lived in London for many years and was at the center of British literary life. He was awarded the Nobel Prize in 1923.

William Butler Yeats
The Lake Isle of Innisfree

I will arise and go now, and go to Innisfree,
And a small cabin build there, of clay and wattles° made:
Nine bean-rows will I have there, a hive for the honey-bee,
And live alone in the bee-loud glade.

And I shall have some peace there, for peace comes dropping slow,   5
Dropping from the veils of the morning to where the cricket sings;
There midnight's all a glimmer, and noon a purple glow,
And evening full of the linnet's wings.

I will arise and go now, for always night and day
I hear lake water lapping with low sounds by the shore;   10
While I stand on the roadway, or on the pavements gray,
I hear it in the deep heart's core.

—1892

Leda° and the Swan

A sudden blow: the great wings beating still
Above the staggering girl, her thighs caressed
By the dark webs, her nape caught in his bill,
He holds her helpless breast upon his breast.

How can those terrified vague fingers push   5
The feathered glory from her loosening thighs?

2 wattles woven poles and reeds
Leda mortal mother of Helen of Troy and Clytemnestra, wife and assassin of Agamemnon

And how can body, laid in that white rush,
But feel the strange heart beating where it lies?

A shudder in the loins engenders there
The broken wall, the burning roof and tower   10
And Agamemnon dead.°
      Being so caught up,
So mastered by the brute blood of the air,
Did she put on his knowledge with his power
Before the indifferent beak could let her drop?

                              —1923

Sailing to Byzantium°

1

That is no country for old men. The young
In one another's arms, birds in the trees
—Those dying generations—at their song,
The salmon-falls, the mackerel-crowded seas,
Fish, flesh, or fowl, commend all summer long   5
Whatever is begotten, born, and dies.
Caught in that sensual music all neglect
Monuments of unaging intellect.

2

An aged man is but a paltry thing,
A tattered coat upon a stick, unless   10
Soul clap its hands and sing, and louder sing
For every tatter in its mortal dress,
Nor is there singing school but studying
Monuments of its own magnificence;
And therefore I have sailed the seas and come   15
To the holy city of Byzantium.

10–11 The broken wall . . . Agamemnon dead events that occurred during and after the
Trojan War
Byzantium Constantinople or Istanbul, capital of the Eastern Roman Empire

3

O sages standing in God's holy fire
As in the gold mosaic of a wall,
Come from the holy fire, perne in a gyre,°
And be the singing-masters of my soul.   *20*
Consume my heart away; sick with desire
And fastened to a dying animal
It knows not what it is; and gather me
Into the artifice of eternity.

4

Once out of nature I shall never take   *25*
My bodily form from any natural thing,
But such a form as Grecian goldsmiths make
Of hammered gold and gold enameling
To keep a drowsy Emperor awake;
Or set upon a golden bough to sing   *30*
To lords and ladies of Byzantium
Of what is past, or passing, or to come.

                                                              —1927

The Second Coming

Turning and turning in the widening gyre°
The falcon cannot hear the falconer;
Things fall apart; the center cannot hold;
Mere anarchy is loosed upon the world,
The blood-dimmed tide is loosed, and everywhere   *5*
The ceremony of innocence is drowned;
The best lack all conviction, while the worst
Are full of passionate intensity.

Surely some revelation is at hand;
Surely the Second Coming is at hand.   *10*
The Second Coming! Hardly are those words out

19 perne in a gyre descend in a spiral; the gyre for Yeats was a private symbol of historical cycles
1 gyre see note to "Sailing to Byzantium"

When a vast image out of *Spiritus Mundi*°
Troubles my sight: somewhere in the sands of the desert
A shape with lion body and the head of a man,
A gaze blank and pitiless as the sun,   15
Is moving its slow thighs, while all about it
Reel shadows of the indignant desert birds.
The darkness drops again; but now I know
That twenty centuries of stony sleep
Were vexed to nightmare by a rocking cradle,   20
And what rough beast, its hour come round at last,
Slouches towards Bethlehem to be born?

—1921

The Song of Wandering Aengus°

I went out to the hazel wood,
Because a fire was in my head,
And cut and peeled a hazel wand,
And hooked a berry to a thread;
And when white moths were on the wing,   5
And moth-like stars were flickering out,
I dropped the berry in a stream
And caught a little silver trout.

When I had laid it on the floor
I went to blow the fire aflame,   10
But something rustled on the floor,
And some one called me by my name:
It had become a glimmering girl
With apple blossom in her hair
Who called me by my name and ran   15
And faded through the brightening air.

---

12 Spiritus Mundi World-Spirit

Aengus Among the Sidhe (native Irish deities), the god of youth, love, beauty, and poetry. Yeats once also called him the "Master of Love." Here, however, he seems mortal.

Though I am old with wandering
Through hollow lands and hilly lands,
I will find out where she has gone,
And kiss her lips and take her hands;   20
And walk among long dappled grass,
And pluck till time and times are done
The silver apples of the moon,
The golden apples of the sun.

—*1899*

Edwin Arlington Robinson (1869–1935) *wrote many poems set in "Tilbury," a recreation of his hometown of Gardiner, Maine. These poems continue to present readers with a memorable cast of eccentric characters who somehow manifest universal human desires. Robinson languished in poverty and obscurity for many years before his reputation began to flourish as a result of the interest taken in his work by President Theodore Roosevelt, who obtained a government job for Robinson and wrote a favorable review of one of his books.*

Edwin Arlington Robinson
Firelight

Ten years together without yet a cloud,
They seek each other's eyes at intervals
Of gratefulness to firelight and four walls
For love's obliteration of the crowd.
Serenely and perennially endowed   5
And bowered as few may be, their joy recalls
No snake, no sword, and over them there falls
The blessing of what neither says aloud.

Wiser for silence, they were not so glad
Were she to read the graven° tale of lines   10
On the wan face of one somewhere alone;

---

10 graven engraved

Nor were they more content could he have had
Her thoughts a moment since of one who shines
Apart, and would be hers if he had known.

—*1920*

Eros Turannos°

She fears him, and will always ask
    What fated her to choose him;
She meets in his engaging mask
    All reasons to refuse him
But what she meets and what she fears   5
Are less than are the downward years,
Drawn slowly to the foamless weirs
    Of age, were she to lose him.

Between a blurred sagacity
    That once had power to sound him,   10
And Love, that will not let him be
    The Judas that she found him,
Her pride assuages her almost,
As if it were alone the cost.—
He sees that he will not be lost,   15
    And waits and looks around him.

A sense of ocean and old trees
    Envelops and allures him;
Tradition, touching all he sees,
    Beguiles and reassures him;   20
And all her doubts of what he says
Are dimmed with what she knows of days—
Till even prejudice delays
    And fades, and she secures him.

The falling leaf inaugurates   25
    The reign of her confusion;

Eros Turannos "Love, the Tyrant"

The pounding wave reverberates
    The dirge of her illusion;
And home, where passion lived and died
Becomes a place where she can hide,   *30*
While all the town and harbor side
    Vibrate with her seclusion.

We tell you, tapping on our brows,
    The story as it should be,—
As if the story of a house   *35*
    Were told, or ever could be;
We'll have no kindly veil between
Her visions and those we have seen,—
As if we guessed what hers have been,
    Or what they are or would be.   *40*

Meanwhile we do no harm; for they
    That with a god have striven,
Not hearing much of what we say
    Take what the god has given;
Though like waves breaking it may be   *45*
Or like a changed familiar tree,
Or like a stairway to the sea
    Where down the blind are driven.

                                —1916

The Mill

The miller's wife had waited long,
    The tea was cold, the fire was dead;
And there might yet be nothing wrong
    In how he went and what he said:
"There are no millers any more,"   *5*
    Was all that she had heard him say;
And he had lingered at the door
    So long that it seemed yesterday.

Sick with a fear that had no form
    She knew that she was there at last;   *10*

And in the mill there was a warm
    And mealy fragrance of the past.
What else there was would only seem
    To say again what he had meant;
And what was hanging from a beam   *15*
    Would not have heeded where she went.

And if she thought it followed her,
    She may have reasoned in the dark
That one way of the few there were
    Would hide her and would leave no mark: *20*
Black water, smooth above the weir
    Like starry velvet in the night,
Though ruffled once, would soon appear
    The same as ever to the sight.

                      —1920

Richard Cory

Whenever Richard Cory went down town,
We people on the pavement looked at him:
He was a gentleman from sole to crown,
Clean favored, and imperially slim.

And he was always quietly arrayed,   *5*
And he was always human when he talked;
But still he fluttered pulses when he said,
"Good-morning," and he glittered when he walked.

And he was rich—yes, richer than a king—
And admirably schooled in every grace: *10*
In fine, we thought that he was everything
To make us wish that we were in his place.

So on we worked, and waited for the light,
And went without the meat, and cursed the bread;
And Richard Cory, one calm summer night,   *15*
Went home and put a bullet through his head.

                      —1896

Stephen Crane (1871–1900) was the brilliant young journalist who wrote The Red Badge of Courage *and was also an unconventional poet whose skeptical epigrams and fables today seem far ahead of their time. In many ways he mirrors the cosmic pessimism of contemporaries like Hardy, Housman, and Robinson, all of whom were influenced by the currents of determinism that ran so strongly at the end of the nineteenth century.*

Stephen Crane
The Black Riders

VI

God fashioned the ship of the world carefully.
With the infinite skill of an All-Master
Made He the hull and the sails,
Held He the rudder
Ready for adjustment.   5
Erect stood He, scanning His work proudly.
Then—at fateful time—a wrong called,
And God turned, heeding.
Lo, the ship, at this opportunity, slipped slyly,
Making cunning noiseless travel down the ways.   10
So that, for ever rudderless, it went upon the seas
Going ridiculous voyages,
Making quaint progress,
Turning as with serious purpose
Before stupid winds.   15
And there were many in the sky
Who laughed at this thing.

—1895

War Is Kind

XXI

A man said to the universe:
"Sir, I exist!"
"However," replied the universe,
"The fact has not created in me
A sense of obligation."   5

—*1899*

Paul Laurence Dunbar (1872–1906), a native of Dayton, Ohio, was one of the first black poets to make a mark in American literature. Many of his dialect poems reflect a sentimentalized view of life in the South, which he did not know directly. However, he was also capable of powerful expressions of racial protest.

Paul Laurence Dunbar
We Wear the Mask

We wear the mask that grins and lies,
It hides our cheeks and shades our eyes,—
This debt we pay to human guile;
With torn and bleeding hearts we smile,
And mouth with myriad subtleties.   5

Why should the world be over-wise,
In counting all our tears and sighs?
Nay, let them only see us, while
        We wear the mask.

We smile, but, O great Christ, our cries   10
To thee from tortured souls arise.
We sing, but oh the clay is vile
Beneath our feet, and long the mile;
But let the world dream otherwise,
        We wear the mask!   15

—*1896*

Robert Frost (1874–1963), during the second half of his long life, was a public figure who attained a popularity unmatched by any American poet of the last century. His reading at the inauguration of John F. Kennedy in 1961 capped an impressive career that included four Pulitzer Prizes. Unattracted by the more exotic aspects of modernism, Frost nevertheless remains a poet who speaks eloquently to contemporary uncertainties about humanity's place in a universe that does not seem to care much for its existence. While Frost is rarely directly an autobiographical poet ("Home Burial" may reflect the death of Frost's son Elliot at age three), his work always bears the stamp of his powerful personality and identification with the New England landscape.

Robert Frost
Acquainted with the Night

I have been one acquainted with the night.
I have walked out in rain—and back in rain.
I have outwalked the furthest city light.

I have looked down the saddest city lane.
I have passed by the watchman on his beat   5
And dropped my eyes, unwilling to explain.

I have stood still and stopped the sound of feet
When far away an interrupted cry
Came over houses from another street,

But not to call me back or say good-bye;   10
And further still at an unearthly height
One luminary clock against the sky

Proclaimed the time was neither wrong nor right.
I have been one acquainted with the night.

—*1928*

After Apple-Picking

My long two-pointed ladder's sticking through a tree
Toward heaven still,
And there's a barrel that I didn't fill
Beside it, and there may be two or three

Apples I didn't pick upon some bough. 5

But I am done with apple-picking now.

Essence of winter sleep is on the night,

The scent of apples: I am drowsing off.

I cannot rub the strangeness from my sight

I got from looking through a pane of glass 10

I skimmed this morning from the drinking trough

And held against the world of hoary grass.

It melted, and I let it fall and break.

But I was well

Upon my way to sleep before it fell, 15

And I could tell

What form my dreaming was about to take.

Magnified apples appear and disappear,

Stem end and blossom end,

And every fleck of russet showing clear. 20

My instep arch not only keeps the ache,

It keeps the pressure of a ladder-round.

I feel the ladder sway as the boughs bend.

And I keep hearing from the cellar bin

The rumbling sound 25

Of load on load of apples coming in.

For I have had too much

Of apple-picking: I am overtired

Of the great harvest I myself desired.

There were ten thousand thousand fruit to touch, 30

Cherish in hand, lift down, and not let fall.

For all

That struck the earth,

No matter if not bruised or spiked with stubble,

Went surely to the cider-apple heap 35

As of no worth.

One can see what will trouble

This sleep of mine, whatever sleep it is.

Were he not gone,

The woodchuck could say whether it's like his 40

Long sleep, as I describe its coming on,

Or just some human sleep.

—1914

Design

I found a dimpled spider, fat and white,
On a white heal-all,° holding up a moth
Like a white piece of rigid satin cloth—
Assorted characters of death and blight
Mixed ready to begin the morning right,   5
Like the ingredients of a witches' broth—
A snow-drop spider, a flower like a froth,
And dead wings carried like a paper kite.

What had that flower to do with being white,
The wayside blue and innocent heal-all?   10
What brought the kindred spider to that height,
Then steered the white moth thither in the night?
What but design of darkness to appall?—
If design govern in a thing so small.

—1936

Home Burial

He saw her from the bottom of the stairs
Before she saw him. She was starting down,
Looking back over her shoulder at some fear.
She took a doubtful step and then undid it
To raise herself and look again. He spoke   5
Advancing toward her: "What is it you see
From up there always?—for I want to know."
She turned and sank upon her skirts at that,
And her face changed from terrified to dull.
He said to gain time: "What is it you see?"   10
Mounting until she cowered under him.
"I will find out now—you must tell me, dear."
She, in her place, refused him any help,
With the least stiffening of her neck and silence.

2 **heal-all** a wildflower, usually blue

She let him look, sure that he wouldn't see,   *15*
Blind creature; and awhile he didn't see.
But at last he murmured, "Oh," and again, "Oh."

"What is it—what?" she said.

                              "Just that I see."

"You don't," she challenged. "Tell me what it is."

"The wonder is I didn't see at once   *20*
I never noticed it from here before.
I must be wonted to it—that's the reason.
The little graveyard where my people are!
So small the window frames the whole of it.
Not so much larger than a bedroom, is it?   *25*
There are three stones of slate and one of marble,
Broad-shouldered little slabs there in the sunlight
On the sidehill. We haven't to mind *those*.
But I understand: it is not the stones,
But the child's mound—"

                              "Don't, don't, don't, don't," she cried.   *30*

She withdrew, shrinking from beneath his arm
That rested on the banister, and slid downstairs;
And turned on him with such a daunting look,
He said twice over before he knew himself:
"Can't a man speak of his own child he's lost?"   *35*

"Not you!—Oh, where's my hat? Oh, I don't need it!
I must get out of here. I must get air.—
I don't know rightly whether any man can."

"Amy! Don't go to someone else this time.
Listen to me. I won't come down the stairs."   *40*
He sat and fixed his chin between his fists.
"There's something I should like to ask you, dear."

"You don't know how to ask it."

                              "Help me, then."

Her fingers moved the latch for all reply.

"My words are nearly always an offense.   45
I don't know how to speak of anything
So as to please you. But I might be taught,
I should suppose. I can't say I see how.
A man must partly give up being a man
With womenfolk. We could have some arrangement   50
By which I'd bind myself to keep hands off
Anything special you're a-mind to name.
Though I don't like such things 'twixt those that love.
Two that don't love can't live together without them.
But two that do can't live together with them."   55
She moved the latch a little. "Don't—don't go.
Don't carry it to someone else this time.
Tell me about it if it's something human.
Let me into your grief. I'm not so much
Unlike other folks as your standing there   60
Apart would make me out. Give me my chance.
I do think, though, you overdo it a little.
What was it brought you up to think it the thing
To take your mother-loss of a first child
So inconsolably—in the face of love.   65
You'd think his memory might be satisfied—"

"There you go sneering now!"

              "I'm not, I'm not!
You make me angry. I'll come down to you.
God, what a woman! And it's come to this,
A man can't speak of his own child that's dead."   70

"You can't because you don't know how to speak.
If you had any feelings, you that dug
With your own hand—how could you?—his little grave;
I saw you from that very window there,
Making the gravel leap and leap in air,   75
Leap up, like that, like that, and land so lightly
And roll back down the mound beside the hole.
I thought, Who is that man? I didn't know you.
And I crept down the stairs and up the stairs
To look again, and still your spade kept lifting.   80

Then you came in. I heard your rumbling voice
Out in the kitchen, and I don't know why,
But I went near to see with my own eyes.
You could sit there with the stains on your shoes
Of the fresh earth from your own baby's grave   *85*
And talk about your everyday concerns.
You had stood the spade up against the wall
Outside there in the entry, for I saw it."

"I shall laugh the worst laugh I ever laughed.
I'm cursed. God, if I don't believe I'm cursed."   *90*
"I can repeat the very words you were saying:
'Three foggy mornings and one rainy day
Will rot the best birch fence a man can build.'
Think of it, talk like that at such a time!
What had how long it takes a birch to rot   *95*
To do with what was in the darkened parlor?
You *couldn't* care! The nearest friends can go
With anyone to death, comes so far short
They might as well not try to go at all.
No, from the time when one is sick to death,   *100*
One is alone, and he dies more alone.
Friends make pretense of following to the grave,
But before one is in it, their minds are turned
And making the best of their way back to life
And living people, and things they understand.   *105*
But the world's evil. I won't have grief so
If I can change it. Oh, I won't, I won't!"

"There, you have said it all and you feel better.
You won't go now. You're crying. Close the door.
The heart's gone out of it: why keep it up?   *110*
Amy! There's someone coming down the road!"

"*You*—oh, you think the talk is all. I must go—
Somewhere out of this house. How can I make you—"

"If—you—do!" She was opening the door wider.
"Where do you mean to go? First tell me that.   *115*
I'll follow and bring you back by force. I *will!*—"

—1914

The Need of Being Versed in Country Things

The house had gone to bring again
To the midnight sky a sunset glow.
Now the chimney was all of the house that stood,
Like a pistil after the petals go.

The barn opposed across the way,   5
That would have joined the house in flame
Had it been the will of the wind, was left
To bear forsaken the place's name.

No more it opened with all one end
For teams that came by the stony road   10
To drum on the floor with scurrying hoofs
And brush the mow with the summer load.

The birds that came to it through the air
At broken windows flew out and in,
Their murmur more like the sigh we sigh   15
From too much dwelling on what has been.

Yet for them the lilac renewed its leaf,
And the aged elm, though touched with fire;
And the dry pump flung up an awkward arm;
And the fence post carried a strand of wire.   20

For them there was really nothing sad.
But though they rejoiced in the nest they kept,
One had to be versed in country things
Not to believe the phoebes wept.

—*1923*

Stopping by Woods on a Snowy Evening

Whose woods these are I think I know.
His house is in the village though;
He will not see me stopping here
To watch his woods fill up with snow.

My little horse must think it queer   5
To stop without a farmhouse near
Between the woods and frozen lake
The darkest evening of the year.

He gives his harness bells a shake
To ask if there is some mistake.   10
The only other sound's the sweep
Of easy wind and downy flake.

The woods are lovely, dark and deep,
But I have promises to keep,
And miles to go before I sleep,   15
And miles to go before I sleep.

—1923

Wallace Stevens (1879–1955) was a lawyer specializing in surety bonds and rose to be a vice-president of the Hartford Accident and Indemnity Company. His poetry was collected for the first time in Harmonium when he was forty-five, and while he published widely during his lifetime, his poetry was only slowly recognized as the work of a major modernist whose originality has not been surpassed. Stevens's idea of poetry as a force taking the place of religion has had a profound influence on poets and critics of this century.

Wallace Stevens

Anecdote of the Jar

I placed a jar in Tennessee,
And round it was, upon a hill.
It made the slovenly wilderness
Surround that hill.

The wilderness rose up to it,   5
And sprawled around, no longer wild.
The jar was round upon the ground
And tall and of a port in air.

It took dominion everywhere.
The jar was gray and bare.   10
It did not give of bird or bush,
Like nothing else in Tennessee.

—1923

Disillusionment of Ten O'Clock

The houses are haunted
By white night-gowns.
None are green,
Or purple with green rings,
Or green with yellow rings,   5
Or yellow with blue rings.
None of them are strange,

With socks of lace
And beaded ceintures.°
People are not going   *10*
To dream of baboons and periwinkles.°
Only, here and there, an old sailor,
Drunk and asleep in his boots,
Catches tigers
In red weather.   *15*

—*1923*

The Snow Man

One must have a mind of winter
To regard the frost and the boughs
Of the pine-trees crusted with snow;

And have been cold a long time
To behold the junipers shagged with ice,   *5*
The spruces rough in the distant glitter

Of the January sun; and not to think
Of any misery in the sound of the wind,
In the sound of a few leaves,

Which is the sound of the land   *10*
Full of the same wind
That is blowing in the same bare place

For the listener, who listens in the snow,
And, nothing himself, beholds
Nothing that is not there and the nothing that is.   *15*

—*1923*

---

9 ceintures sashes   **11 periwinkles** either wildflowers or small mollusks

Sunday Morning

I

Complacencies of the peignoir,° and late
Coffee and oranges in a sunny chair,
And the green freedom of a cockatoo
Upon a rug mingle to dissipate
The holy hush of ancient sacrifice.   5
She dreams a little, and she feels the dark
Encroachment of that old catastrophe,
As a calm darkens among water-lights.
The pungent oranges and bright, green wings
Seem things in some procession of the dead,   10
Winding across wide water, without sound.
The day is like wide water, without sound,
Stilled for the passing of her dreaming feet
Over the seas, to silent Palestine,
Dominion of the blood and sepulchre.   15

II

Why should she give her bounty to the dead?
What is divinity if it can come
Only in silent shadows and in dreams?
Shall she not find in comforts of the sun,
In pungent fruit and bright, green wings, or else   20
In any balm or beauty of the earth,
Things to be cherished like the thought of heaven?
Divinity must live within herself:
Passions of rain, or moods in falling snow;
Grievings in loneliness, or unsubdued   25
Elations when the forest blooms; gusty
Emotions on wet roads on autumn nights;
All pleasures and all pains, remembering
The bough of summer and the winter branch.
These are the measures destined for her soul.   30

1 peignoir woman's dressing gown

III

Jove° in the clouds had his inhuman birth.
No mother suckled him, no sweet land gave
Large-mannered motions to his mythy mind.
He moved among us, as a muttering king,
Magnificent, would move among his hinds,°   35
Until our blood, commingling, virginal,
With heaven, brought such requital to desire
The very hinds discerned it, in a star.
Shall our blood fail? Or shall it come to be
The blood of paradise? And shall the earth   40
Seem all of paradise that we shall know?
The sky will be much friendlier then than now,
A part of labor and a part of pain,
And next in glory to enduring love,
Not this dividing and indifferent blue.   45

IV

She says, "I am content when wakened birds,
Before they fly, test the reality
Of misty fields, by their sweet questionings;
But when the birds are gone, and their warm fields
Return no more, where, then, is paradise?"   50
There is not any haunt of prophecy,
Nor any old chimera° of the grave,
Neither the golden underground, nor isle
Melodious, where spirits gat them home,
Nor visionary south, nor cloudy palm   55
Remote on heaven's hill, that has endured
As April's green endures; or will endure
Like her remembrance of awakened birds,
Or her desire for June and evening, tipped
By the consummation of the swallow's wings.   60

---

31 Jove Roman name of Zeus   **35 hinds** inferiors or shepherds who saw the star of the nativity
52 chimera imagined monster

V

She says, "But in contentment I still feel
The need of some imperishable bliss."
Death is the mother of beauty; hence from her,
Alone, shall come fulfilment to our dreams
And our desires. Although she strews the leaves   65
Of sure obliteration on our paths,
The path sick sorrow took, the many paths
Where triumph rang its brassy phrase, or love
Whispered a little out of tenderness,
She makes the willow shiver in the sun   70
For maidens who were wont to sit and gaze
Upon the grass, relinquished to their feet.
She causes boys to pile new plums and pears
On disregarded plate. The maidens taste
And stray impassioned in the littering leaves.   75

VI

Is there no change of death in paradise?
Does ripe fruit never fall? Or do the boughs
Hang always heavy in that perfect sky,
Unchanging, yet so like our perishing earth,
With rivers like our own that seek for seas   80
They never find, the same receding shores
That never touch with inarticulate pang?
Why set the pear upon those river-banks
Or spice the shores with odors of the plum?
Alas, that they should wear our colors there,   85
The silken weavings of our afternoons,
And pick the strings of our insipid lutes!
Death is the mother of beauty, mystical,
Within whose burning bosom we devise
Our earthly mothers waiting, sleeplessly.   90

VII

Supple and turbulent, a ring of men
Shall chant in orgy on a summer morn
Their boisterous devotion to the sun,

Not as a god, but as a god might be,
Naked among them, like a savage source.   *95*
Their chant shall be a chant of paradise,
Out of their blood, returning to the sky;
And in their chant shall enter, voice by voice,
The windy lake wherein their lord delights,
The trees, like serafin,° and echoing hills,   *100*
That choir among themselves long afterward.
They shall know well the heavenly fellowship
Of men that perish and of summer morn.
And whence they came and whither they shall go
The dew upon their feet shall manifest.   *105*

VIII

She hears, upon that water without sound,
A voice that cries, "The tomb in Palestine
Is not the porch of spirits lingering.
It is the grave of Jesus, where he lay."
We live in an old chaos of the sun,   *110*
Or old dependency of day and night,
Or island solitude, unsponsored, free,
Of that wide water, inescapable.
Deer walk upon our mountains, and the quail
Whistle about us their spontaneous cries;   *115*
Sweet berries ripen in the wilderness;
And, in the isolation of the sky,
At evening, casual flocks of pigeons make
Ambiguous undulations as they sink,
Downward to darkness, on extended wings.   *120*

—1923

---

100 serafin seraphim, a type of angel

William Carlos Williams (1883–1963), like his friend Wallace Stevens, followed an unconventional career for a poet, working until his death as a pediatrician in Rutherford, New Jersey. Williams is modern poetry's greatest proponent of the American idiom. His plainspoken poems have been more widely imitated than those of any other American poet of this century, perhaps because he represents a home-grown modernist alternative to the intellectualized Europeanism of Eliot and Ezra Pound (a friend of his from college days). In his later years, Williams assisted many younger poets, among them Allen Ginsberg, for whose controversial book Howl *he wrote an introduction.*

William Carlos Williams
The Last Words of My English Grandmother

There were some dirty plates
and a glass of milk
beside her on a small table
near the rank, disheveled bed—

Wrinkled and nearly blind   5
she lay and snored
rousing with anger in her tones
to cry for food,

Gimme something to eat—
They're starving me—   10
I'm all right—I won't go
to the hospital. No, no, no

Give me something to eat!
Let me take you
to the hospital, I said   15
and after you are well

you can do as you please.
She smiled, Yes
you do what you please first
then I can do what I please—   20

Oh, oh, oh! she cried
as the ambulance men lifted
her to the stretcher—
Is this what you call

making me comfortable?   25
By now her mind was clear—
Oh you think you're smart
you young people,

she said, but I'll tell you
you don't know anything.   30
Then we started.
On the way

We passed a long row
of elms. She looked at them
awhile out of   35
the ambulance window and said,

What are all those
fuzzy-looking things out there?
Trees? Well, I'm tired
of them and rolled her head away.   40

—1920

The Red Wheelbarrow

so much depends
upon

a red wheel
barrow

glazed with rain   5
water

beside the white
chickens.

—1923

Spring and All

By the road to the contagious hospital°
under the surge of the blue
mottled clouds driven from the
northeast—a cold wind. Beyond, the
waste of broad, muddy fields   5
brown with dried weeds, standing and fallen

patches of standing water
the scattering of tall trees

All along the road the reddish
purplish, forked, upstanding, twiggy   10
stuff of bushes and small trees
with dead, brown leaves under them
leafless vines—

Lifeless in appearance, sluggish
dazed spring approaches—   15

They enter the new world naked,
cold, uncertain of all
save that they enter. All about them
the cold, familiar wind—

Now the grass, tomorrow   20
the stiff curl of wildcarrot leaf
One by one objects are defined—
It quickens: clarity, outline of leaf

But now the stark dignity of
entrance—Still, the profound change   25
has come upon them: rooted, they
grip down and begin to awaken

—*1923*

---

1 **contagious hospital** a hospital for quarantined patients

Ezra Pound (1885–1972) was the greatest international proponent of modern poetry. Born in Idaho and reared in Philadelphia, he emigrated to England in 1909, where he befriended Yeats, promoted the early work of Frost, and discovered Eliot. Pound's early promotion of the imagist movement assisted a number of important poetic principles and reputations, including those of H. D. (Hilda Doolittle) and, later, William Carlos Williams. Pound's support of Mussolini during World War II, expressed in controversial radio broadcasts, caused him to be held for over a decade after the war as a mental patient in the United States, after which he returned to Italy for the final years of his long and controversial life.

Ezra Pound

In a Station of the Metro

The apparition of these faces in the crowd;
Petals on a wet, black bough.

—1916

Portrait d'une Femme°

Your mind and you are our Sargasso Sea,°
London has swept about you this score years
And bright ships left you this or that in fee:
Ideas, old gossip, oddments of all things,
Strange spars of knowledge and dimmed wares of price.   5
Great minds have sought you—lacking someone else.
You have been second always. Tragical?
No. You preferred it to the usual thing:
One dull man, dulling and uxorious,°
One average mind—with one thought less, each year   10
Oh, you are patient, I have seen you sit
Hours, where something might have floated up.
And now you pay one. Yes, you richly pay.

Portrait d'une Femme Portrait of a Lady   **1 Sargasso Sea** area of seaweed in the mid-Atlantic where flotsam accumulates   **9 uxorious** doting and submissive

You are a person of some interest, one comes to you
And takes strange gain away: *15*
Trophies fished up; some curious suggestion;
Fact that leads nowhere; and a tale or two,
Pregnant with mandrakes,° or with something else
That might prove useful and yet never proves,
That never fits a corner or shows use,   *20*
Or finds its hour upon the loom of days:
That tarnished, gaudy, wonderful old work;
Idols and ambergris° and rare inlays,
These are your riches, your great store; and yet
For all this sea-hoard of deciduous things,   *25*
Strange woods half sodden, and new brighter stuff:
In the slow float of differing light and deep,
No! there is nothing! In the whole and all,
Nothing that's quite your own.
            Yet this is you

                —1912

The River-Merchant's Wife: A Letter°

While my hair was still cut straight across my forehead
I played about the front gate, pulling flowers.
You came by on bamboo stilts, playing horse,
You walked about my seat, playing with blue plums.
And we went on living in the village of Chokan: *5*
Two small people, without dislike or suspicion.
At fourteen I married My Lord you.
I never laughed, being bashful.
Lowering my head, I looked at the wall.
Called to, a thousand times, I never looked back.   *10*

---

18 mandrakes plants with roots shaped like the lower half of the human body   **23 ambergris** intestinal secretion of the sperm whale; valuable and used in making perfumes
The River-Merchant's Wife: A Letter imitation of a poem by Li-Po (A.D. 701–762)

At fifteen I stopped scowling,
I desired my dust to be mingled with yours
Forever and forever and forever.
Why should I climb the lookout?

At sixteen you departed,   *15*
You went into far Ku-to-yen, by the river of swirling eddies,
And you have been gone five months.
The monkeys make sorrowful noise overhead.

You dragged your feet when you went out.
By the gate now, the moss is grown, the different mosses,   *20*
Too deep to clear them away!
The leaves fall early this autumn, in wind.
The paired butterflies are already yellow with August
Over the grass in the West garden;
They hurt me. I grow older.   *25*
If you are coming down through the narrows of the river Kiang,
Please let me know beforehand,
And I will come out to meet you
    As far as Cho-Fu-Sa.

—1915

Elinor Wylie (1885–1928), whose considerable lyrical skills found wide popularity during her relatively brief career, has recently come to the notice of the present generation. For many readers in the post-World War I era, Wylie, along with her slightly younger contemporary Edna St. Vincent Millay, helped to define the literary role of the New Woman of the 1920s. A poetic traditionalist whose lifestyle was thoroughly modern, Wylie now seems overdue for a serious reassessment of her place in the development of twentieth-century women's poetry.

Elinor Wylie
Let No Charitable Hope

Now let no charitable hope
Confuse my mind with images
Of eagle and of antelope:
I am in nature none of these.

I was, being human, born alone;   5
I am, being woman, hard beset;
I live by squeezing from a stone
The little nourishment I get.

In masks outrageous and austere
The years go by in single file;   10
But none has merited my fear,
And none has quite escaped my smile.

—*1923*

H. D. (Hilda Doolittle) (1886–1961) was born in Bethlehem, Pennsylvania.
Hilda Doolittle was a college friend of both Williams and Pound and moved to
Europe permanently in 1911. With her husband Richard Aldington, H. D. was an
important member of the imagist group promoted by Pound.

H. D. (Hilda Doolittle)
Pear Tree

Silver dust,
lifted from the earth,
higher than my arms reach,
you have mounted,
O, silver,   5
higher than my arms reach,
you front us with great mass;

no flower ever opened
so staunch a white leaf,
no flower ever parted silver   10
from such rare silver;

O, white pear,
your flower-tufts
thick on the branch
bring summer and ripe fruits   15
in their purple hearts.

—*1916*

Sea Rose

Rose, harsh rose,
marred and with stint of petals,
meager flower, thin,
sparse of leaf,

more precious   5
than a wet rose
single on a stem—
you are caught in the drift.

Stunted, with small leaf,
you are flung on the sand,   10
you are lifted
in the crisp sand
that drives in the wind.

Can the spice-rose
drip such acrid fragrance   15
hardened in a leaf?

—*1916*

Siegfried Sassoon (1886–1967) *was a decorated hero who publicly denounced World War I and became a friend and supporter of other British war poets, including Robert Graves and Wilfred Owen. His sardonic, anti-heroic war poems owe much to Thomas Hardy, whom he acknowledged as his chief poetic influence.*

Siegfried Sassoon
Dreamers

Soldiers are citizens of death's grey land,
    Drawing no dividend from time's tomorrows.
In the great hour of destiny they stand,
    Each with his feuds, and jealousies, and sorrows.

Soldiers are sworn to action; they must win   5
    Some flaming, fatal climax with their lives.
Soldiers are dreamers, when the guns begin
    They think of firelit homes, clean beds, and wives.

I see them in foul dug-outs, gnawed by rats,
    And in the ruined trenches, lashed with rain,   *10*
Dreaming of things they did with balls and bats,
    And mocked by hopeless longing to regain
Bank-holidays, and picture shows, and spats,
    And going to the office in the train.

                        —1918

Robinson Jeffers (1887–1962) lived with his wife and children for many years in Carmel, California, in a rock house that he built himself by the sea. Many of his ideas about man's small place in the larger world of nature have gained in relevance through the years since his death. Largely forgotten for many years, his poetry, particularly his book-length verse narratives, is once more regaining the attention of serious readers.

Robinson Jeffers
The Purse-Seine°

Our sardine fishermen work at night in the dark of the moon; daylight
    or moonlight
They could not tell where to spread the net, unable to see the
    phosphorescence of the shoals of fish.
They work northward from Monterey, coasting Santa Cruz; off New
    Year's Point or off Pigeon Point
The look-out man will see some lakes of milk-color light on the
    sea's night-purple; he points, and the helmsman
Turns the dark prow, the motorboat circles the gleaming shoal
    and drifts out her seine-net. They close the circle   *5*
and purse the bottom of the net, then with great labor haul it in.

                          I cannot tell you

How beautiful the scene is, and a little terrible, then, when the
    crowded fish
Know they are caught, and wildly beat from one wall to the other of
    their closing destiny the phosphorescent

Purse-Seine large circular fishing net; the bottom is closed (or pursed) before it is hauled in

Water to a pool of flame, each beautiful slender body sheeted
  with flame, like a live rocket   10
A comet's tail wake of clear yellow flame; while outside the
  narrowing
Floats and cordage of the net great sea-lions come up to watch,
  sighing in the dark; the vast walls of night
Stand erect to the stars.

                      Lately I was looking from a night mountain-top
On a wide city, the colored splendor, galaxies of light: how could
  I help but recall the seine-net   15
Gathering the luminous fish? I cannot tell you how beautiful the
  city appeared, and a little terrible.
I thought, We have geared the machines and locked all together
  into interdependence; we have built the great cities; now
There is no escape. We have gathered vast populations incapable
  of free survival, insulated
From the strong earth, each person in himself helpless, on all
  dependent. The circle is closed, and the net
Is being hauled in. They hardly feel the cords drawing, yet they
  shine already. The inevitable mass-disasters   20
Will not come in our time nor in our children's, but we and our
  children
Must watch the net draw narrower, government take all powers—
  or revolution, and the new government
Take more than all, add to kept bodies kept souls—or anarchy,
  the mass-disasters.

                      These things are Progress;
Do you marvel our verse is troubled or frowning, while it keeps
  its reason? Or it lets go, lets the mood flow   25
In the manner of the recent young men into mere hysteria,
  splintered gleams, crackled laughter. But they are quite wrong.
There is no reason for amazement: surely one always knew that
  cultures decay, and life's end is death.

                                  —1937

Marianne Moore (1887–1972) called her own work poetry—unconventional and marked with the stamp of a rare personality—because, as she put it, there was no other category for it. For four years she was editor of the Dial, one of the chief modernist periodicals. Moore's wide range of reference, which can leap from the commonplace to the wondrous within a single poem, reflects her unique set of personal interests—which range from exotic natural species to baseball.

Marianne Moore

The Fish

wade
through black jade.
    Of the crow-blue mussel-shells, one keeps
    adjusting the ash-heaps;
        opening and shutting itself like   5

an
injured fan.
    The barnacles which encrust the side
    of the wave, cannot hide
        there for the submerged shafts of the   10

sun,
split like spun
    glass, move themselves with spotlight swiftness
    into the crevices—
        in and out, illuminating   15

the
turquoise sea
of bodies. The water drives a wedge
of iron through the iron edge
        of the cliff; whereupon the stars,   20

pink
rice-grains, ink-
    bespattered jelly-fish, crabs like green
    lilies, and submarine
        toadstools, slide each on the other.   25

All
external
    marks of abuse are present on this
    defiant edifice—
        all the physical features of   30
ac-
cident—lack
    of cornice, dynamite grooves, burns, and
    hatchet strokes, these things stand
        out on it; the chasm-side is   35
dead.
Repeated
    evidence has proved that it can live
    on what can not revive
        its youth. The sea grows old in it.

—1921

Silence

My father used to say,
"Superior people never make long visits,
have to be shown Longfellow's grave
or the glass flowers at Harvard.
Self-reliant like the cat—   5
that takes its prey to privacy,
the mouse's limp tail hanging like a shoelace from its mouth—
they sometimes enjoy solitude
and can be robbed of speech
by speech which has delighted them.   10
The deepest feeling always shows itself in silence;
not in silence, but restraint."
Nor was he insincere in saying, "Make my house your inn."
Inns are not residences.

—1935

T. S. Eliot (1888–1965) was the author of The Waste Land, *one of the most famous and difficult modernist poems, and became an international figure. Born in St. Louis and educated at Harvard, he moved to London in 1914, where he remained for the rest of his life, becoming a British subject in 1927. This chief prophet of modern despair turned to the Church of England in later life, and wrote successful dramas on religious themes. As a critic and influential editor, Eliot dominated poetic taste in England and America for over twenty-five years. He was awarded the Nobel Prize in 1948.*

T. S. Eliot
Journey of the Magi°

'A cold coming we had of it,
Just the worst time of the year
For a journey, and such a long journey:
The ways deep and the weather sharp,
The very dead of winter.'°   5
And the camels galled, sore-footed, refractory,
Lying down in the melting snow.
There were times we regretted
The summer palaces on slopes, the terraces,
And the silken girls bringing sherbet.   10
Then the camel men cursing and grumbling
And running away, and wanting their liquor and women,
And the night-fires going out, and the lack of shelters,
And the cities hostile and the towns unfriendly
And the villages dirty and charging high prices: 15
A hard time we had of it.
At the end we preferred to travel all night,
Sleeping in snatches,
With the voices singing in our ears, saying
That this was all folly.   20

Then at dawn we came down to a temperate valley,
Wet, below the snow line, smelling of vegetation;
With a running stream and a water-mill beating the darkness,

Magi Wise Men mentioned in Matthew 2:1-2   **1-5 'A cold . . . winter'** The quotation marks indicated Eliot's source, a sermon by Lancelot Andrewes (1555–1626).

And three trees on the low sky.
And an old white horse galloped away in the meadow.   25
Then we came to a tavern with vine-leaves over the lintel,
Six hands at an open door dicing for pieces of silver,
And feet kicking the empty wine-skins.
But there was no information, and so we continued
And arrived at evening, not a moment too soon   30
Finding the place; it was (you may say) satisfactory.

All this was a long time ago, I remember,
And I would do it again, but set down
This° set down
This: were we led all that way for   35
Birth or Death? There was a Birth, certainly,
We had evidence and no doubt. I had seen birth and death,
But had thought they were different; this Birth was
Hard and bitter agony for us, like Death, our death.
We returned to our places, these Kingdoms,   40
But no longer at ease here, in the old dispensation,°
With an alien people clutching their gods.
I should be glad of another death.

—*1927*

The Love Song of J. Alfred Prufrock

S'io credesse che mia risposta fosse
A persona che mai tornasse al mondo,
Questa fiamma staria senza più scosse.
Ma perciocche giammai di questo fondo
Non tornò vivo alcun, s'i'odo il vero,
Senza tema d'infamia ti rispondo.°

33-34 set down . . . This The Magus is dictating his memoirs to a scribe   **41 old dispensation**
world before the birth of Christ

S'io credesse . . . rispondo From Dante's *Inferno* (Canto 27). The speaker is Guido da Montefeltro:
"If I thought I spoke to someone who would return to the world, this flame would tremble no longer.
But, if what I hear is true, since no one has ever returned alive from this place I can answer you with-
out fear of infamy."

Let us go then, you° and I,
When the evening is spread out against the sky
Like a patient etherised upon a table;
Let us go, through certain half-deserted streets,
The muttering retreats   5
Of restless nights in one-night cheap hotels
And sawdust restaurants with oyster-shells:
Streets that follow like a tedious argument
Of insidious intent
To lead you to an overwhelming question . . .   10
Oh, do not ask, "What is it?"
Let us go and make our visit.

In the room the women come and go
Talking of Michelangelo.°

The yellow fog that rubs its back upon the window-panes,   15
The yellow smoke that rubs its muzzle on the window-panes,
Licked its tongue into the corners of the evening,
Lingered upon the pools that stand in drains,
Let fall upon its back the soot that falls from chimneys,
Slipped by the terrace, made a sudden leap,   20
And seeing that it was a soft October night,
Curled once about the house, and fell asleep.

And indeed there will be time
For the yellow smoke that slides along the street,
Rubbing its back upon the window-panes;   25
There will be time, there will be time
To prepare a face to meet the faces that you meet;
There will be time to murder and create,
And time for all the works and days of hands
That lift and drop a question on your plate: 30
Time for you and time for me,
And time yet for a hundred indecisions,
And for a hundred visions and revisions,
Before the taking of a toast and tea.

---

1 you Eliot said that the auditor of the poem was a male friend of Prufrock.   **14 Michelangelo**
Italian painter and sculptor (1475–1564)

In the room the women come and go   35
Talking of Michelangelo.

And indeed there will be time
To wonder, "Do I dare?" and, "Do I dare?"—
Time to turn back and descend the stair,
With a bald spot in the middle of my hair—   40
(They will say: "How his hair is growing thin!")
My morning coat, my collar mounting firmly to the chin,
My necktie rich and modest, but asserted by a simple pin—
(They will say: "But how his arms and legs are thin!")
Do I dare
Disturb the universe?   45
In a minute there is time
For decisions and revisions which a minute will reverse.

For I have known them all already, known them all:
Have known the evenings, mornings, afternoons,
I have measured out my life with coffee spoons;   50
I know the voices dying with a dying fall
Beneath the music from a farther room.
　　　So how should I presume?

And I have known the eyes already, known them all—   55
The eyes that fix you in a formulated phrase,
And when I am formulated, sprawling on a pin,
When I am pinned and wriggling on the wall,
Then how should I begin
To spit out all the butt-ends of my days and ways?   60
　　　And how should I presume?

And I have known the arms already, known them all—
Arms that are braceleted and white and bare
(But in the lamplight, downed with light brown hair!)
Is it perfume from a dress
That makes me so digress?   65
Arms that lie along a table, or wrap about a shawl.
　　And should I then presume?
　　And how should I begin?

　　　. . . . .

Shall I say, I have gone at dusk through narrow streets,   70
And watched the smoke that rises from the pipes
Of lonely men in shirtsleeves, leaning out of windows? . . .

I should have been a pair of ragged claws
Scuttling across the floors of silent seas.

    . . . . .

And the afternoon, the evening, sleeps so peacefully!   75
Smoothed by long fingers,
Asleep . . . tired . . . or it malingers,
Stretched on the floor, here beside you and me.
Should I, after tea and cakes and ices,
Have the strength to force the moment to its crisis?   80
But though I have wept and fasted, wept and prayed,
Though I have seen my head (grown slightly bald) brought in
    upon a platter,
I am no prophet°—and here's no great matter;
I have seen the moment of my greatness flicker,
And I have seen the eternal Footman hold my coat, and   85
    snicker,
       And in short, I was afraid.

And would it have been worth it, after all,
After the cups, the marmalade, the tea,
Among the porcelain, among some talk of you and me,
Would it have been worth while,   90
To have bitten off the matter with a smile,
To have squeezed the universe into a ball
To roll it towards some overwhelming question,
To say: "I am Lazarus,° come from the dead,
Come back to tell you all, I shall tell you all"—   95
If one, settling a pillow by her head,
    Should say: "That is not what I meant at all;
    That is not it, at all."

82-83 my head . . . no prophet allusion to John the Baptist   **94 Lazarus** raised from the dead in
John 11:1-44

And would it have been worth it, after all,
Would it have been worth while,   *100*
After the sunsets and the dooryards and the sprinkled streets,
After the novels, after the teacups, after the skirts that trail
    along the floor—
And this, and so much more?—
It is impossible to say just what I mean!
But as if a magic lantern° threw the nerves in patterns on
    a screen: *105*
Would it have been worth while
If one, settling a pillow or throwing off a shawl,
And turning toward the window, should say:
    "That is not it at all,
    That is not what I meant, at all."   *110*

    . . . . .

No! I am not Prince Hamlet, nor was meant to be;
Am an attendant lord, one that will do
To swell a progress, start a scene or two,
Advise the prince; no doubt, an easy tool,
Deferential, glad to be of use,   *115*
Politic, cautious, and meticulous;
Full of high sentence, but a bit obtuse;
At times, indeed, almost ridiculous—
Almost, at times, the Fool.°

I grow old . . . I grow old . . .   *120*
I shall wear the bottoms of my trousers rolled.

Shall I part my hair behind? Do I dare to eat a peach?
I shall wear white flannel trousers, and walk upon the beach.
I have heard the mermaids singing, each to each.

I do not think that they will sing to me.   *125*

I have seen them riding seaward on the waves
Combing the white hair of the waves blown back

---

105 magic lantern old-fashioned slide projector   **111-119 not Prince Hamlet . . . the Fool** The allusion is probably to Polonius, a character in *Hamlet*.

When the wind blows the water white and black.
We have lingered in the chambers of the sea
By sea-girls wreathed with seaweed red and brown   *130*
Till human voices wake us, and we drown.

—1917

John Crowe Ransom (1888–1974), *as a professor at Vanderbilt University in Nashville, began a little magazine called the* Fugitive, *which lent its name to a group of young southern poets who published in it. Later he moved to Kenyon College, where he was editor of the* Kenyon Review *for many years. Ransom was influential as both a poet and a critic.*

John Crowe Ransom
Bells for John Whiteside's Daughter

There was such speed in her little body,
And such lightness in her footfall,
It is no wonder her brown study°
Astonishes us all.

Her wars were bruited° in our high window.   *5*
We looked among orchard trees and beyond
Where she took arms against her shadow,
Or harried unto the pond

The lazy geese, like a snow cloud
Dripping their snow on the green grass,   *10*
Tricking and stopping, sleepy and proud,
Who cried in goose, Alas,

For the tireless heart within the little
Lady with rod that made them rise
From their noon apple-dreams and scuttle   *15*
Goose-fashion under the skies!

---

3 brown study appearance of deep concentration   **5 bruited** shouted

But now go the bells, and we are ready,
In one house we are sternly stopped
To say we are vexed at her brown study,
Lying so primly propped.

20

—1924

Piazza° Piece

—I am a gentleman in a dustcoat° trying
To make you hear. Your ears are soft and small
And listen to an old man not at all.
They want the young men's whispering and sighing.
But see the roses on your trellis dying
And hear the spectral singing of the moon;
For I must have my lovely lady soon,
I am a gentleman in a dustcoat trying.

5

—I am a lady young in beauty waiting
Until my truelove comes, and then we kiss.
But what grey man among the vines is this
Whose words are dry and faint as in a dream?
Back from my trellis, Sir, before I scream!
I am a lady young in beauty waiting.

10

—1927

Piazza courtyard   **1 dustcoat** old-fashioned coat worn while driving an open car

Edna St. Vincent Millay (1892–1950) was extremely popular in the 1920s, when her sonnets seemed the ultimate expression of the liberated sexuality of what was then called the New Woman. Neglected for many years, her poems have recently generated renewed interest, and it seems likely that she will eventually regain her status as one of the most important female poets of the twentieth century.

Edna St. Vincent Millay
If I Should Learn, in Some Quite Casual Way

If I should learn, in some quite casual way,
That you were gone, not to return again—
Read from the back-page of a paper, say,
Held by a neighbor in a subway train,
How at the corner of this avenue   5
And such a street (so are the papers filled)
A hurrying man, who happened to be you,
At noon today had happened to be killed—
I should not cry aloud—I could not cry
Aloud, or wring my hands in such a place—   10
I should but watch the station lights rush by
With a more careful interest on my face;
Or raise my eyes and read with greater care
Where to store furs and how to treat the hair.

—1917

Not in a Silver Casket

Not in a silver casket cool with pearls
Or rich with red corundum° or with blue,
Locked, and the key withheld, as other girls
Have given their loves, I give my love to you;

---

2 **red corundum** ruby-like gemstone

Not in a lovers'-knot, not in a ring   5
Worked in such fashion, and the legend plain—
Semper fidelis,° where a secret spring
Kennels a drop of mischief for the brain:
Love in the open hand, no thing but that,
Ungemmed, unhidden, wishing not to hurt,   10
As one should bring you cowslips in a hat
Swung from the hand, or apples in her skirt,
I bring you, calling out as children do:
"Look what I have!—And these are all for you."

—*1931*

Oh, Oh, You Will Be Sorry for that Word

Oh, oh, you will be sorry for that word!
Give back my book and take my kiss instead.
Was it my enemy or my friend I heard,
"What a big book for such a little head!"
Come, I will show you now my newest hat,   5
And you may watch me purse my mouth and prink!°
Oh, I shall love you still, and all of that.
I never again shall tell you what I think.
I shall be sweet and crafty, soft and sly;
You will not catch me reading any more: 10
I shall be called a wife to pattern by;
And some day when you knock and push the door,
Some sane day, not too bright and not too stormy,
I shall be gone, and you may whistle for me.

—*1923*

7 *Semper fidelis* always faithful
6 **prink** primp

What Lips My Lips Have Kissed, and Where, and Why

What lips my lips have kissed, and where, and why,
I have forgotten, and what arms have lain
Under my head till morning; but the rain
Is full of ghosts tonight, that tap and sigh
Upon the glass and listen for reply,   5
And in my heart there stirs a quiet pain
For unremembered lads that not again
Will turn to me at midnight with a cry.
Thus in the winter stands the lonely tree,
Nor knows what birds have vanished one by one,   10
Yet knows its boughs more silent than before:
I cannot say what loves have come and gone,
I only know that summer sang in me
A little while, that in me sings no more.

—1923

Wilfred Owen (1893–1918) was killed in the trenches only a few days before the armistice that ended World War I. Owen showed more promise than any other English poet of his generation. A decorated officer whose nerves broke down after exposure to battle, he met Siegfried Sassoon at Craiglockhart military hospital. His work was posthumously collected by his friend. A novel by Pat Barker, Regeneration *(also made into a film), deals with their poetic and personal relationship.*

Wilfred Owen
Dulce et Decorum Est°

Bent double, like old beggars under sacks,
Knock-kneed, coughing like hags, we cursed through sludge,
Till on the haunting flares we turned our backs

Dulce et Decorum Est (pro patria mori) from the Roman poet Horace: "It is sweet and proper to die for one's country"

And towards our distant rest began to trudge.
Men marched asleep. Many had lost their boots   5
But limped on, blood-shod. All went lame; all blind;
Drunk with fatigue; deaf even to the hoots
Of tired, outstripped Five-Nines° that dropped behind.

Gas! Gas! Quick, boys!—An ecstasy of fumbling
Fitting the clumsy helmets just in time;   10
But someone still was yelling out and stumbling
And flound'ring like a man in fire or lime . . .
Dim, through the misty panes and thick green light,°
As under a green sea, I saw him drowning.

In all my dreams, before my helpless sight,   15
He plunges at me, guttering, choking, drowning.

If in some smothering dreams you too could pace
Behind the wagon that we flung him in,
And watch the white eyes writhing in his face,
His hanging face, like a devil's sick of sin;   20
If you could hear, at every jolt, the blood
Come gargling from the froth-corrupted lungs,
Obscene as cancer, bitter as the cud
Of vile, incurable sores on innocent tongues,—
My friend,° you would not tell with such high zest   25
To children ardent for some desperate glory,
The old Lie: Dulce et decorum est
Pro patria mori.

                                                          —1920

---

8 **Five-Nines** German artillery shells (59 mm)   13 **misty panes and thick green light** i.e., through the gas mask   25 **my friend** The poem was originally addressed to Jessie Pope, a writer of patriotic verse.

Dorothy Parker (1893–1967), *as a humorist, journalist, and poet, was for many years associated with* The New Yorker *as both author and critic. Along with Robert Benchley, James Thurber, and E. B. White, she epitomizes the hard-edged humor that made that magazine unique among American periodicals.*

Dorothy Parker
One Perfect Rose

A single flow'r he sent me, since we met.
All tenderly his messenger he chose;
Deep-hearted, pure, with scented dew still wet—
One perfect rose.

I knew the language of the floweret;   5
"My fragile leaves," it said, "his heart enclose."
Love long has taken for his amulet
One perfect rose.

Why is it no one sent me yet
One perfect limousine, do you suppose?   10
Ah no, it's always just my luck to get
One perfect rose.

                                                          —1926

Résumé

Razors pain you;
Rivers are damp;
Acids stain you;
And drugs cause cramp.
Guns aren't lawful;   5
Nooses give;
Gas smells awful;
You might as well live.

                                                          —1926

e. e. cummings (1894–1962) was the son of a Harvard professor and Unitarian clergyman. Edward Estlin Cummings served as a volunteer ambulance driver in France during World War I. cummings's experimentation with the typographical aspects of poetry reveals his serious interest in cubist painting, which he studied in Paris in the 1920s. A brilliant satirist, he also excelled as a writer of lyrical poems whose unusual appearance and idiosyncratic grammar, spelling, and punctuation often overshadow their traditional themes.

e. e. cummings
nobody loses all the time

i had an uncle named
Sol who was a born failure and
nearly everybody said he should have gone
into vaudeville perhaps because my Uncle Sol could
sing McCann He Was a Diver on Xmas Eve like Hell Itself which   5
may or may not account for the fact that my Uncle

Sol indulged in that possibly most inexcusable
of all to use a highfalootin phrase
luxuries that is or to
wit farming and be   10
it needlessly
added

my Uncle Sol's farm
failed because the chickens
ate the vegetables so   15
my Uncle Sol had a
chicken farm till the
skunks ate the chickens when

my Uncle Sol
had a skunk farm but   20
the skunks caught cold and
died and so
my Uncle Sol imitated the
skunks in a subtle manner

or by drowning himself in the watertank   25
but somebody who'd given my Uncle Sol a Victor
Victrola and records while he lived presented to
him upon the auspicious occasion of his decrease a
scrumptious not to mention splendiferous funeral with
tall boys in black gloves and flowers and everything and   30

i remember we all cried like the Missouri
when my Uncle Sol's coffin lurched because
somebody pressed a button
(and down went
my Uncle   35
Sol

and started a worm farm)

                                                                        —1926

pity this busy
monster,manunkind

pity this busy monster,manunkind,

not. Progress is a comfortable disease:
your victim (death and life safely beyond)

plays with the bigness of his littleness
—electrons° deify one razorblade   5
into a mountainrange; lenses extend

unwish through curving wherewhen till unwish
returns on its unself.
                                        A world of made

is not a world of born—pity poor flesh

and trees,poor stars and stones,but never this   10
fine specimen of hypermagical

___

5 electrons in an electron microscope

ultraomnipotence. We doctors know

a hopeless case if—listen: there's a hell
of a good universe next door; let's go

—1944

r-p-o-p-h-e-s-s-a-g-r

r-p-o-p-h-e-s-s-a-g-r

           who

a)s w(e loo)k
upnowgath

        PPEGORHRASS   5
               eringint(o-
aThe):l
    eA
    !p:
S
                            a   10
            (r
rIvInG   .gRrEaPsPhOs)
                       to
rea(be)rran(com)gi(e)ngly
,grasshopper;

15

—1932

Jean Toomer (1894–1967) was born in Washington, D.C., the grandson of a black man who served as governor of Louisiana during Reconstruction. His book Cane *(1923) is a mixed collection of prose and verse based on his observations of life in rural Georgia, where he was a schoolteacher. A complete edition of his poetry, most of it unpublished during his life, was assembled over twenty years after his death.*

Jean Toomer
Reapers

Black reapers with the sound of steel on stones
Are sharpening scythes. I see them place the hones
In their hip-pockets as a thing that's done,
And start their silent swinging, one by one.
Black horses drive a mower through the weeds,   5
And there, a field rat, startled, squealing bleeds,
His belly close to ground. I see the blade,
Blood-stained, continue cutting weeds and shade.

—1923

Louise Bogan (1897–1970) was for many years the poetry editor and resident critic of The New Yorker, *and the opinions expressed in her many book reviews have held up well in the years since her death. In her later years Bogan suffered from severe bouts of clinical depression and wrote little poetry, but her relatively slim output reveals a unique poetic voice.*

Louise Bogan
Women

Women have no wilderness in them,
They are provident instead,
Content in the tight hot cell of their hearts
To eat dusty bread.

They do not see cattle cropping red winter grass,   5
They do not hear

Snow water going down under culverts
Shallow and clear.

They wait, when they should turn to journeys,
They stiffen, when they should bend.
They use against themselves that benevolence
To which no man is friend.

10

They cannot think of so many crops to a field
Or of clean wood cleft by an axe.
Their love is an eager meaninglessness
Too tense, or too lax.

15

They hear in every whisper that speaks to them
A shout and a cry.
As like as not, when they take life over their door-sills
They should let it go by.

20

—1923

Hart Crane (1899–1933) is one of the first modernists to make extensive poetic use of the artifacts —advertising slogans, motion picture lore, trade names —of American popular culture. Much of this material surfaces in The Bridge *(1930), his book-length attempt to write an epic sequence about modern America. Crane committed suicide by leaping from a ship returning from the Yucatán, where he spent his last year on a Guggenheim Fellowship attempting to write an epic poem about the conquest of Mexico.*

Hart Crane
Chaplinesque°

We make our meek adjustments,
Contented with such random consolations
As the wind deposits
In slithered and too ample pockets.

Chaplinesque after Charlie Chaplin, silent-film comedian

For we can still love the world, who find   5
A famished kitten on the step, and know
Recesses for it from the fury of the street,
Or warm torn elbow coverts.

We will sidestep, and to the final smirk
Dally the doom of that inevitable thumb   10
That slowly chafes its puckered index toward us,
Facing the dull squint with what innocence
And what surprise!

And yet these fine collapses are not lies
More than the pirouettes of any pliant cane;   15
Our obsequies are in a way, no enterprise.
We can evade you, and all else but the heart:
What blame to us if the heart live on.

The game enforces smirks; but we have seen
The moon in lonely alleys make   20
A grail of laughter of an empty ash can,
And through all sound of gaiety and quest
Have heard a kitten in the wilderness.

                                                                        —1926

Langston Hughes (1902–1967) was a leading figure in the Harlem Renaissance of the 1920s, and he became the most famous black writer of his day. Phrases from his poems and other writings have become deeply ingrained in the American consciousness. An important experimenter with poetic form, Hughes is credited with incorporating the rhythms of jazz into poetry.

Langston Hughes
Dream Boogie

Good morning, daddy!
Ain't you heard
The boogie-woogie rumble
Of a dream deferred?

Listen closely: 5
You'll hear their feet
Beating out and beating out a—

> *You think*
> *It's a happy beat?*

Listen to it closely: 10
Ain't you heard
something underneath
like a—

> *What did I say?*

Sure,
I'm happy!   15
Take it away!

> *Hey, pop!*
> *Re-bop!*
> *Mop!*   20

>   *Y-e-a-h!*

—*1951*

Theme for English B

The instructor said,

> *Go home and write*
> *a page tonight.*
> *And let that page come out of you—*
> *Then, it will be true.*   5

I wonder if it's that simple?
I am twenty-two, colored, born in Winston-Salem.
I went to school there, then Durham, then here
to this college on the hill above Harlem.
I am the only colored student in my class.   10
The steps from the hill lead down into Harlem,
through a park, then I cross St. Nicholas,

Eighth Avenue, Seventh, and I come to the Y,
the Harlem Branch Y, where I take the elevator
up to my room, sit down, and write this page: *15*

It's not easy to know what is true for you or me
at twenty-two, my age. But I guess I'm what
I feel and see and hear, Harlem, I hear you:
hear you, hear you—we two—you, me, talk on this page.
(I hear New York, too.) Me—who?   *20*
Well, I like to eat, sleep, drink, and be in love.
I like to work, read, learn, and understand life.
I like a pipe for a Christmas present,
or records—Bessie,° bop, or Bach.
I guess being colored doesn't make me *not* like   *25*
the same things other folks like who are other races.
So will my page be colored that I write?
Being me, it will not be white.
But it will be
a part of you, instructor.   *30*
You are white—
yet a part of me, as I am a part of you.
That's American.
Sometimes perhaps you don't want to be a part of me.
Nor do I often want to be a part of you.   *35*
But we are, that's true!
I guess you learn from me—
although you're older—and white—
and somewhat more free.

This is my page for English B.   *40*

—*1951*

24 **Bessie** Bessie Smith (1898–1937), blues singer

Countee Cullen (1903–1946), among black writers of the first half of the twenti-eth century, crafted poetry representing a more conservative style than that of his contemporary, Hughes. Although he wrote a number of lyrics on standard poetic themes, he is best remembered for his eloquent poems on racial subjects.

Countee Cullen
Incident

Once riding in old Baltimore,
  Heart-filled, head-filled with glee,
I saw a Baltimorean
  Keep looking straight at me.

Now I was eight and very small,   5
  And he was no whit bigger,
And so I smiled, but he poked out
  His tongue, and called me, "Nigger."

I saw the whole of Baltimore
  From May until December;   10
Of all the things that happened there
  That's all that I remember.

—1963

Yet Do I Marvel

I doubt not God is good, well-meaning, kind,
And did He stoop to quibble could tell why
The little buried mole continues blind,
Why flesh that mirrors Him must some day die,
Make plain the reason tortured Tantalus°   5
Is baited by the fickle fruit, declare
If merely brute caprice dooms Sisyphus°
To struggle up a never-ending stair.
Inscrutable His ways are, and immune

---

5 Tantalus mythological character tortured by unreachable fruit   **7 Sisyphus** figure in myth who endlessly rolls a boulder uphill

To catechism by a mind too strewn   10
With petty cares to slightly understand
What awful brain compels His awful hand.
Yet do I marvel at this curious thing:
To make a poet black and bid him sing!

—1963

Stanley Kunitz (b. 1905) witnessed the approach of Halley's Comet as a child of five and wrote his poem about it seventy-five years later on the comet's next visit. Kunitz won the Pulitzer Prize for his Selected Poems: 1928–1958, *and also was awarded the National Book Award for* Passing Through *in 1995. In 2000, at the age of ninety-five, Kunitz was appointed poet laureate of the United States.*

Stanley Kunitz
Halley's Comet

Miss Murphy in first grade
wrote its name in chalk
across the board and told us
it was roaring down the stormtracks
of the Milky Way at frightful speed   5
and if it wandered off its course
and smashed into the earth
there'd be no school tomorrow.
A red-bearded preacher from the hills
with a wild look in his eyes   10
stood in the public square
at the playground's edge
proclaiming he was sent by God
to save every one of us,
even the little children.   15
"Repent, ye sinners!" he shouted,
waving his hand-lettered sign.
At supper I felt sad to think
that it was probably
the last meal I'd share   20

with my mother and my sisters;
but I felt excited too
and scarcely touched my plate.
So mother scolded me
and sent me early to my room.   25
The whole family's asleep
except for me. They never heard me steal
into the stairwell hall and climb
the ladder to the fresh night air.
Look for me, Father, on the roof   30
of the red brick building
at the foot of Green Street—
that's where we live, you know, on the top floor.
I'm the boy in the white flannel gown
sprawled on this coarse gravel bed   35
searching the starry sky,
waiting for the world to end.

—1995

A. D. Hope (1907–2000) was the first unquestionably major poet to emerge from Australia. Hope waited until he was almost fifty to publish his first collection of poetry. Even then, the sexual frankness of poems like "Imperial Adam" proved controversial in the conservative climate of mid-1950s Australia. A poet who strongly rejects most of the tendencies of modernism (most prominently free verse), Hope seems closer in spirit to eighteenth-century satirists like Swift and Pope, whom he obviously admires, and to his exact contemporary, W. H. Auden.

A. D. Hope
Imperial Adam

Imperial Adam, naked in the dew,
Felt his brown flanks and found the rib was gone.
Puzzled he turned and saw where, two and two,
The mighty spoor of Jahweh marked the lawn.

Then he remembered through mysterious sleep   5
The surgeon fingers probing at the bone,

The voice so far away, so rich and deep:
"It is not good for him to live alone."

Turning once more he found Man's counterpart
In tender parody breathing at his side.   10
He knew her at first sight, he knew by heart
Her allegory of sense unsatisfied.

The pawpaw drooped its golden breasts above
Less generous than the honey of her flesh;
The innocent sunlight showed the place of love;   15
The dew on its dark hairs winked crisp and fresh.

This plump gourd severed from his virile root,
She promised on the turf of Paradise
Delicious pulp of the forbidden fruit;
Sly as the snake she loosed her sinuous thighs,   20

And waking, smiled up at him from the grass;
Her breasts rose softly and he heard her sigh—
From all the beasts whose pleasant task it was
In Eden to increase and multiply

Adam had learned the jolly deed of kind: 25
He took her in his arms and there and then,
Like the clean beasts, embracing from behind,
Began in joy to found the breed of men.

Then from the spurt of seed within her broke
Her terrible and triumphant female cry,   30
Split upward by the sexual lightning stroke.
It was the beasts now who stood watching by:

The gravid elephant, the calving hind,
The breeding bitch, the she-ape big with young
Were the first gentle midwives of mankind;   35
The teeming lioness rasped her with her tongue;

The proud vicuña nuzzled her as she slept
Lax on the grass; and Adam watching too
Saw how her dumb breasts at their ripening wept,
The great pod of her belly swelled and grew,   40

And saw its water break, and saw, in fear,
Its quaking muscles in the act of birth,
Between her legs a pigmy face appear,
And the first murderer lay upon the earth.

—1955

W. H. Auden (1907–1973) was already established as an important younger British poet before he moved to America in 1939 (he later became a U.S. citizen). As an important transatlantic link between two literary cultures, Auden was one of the most important literary figures and cultural spokespersons in the English-speaking world for almost forty years, giving a name to the postwar era when he dubbed it "The Age of Anxiety" in a poem. In his last years he returned briefly to Oxford, where he occupied the poetry chair.

W. H. Auden
As I Walked Out One Evening

As I walked out one evening,
    Walking down Bristol Street,
The crowds upon the pavement
    Were fields of harvest wheat.

And down by the brimming river
    I heard a lover sing   5
Under an arch of the railway:
    "Love has no ending.

"I'll love you, dear, I'll love you
    Till China and Africa meet,
And the river jumps over the mountain   10
    And the salmon sing in the street.

"I'll love you till the ocean
    Is folded and hung up to dry,
And the seven stars go squawking
    Like geese about the sky.   15

"The years shall run like rabbits,
 For in my arms I hold
The Flower of the Ages,
 And the first love of the world."   20

But all the clocks in the city
 Began to whirr and chime:
"O let not Time deceive you,
 You cannot conquer Time.

"In the burrows of the Nightmare   25
 Where Justice naked is,
Time watches from the shadow
 And coughs when you would kiss.

"In headaches and in worry
 Vaguely life leaks away,   30
And Time will have his fancy
 Tomorrow or to-day.

"Into many a green valley
 Drifts the appalling snow;
Time breaks the threaded dances   35
 And the diver's brilliant bow.

"O plunge your hands in water,
 Plunge them in up to the wrist;
Stare, stare in the basin
 And wonder what you've missed.   40

"The glacier knocks in the cupboard,
 The desert sighs in the bed,
And the crack in the tea-cup opens
 A lane to the land of the dead.

"Where the beggars raffle the banknotes   45
 And the Giant is enchanting to Jack,
And the Lily-white Boy is a Roarer,
 And Jill goes down on her back.

"O look, look in the mirror,
 O look in your distress;   50

Life remains a blessing
    Although you cannot bless.

"O stand, stand at the window
    As the tears scald and start;
You shall love your crooked neighbor   55
    With your crooked heart."

It was late, late in the evening,
    The lovers they were gone;
The clocks had ceased their chiming,
    And the deep river ran on.   60

         —1940

Musée des Beaux Arts°

About suffering they were never wrong,
The Old Masters: how well they understood
Its human position; how it takes place
While someone else is eating or opening a window or just
    walking dully along;
How, when the aged are reverently, passionately waiting   5
For the miraculous birth, there always must be
Children who did not specially want it to happen, skating
On a pond at the edge of the wood:
They never forgot
That even the dreadful martyrdom must run its course   10
Anyhow in a corner, some untidy spot
Where the dogs go on with their doggy life and the torturer's
    horse
Scratches its innocent behind on a tree.

In Brueghel's *Icarus*,° for instance: how everything turns away
Quite leisurely from the disaster; the ploughman may   15
Have heard the splash, the forsaken cry,

Musée des Beaux Arts Museum of Fine Arts   **14 Brueghel's *Icarus*** In this painting (c. 1550) the famous event from Greek myth is almost inconspicuous among the other details Auden mentions.

But for him it was not an important failure; the sun shone
As it had to on the white legs disappearing into the green
Water; and the expensive delicate ship that must have seen
Something amazing, a boy falling out of the sky,   20
Had somewhere to get to and sailed calmly on.

                                                        —1938

The Unknown Citizen

To JS/07/M/378
This Marble Monument Is Erected by the State

He was found by the Bureau of Statistics to be
One against whom there was no official complaint,
And all the reports on his conduct agree
That, in the modern sense of an old-fashioned word, he was a
    saint,
For in everything he did he served the Greater Community.   5
Except for the War till the day he retired
He worked in a factory and never got fired,
But satisfied his employers, Fudge Motors Inc.
Yet he wasn't a scab or odd in his views,
For his Union reports that he paid his dues,   10
(Our report on his Union shows it was sound)
And our Social Psychology workers found
That he was popular with his mates and liked a drink.
The Press are convinced that he bought a paper every day
And that his reactions to advertisements were normal in every
    way.   15
Policies taken out in his name prove that he was fully insured,
And his Health-card shows he was once in hospital but left it cured.
Both Producers Research and High-Grade Living declare
He was fully sensible to the advantages of the Installment Plan
And had everything necessary to the Modern Man,   20
A phonograph, a radio, a car and a frigidaire.
Our researchers into Public Opinion are content
That he held the proper opinions for the time of year;
When there was peace, he was for peace; when there was war,
    he went.

He was married and added five children to the population,   25
Which our Eugenist says was the right number for a parent of
    his generation,
And our teachers report that he never interfered with their
    education.
Was he free? Was he happy? The question is absurd:
Had anything been wrong, we should certainly have heard.

—1939

Theodore Roethke (1908–1963) was born in Michigan. Roethke was an influential teacher of poetry at the University of Washington for many years. His father was the owner of a greenhouse, and Roethke's childhood closeness to nature was an important influence on his mature poetry. His periodic nervous breakdowns, the result of bipolar manic-depression, presaged his early death.

Theodore Roethke
Dolor°

I have known the inexorable sadness of pencils,
Neat in their boxes, dolor of pad and paper-weight,
All of the misery of manilla folders and mucilage,
Desolation in immaculate public places,
Lonely reception room, lavatory, switchboard,   5
The unalterable pathos of basin and pitcher,
Ritual of multigraph, paper-clip, comma,
Endless duplication of lives and objects.
And I have seen dust from the walls of institutions,
Finer than flour, alive, more dangerous than silica,°   10
Sift, almost invisible, through long afternoons of tedium,
Dropping a fine film on nails and delicate eyebrows,
Glazing the pale hair, the duplicate grey standard faces.

—1948

Dolor sadness   **10 silica** rock dust, a cause of silicosis, an occupational disease of miners and quarry workers

My Papa's Waltz

The whiskey on your breath
Could make a small boy dizzy;
But I hung on like death:
Such waltzing was not easy.

We romped until the pans   5
Slid from the kitchen shelf;
My mother's countenance
Could not unfrown itself.

The hand that held my wrist
Was battered on one knuckle;   10
At every step you missed
My right ear scraped a buckle.

You beat time on my head
With a palm caked hard by dirt,
Then waltzed me off to bed   15
Still clinging to your shirt.

—1948

Root Cellar

Nothing would sleep in that cellar, dank as a ditch,
Bulbs broke out of boxes hunting for chinks in the dark,
Shoots dangled and drooped,
Lolling obscenely from mildewed crates,
Hung down long yellow evil necks, like tropical snakes.   5
And what a congress of stinks!—
Roots ripe as old bait,
Pulpy stems, rank, silo-rich,
Leaf-mold, manure, lime, piled against slippery planks.
Nothing would give up life: 10
Even the dirt kept breathing a small breath.

—1948

Elizabeth Bishop (1911–1979) *for most of her life was highly regarded as a "poet's poet," winning the Pulitzer Prize for* North and South *in 1956, but in the years since her death she has gained a wider readership. She traveled widely and lived in Brazil for a number of years before returning to the United States to teach at Harvard during the last years of her life.*

Elizabeth Bishop
The Fish

I caught a tremendous fish
and held him beside the boat
half out of water, with my hook
fast in a corner of his mouth.
He didn't fight.   5
He hadn't fought at all.
He hung a grunting weight,
battered and venerable
and homely. Here and there
his brown skin hung in strips   10
like ancient wallpaper,
and its pattern of darker brown
was like wallpaper:
shapes like full-blown roses
stained and lost through age.   15
He was speckled with barnacles,
fine rosettes of lime,
and infested
with tiny white sea-lice,
and underneath two or three   20
rags of green weed hung down.
While his gills were breathing in
the terrible oxygen
—the frightening gills,
fresh and crisp with blood,   25
that can cut so badly—
I thought of the coarse white flesh
packed in like feathers,

the big bones and the little bones,
the dramatic reds and blacks   *30*
of his shiny entrails,
and the pink swim-bladder
like a big peony.
I looked into his eyes
which were far larger than mine   *35*
but shallower, and yellowed,
the irises backed and packed
with tarnished tinfoil
seen through the lenses
of old scratched isinglass.°   *40*
They shifted a little, but not
to return my stare.
—It was more like the tipping
of an object toward the light.
I admired his sullen face,   *45*
the mechanism of his jaw,
and then I saw
that from his lower lip
—if you could call it a lip—
grim, wet, and weapon-like,   *50*
hung five old pieces of fish-line,
or four and a wire leader
with the swivel still attached,
with all their five big hooks
grown firmly in his mouth.   *55*
A green line, frayed at the end
where he broke it, two heavier lines,
and a fine black thread
still crimped from the strain and snap
when it broke and he got away.   *60*
Like medals with their ribbons
frayed and wavering,
a five-haired beard of wisdom
trailing from his aching jaw.

40 isinglass semi-transparent material made from fish bladders

I stared and stared   *65*
and victory filled up
the little rented boat,
from the pool of bilge
where oil had spread a rainbow
around the rusted engine
to the bailer° rusted orange,   *70*
the sun-cracked thwarts,
the oarlocks on their strings,
the gunnels°—until everything
was rainbow, rainbow, rainbow!   *75*
and I let the fish go.

                                            —1946

One Art

The art of losing isn't hard to master;
so many things seem filled with the intent
to be lost that their loss is no disaster.

Lose something every day. Accept the fluster
of lost door keys, the hour badly spent.   *5*
The art of losing isn't hard to master.

Then practice losing farther, losing faster:
places, and names, and where it was you meant
to travel. None of these will bring disaster.

I lost my mother's watch. And look! my last, or   *10*
next-to-last, of three loved houses went.
The art of losing isn't hard to master.

I lost two cities, lovely ones. And, vaster,
some realms I owned, two rivers, a continent.
I miss them, but it wasn't a disaster.   *15*

---

71 bailer bucket   **74 gunnels** gunwales

—Even losing you (the joking voice, a gesture
I love) I shan't have lied. It's evident
the art of losing's not too hard to master
though it may look like *(Write* it!) like disaster.

—*1976*

May Sarton (1912–1995) was born in Belgium. Sarton succeeded equally in poetry and prose. The journals and memoirs she produced in her last two decades added considerably to the literature of aging and won her readers perhaps more numerous than the many admirers of her poetry. Her feminism and lesbianism, made public long before doing so was either fashionable or prudent, rarely overshadow her skills at evoking the New England landscape she passionately loved.

May Sarton
A Guest

My woods belong to woodcock and to deer;
For them, it is an accident I'm here.

If, for the plump raccoon, I represent
An ash can that was surely heaven-sent,

The bright-eyed mask, the clever little paws   5
Obey not mine, but someone else's laws.

The young buck takes me in with a long glance
That says that I, not he, am here by chance.

And they all go their ways, as I must do,
Up through the green and down again to snow,   10

No one of us responsible or near,
But each himself and in the singular.

When we do meet, I am the one to stare
As if an angel had me by the hair,

As I am flooded by some ancient bliss   15
Before all I possess and can't possess.

So when a stranger knocks hard at the door,
He cannot know what I am startled for—

To see before me an unfurry face,
A creature like myself in this wild place. 20

Our wilderness gets wilder every day
And we intend to keep the tamed at bay.

Robert Hayden (1913–1980) named Countee Cullen as one of the chief early influences on his poetry. A native of Michigan, he taught for many years at Fisk University in Nashville and at the University of Michigan. Although many of Hayden's poems are on African American subjects, he wished to be considered a poet with strong links to the mainstream English tradition.

Robert Hayden
Those Winter Sundays

Sundays too my father got up early
and put his clothes on in the blueblack cold,
then with cracked hands that ached
from labor in the weekday weather made
banked fires blaze. No one ever thanked him. 5

I'd wake and hear the cold splintering, breaking.
When the rooms were warm, he'd call,
and slowly I would rise and dress,
fearing the chronic angers of that house,

Speaking indifferently to him, 10
who had driven out the cold
and polished my good shoes as well.
What did I know, what did I know
of love's austere and lonely offices?°

—1962

14 offices daily religious ceremonies

Dudley Randall (1914—2000) was the founder of Broadside Press, a black-owned publishing firm that eventually attracted important writers like Gwendolyn Brooks and Don L. Lee. For most of his life a resident of Detroit, Randall spent many years working in that city's library system before taking a similar position at the University of Detroit.

Dudley Randall
Ballad of Birmingham

*(On the Bombing of a Church in
Birmingham, Alabama, 1963)°*

"Mother dear, may I go downtown
Instead of out to play,
And march the streets of Birmingham
In a Freedom March today?"

"No, baby, no, you may not go, 5
For the dogs are fierce and wild,
And clubs and hoses, guns and jail
Aren't good for a little child."

"But, mother, I won't be alone.
Other children will go with me, 10
And march the streets of Birmingham
To make our country free."

"No, baby, no, you may not go,
For I fear those guns will fire.
But you may go to church instead 15
And sing in the children's choir."

She has combed and brushed her night-dark hair,
And bathed rose petal sweet,
And drawn white gloves on her small brown hands,
And white shoes on her feet. 20

Birmingham, Alabama, 1963 during the height of the civil rights movement

The mother smiled to know her child
Was in the sacred place,
But that smile was the last smile
To come upon her face.

For when she heard the explosion,   25
Her eyes grew wet and wild.
She raced through the streets of Birmingham
Calling for her child.

She clawed through bits of glass and brick,
Then lifted out a shoe.   30
"O, here's the shoe my baby wore,
But, baby, where are you?"

—*1969*

***William Stafford** (1914–1993) was one of the most prolific poets of the postwar era. Stafford published in virtually every magazine in the United States. Raised in Kansas as a member of the pacifist Church of the Brethren, Stafford served in a camp for conscientious objectors during World War II. His first book did not appear until he was in his forties, but he published over thirty collections before his death at age seventy nine.*

William Stafford
Traveling Through the Dark

Traveling through the dark I found a deer
dead on the edge of the Wilson River road.
It is usually best to roll them into the canyon:
that road is narrow; to swerve might make more dead.

By glow of the tail-light I stumbled back of the car   5
and stood by the heap, a doe, a recent killing;
she had stiffened already, almost cold.
I dragged her off; she was large in the belly.

My fingers touching her side brought me the reason—
her side was warm; her fawn lay there waiting,   10
alive, still, never to be born.
Beside that mountain road I hesitated.

The car aimed ahead its lowered parking lights;
under the hood purred the steady engine.
I stood in the glare of the warm exhaust turning red;   15
around our group I could hear the wilderness listen.

I thought hard for us all—my only swerving—
then pushed her over the edge into the river.

—*1960*

Dylan Thomas (1914–1953) *was a legendary performer of his and others' poetry. His popularity in the United States led to several collegiate reading tours, punctuated with outrageous behavior and self-destructive drinking that led to his early death in New York City, the victim of what the autopsy report labeled "insult to the brain." The Wales of his childhood remained a constant source of inspiration for his poetry and for radio dramas like* Under Milk Wood, *which was turned into a film by fellow Welshman Richard Burton and his then-wife, Elizabeth Taylor.*

Dylan Thomas
Do Not Go Gentle into That Good Night

Do not go gentle into that good night,
Old age should burn and rave at close of day;
Rage, rage against the dying of the light.

Though wise men at their end know dark is right,
Because their words had forked no lightning they   5
Do not go gentle into that good night.

Good men, the last wave by, crying how bright
Their frail deeds might have danced in a green bay,
Rage, rage against the dying of the light.

Wild men who caught and sang the sun in flight,   *10*
And learn, too late, they grieved it on its way,
Do not go gentle into that good night.

Grave men, near death, who see with blinding sight
Blind eyes could blaze like meteors and be gay,
Rage, rage against the dying of the light.   *15*

And you, my father, there on the sad height,
Curse, bless, me now with your fierce tears, I pray,
Do not go gentle into that good night.
Rage, rage against the dying of the light.

                                                          —1952

Fern Hill

Now as I was young and easy under the apple boughs
About the lilting house and happy as the grass was green,
   The night above the dingle starry,
     Time let me hail and climb
   Golden in the heydays of his eyes,   *5*
And honored among wagons I was prince of the apple towns
And once below a time I lordly had the trees and leaves
     Trail with daisies and barley
   Down the rivers of the windfall light.

And as I was green and carefree, famous among the barns   *10*
About the happy yard and singing as the farm was home,
   In the sun that is young once only,
     Time let me play and be
   Golden in the mercy of his means,
And green and golden I was huntsman and herdsman, the calves *15*
Sang to my horn, the foxes on the hills barked clear and cold,
     And the sabbath rang slowly
   In the pebbles of the holy streams.

All the sun long it was running, it was lovely, the hay
Fields high as the house, the tunes from the chimneys, it was air *20*
     And playing, lovely and watery

And fire green as grass.
And nightly under the simple stars
As I rode to sleep the owls were bearing the farm away,
All the moon long I heard, blessed among stables, the night-jars   25
    Flying with the ricks, and the horses
        Flashing into the dark.

And then to awake, and the farm, like a wanderer white
With the dew, come back, the cock on his shoulder: it was all
    Shining, it was Adam and maiden,   30
        The sky gathered again
    And the sun grew round that very day.
So it must have been after the birth of the simple light
In the first, spinning place, the spellbound horses walking warm
    Out of the whinnying green stable   35
        On to the fields of praise.

And honored among foxes and pheasants by the gay house
Under the new made clouds and happy as the heart was long,
    In the sun born over and over,
        I ran my heedless ways,   40
    My wishes raced through the house high hay
And nothing I cared, at my sky blue trades, that time allows
In all his tuneful turning so few and such morning songs
    Before the children green and golden
        Follow him out of grace,   45

Nothing I cared, in the lamb white days, that time would take me
Up to the swallow thronged loft by the shadow of my hand,
    In the moon that is always rising,
        Nor that riding to sleep
    I should hear him fly with the high fields   50
And wake to the farm forever fled from the childless land.
Oh as I was young and easy in the mercy of his means,
        Time held me green and dying
    Though I sang in my chains like the sea.

                                                        —1946

Weldon Kees (1914–1955) *was a multitalented poet, painter, jazz musician, and filmmaker who went from the University of Nebraska to New York to California. His reputation, aided by posthumous publication of his stories, criticism, letters, and novels, has grown steadily since his apparent suicide by leaping from the Golden Gate Bridge.*

Weldon Kees
For My Daughter

Looking into my daughter's eyes I read
Beneath the innocence of morning flesh
Concealed, hintings of death she does not heed.
Coldest of winds have blown this hair, and mesh
Of seaweed snarled these miniatures of hands;   5
The night's slow poison, tolerant and bland,
Has moved her blood. Parched years that I have seen
That may be hers appear; foul, lingering
Death in certain war, the slim legs green.
Or, fed on hate, she relishes the sting   10
Of others' agony; perhaps the cruel
Bride of a syphilitic or a fool.
These speculations sour in the sun.
I have no daughter. I desire none.

—1943

Randall Jarrell (1914–1965) excelled as both a poet and a (sometimes brutally honest) reviewer of poetry. Ironically, the author of what is perhaps the best-known poem to have emerged from World War II did not see combat during the war: he served as a control tower officer in stateside bases. A native of Nashville, Kentucky, Jarrell studied at Vanderbilt University and followed his mentor, John Crowe Ransom, to Kenyon College in 1937, where he befriended another student, Robert Lowell.

Randall Jarrell

The Death of the Ball Turret° Gunner

From my mother's sleep I fell into the State,
And I hunched in its belly till my wet fur froze.
Six miles from earth, loosed from its dream of life,
I woke to black flak and the nightmare fighters.
When I died they washed me out of the turret with a hose.   5

—1945

Margaret Walker (1915–1998), as a female African-American poet, was perhaps overshadowed by Gwendolyn Brooks, even though Walker's receipt of the Yale Younger Poets Award in 1942 for For My People *came some years before Brooks's own recognition. A longtime teacher at Jackson State University, she influenced several generations of young writers.*

Margaret Walker

For Malcolm X

All you violated ones with gentle hearts;
You violent dreamers whose cries shout heartbreak;
Whose voices echo clamors of our cool capers,
And whose black faces have hollowed pits for eyes.
All you gambling sons and hooked children and bowery bums   5

Ball Turret A Plexiglas sphere set into the belly of a heavy bomber; Jarrell noted the similarity between the gunner and a fetus in the womb.

Hating white devils and black bourgeoisie,
Thumbing your noses at your burning red suns,
Gather round this coffin and mourn your dying swan.

Snow-white moslem head-dress around a dead black face!
Beautiful were your sand-papering words against our skins!   10
Our blood and water pour from your flowing wounds.
You have cut open our breasts and dug scalpels in our brains.
When and Where will another come to take your holy place?
Old man mumbling in his dotage, or crying child, unborn?

—1970

Gwendolyn Brooks (1917–2000) *was the first African American to win a Pulitzer Prize for poetry. Brooks reflected many changes in black culture during her long career, and she wrote about the stages of her own life candidly in* From the Mecca, *her literary autobiography. Brooks was the last poetry consultant of the Library of Congress before that position became poet laureate of the United States. At the end of her life Brooks was one of the most honored and beloved of American poets.*

Gwendolyn Brooks
the mother

Abortions will not let you forget.
You remember the children you got that you did not get,
The damp small pulps with a little or with no hair,
The singers and workers that never handled the air.
You will never neglect or beat   5
them, or silence or buy with a sweet.
You will never wind up the sucking-thumb
Or scuttle off ghosts that come.
You will never leave them, controlling your luscious sigh,
Return for a snack of them, with gobbling mother-eye.   10

I have heard in the voices of the wind the voices of my dim killed
   children.
I have contracted. I have eased
My dim dears at the breasts they could never suck.
I have said, Sweets, if I sinned, if I seized

Your luck   15
And your lives from your unfinished reach,
If I stole your births and your names,
Your straight baby tears and your games,
Your stilted or lovely loves, your tumults, your marriages, aches, and
    your deaths,
If I poisoned the beginnings of your breaths,   20
Believe that even in my deliberateness I was not deliberate.
Though why should I whine,
Whine that the crime was other than mine?—
Since anyhow you are dead.
Or rather, or instead,   25
You were never made.
But that too, I am afraid,
Is faulty: oh, what shall I say, how is the truth to be said?
You were born, you had body, you died.
It is just that you never giggled or planned or cried.   30
Believe me, I loved you all.
Believe me, I knew you, though faintly, and I loved, I loved you
All.

                                                             —*1945*

We Real Cool

    The Pool Players.
    Seven at the Golden Shovel.

We real cool. We
Left school. We

Lurk late. We
Strike straight. We

Sing sin. We   5
Thin gin. We

Jazz June. We
Die soon.

                                                             —*1960*

Robert Lowell (1917–1977) *is noted as one of the chief confessional poets because of the immense influence of his nakedly autobiographical collection of 1959,* Life Studies. *His literary career covered many bases—complex, formal early work; poetic dramas and translations; public figure—and he had, as the scion of one of Boston's oldest families, a ready-made stature that made him a public figure for most of his adult life.*

Robert Lowell
For the Union Dead

"Relinquunt Omnia Servare Rem Publicam"°

The old South Boston Aquarium stands
in a Sahara of snow now. Its broken windows are boarded.
The bronze weathervane cod has lost half its scales.
The airy tanks are dry.

Once my nose crawled like a snail on the glass;   5
my hand tingled
to burst the bubbles
drifting from the noses of the cowed, compliant fish.

My hand draws back. I often sigh still
for the dark downward and vegetating kingdom   10
of the fish and reptile. One morning last March,
I pressed against the new barbed and galvanized

fence on the Boston Common. Behind their cage,
yellow dinosaur steamshovels were grunting
as they cropped up tons of mush and grass   15
to gouge their underworld garage.

Parking spaces luxuriate like civic
sandpiles in the heart of Boston.
A girdle of orange, Puritan-pumpkin colored girders
braces the tingling Statehouse,   20

Relinquunt . . . Publicam "They sacrificed everything to serve the state"

shaking over the excavations, as it faces Colonel Shaw°
and his bell-cheeked Negro infantry
on St. Gaudens'° shaking Civil War relief,
propped by a plank splint against the garage's earthquake.

Two months after marching through Boston,   25
half the regiment was dead;
at the dedication,
William James° could almost hear the bronze Negroes breathe.

Their monument sticks like a fishbone
in the city's throat.   30
Its Colonel is as lean
as a compass-needle.

He has an angry wrenlike vigilance,
a greyhound's gentle tautness;
he seems to wince at pleasure,   35
and suffocate for privacy.

He is out of bounds now. He rejoices in man's lovely,
peculiar power to choose life and die—
when he leads his black soldiers to death,
he cannot bend his back.   40

On a thousand small town New England greens,
the old white churches hold their air
of sparse, sincere rebellion; frayed flags
quilt the graveyards of the Grand Army of the Republic.

The stone statues of the abstract Union Soldier   45
grow slimmer and younger each year—
wasp-waisted, they doze over muskets
and muse through their sideburns . . .

Shaw's father wanted no monument
except the ditch,   50
where his son's body was thrown
and lost with his "niggers."

21 Colonel Shaw Robert Gould Shaw (1837–1863) led the black troops of the Massachusetts 54th regiment and died with many of them during the attack on Fort Wagner, S.C. *Glory*, a recent film, was based on these events.   **23 St. Gaudens** American sculptor (1848–1907)   **28 William James** American philosopher (1842–1910) who gave a dedication speech for the monument

The ditch is nearer.
There are no statues for the last war here;
on Boylston Street, a commercial photograph   55
shows Hiroshima boiling

over a Mosler Safe, the "Rock of Ages"
that survived the blast. Space is nearer.
When I crouch to my television set,
the drained faces of Negro school-children° rise like balloons.   60

Colonel Shaw
is riding on his bubble,
he waits
for the blessèd break.

The Aquarium is gone. Everywhere,   65
giant finned cars nose forward like fish;
a savage servility
slides by on grease.

—1959

Lawrence Ferlinghetti (b. 1919), *first owner of a literary landmark, San Francisco's City Lights Bookstore, has promoted and published the voice of the American avant-garde since the early 1950s. His own output has been relatively small, but Ferlinghetti's* A Coney Island of the Mind *remains one of the quintessential documents of the Beat Generation.*

Lawrence Ferlinghetti
A Coney Island of the Mind, #15

Constantly risking absurdity
                    and death
        whenever he performs
                    above the heads
                        of his audience   5

---

60 **Negro school-children** refers to protesters during the early days of the civil rights movement

the poet like an acrobat
           climbs on rime
                to a high wire of his own making
and balancing on eyebeams
               above a sea of faces   *10*
        paces his way
             to the other side of day
     performing entrechats
           and sleight-of-foot tricks
and other high theatrics   *15*
           and all without mistaking
     any thing
          for what it may not be

    For he's the super realist
           who must perforce perceive   *20*
     taut truth
       before the taking of each stance or step
in his supposed advance
        toward that still higher perch
where Beauty stands and waits   *25*
        with gravity
          to start her death-defying leap

    And he
     a little charleychaplin man
         who may or may not catch   *30*
her fair eternal form
       spreadeagled in the empty air
  of existence

                        —*1958*

May Swenson (1919–1989) *displayed an inventiveness in poetry that ranges from traditional formalism to many spatial or concrete poems. A careful observer of the natural world, Swenson often attempts to mimic directly the rhythms of the physical universe in her self-labeled "iconographs."*

May Swenson
How Everything Happens

(BASED ON A STUDY OF THE WAVE)

```
                                              happen.
                                        to
                                        up
                              stacking
                            is
                        something
When nothing is happening
When it happens
                something
                        pulls
                            back
                                not
                                    to
                                        happen.
When                                has happened.
        pulling back          stacking up
                    happens
        has happened                              stacks up.
When it            something              nothing
                        pulls back while
Then nothing is happening

                                        happens.
                                    and
                            forward
                        pushes
                    up
                stacks
        something
Then
```

—*1967*

Howard Nemerov (1920–1991) served as poet laureate of the United States during 1988 and 1989. A poet of brilliant formal inventiveness, he was also a skilled satirist and observer of the American scene. His sister, Diane Arbus, was a famous photographer. His Collected Poems *won the Pulitzer Prize in 1978.*

Howard Nemerov

A Primer of the Daily Round

A peels an apple, while B kneels to God,
C telephones to D, who has a hand
On E's knee, F coughs, G turns up the sod
For H's grave, I do not understand
But J is bringing one clay pigeon down   5
While K brings down a nightstick on L's head,
And M takes mustard, N drives into town,
O goes to bed with P, and Q drops dead,
R lies to S, but happens to be heard
By T, who tells U not to fire V   10
For having to give W the word
That X is now deceiving Y with Z,
    Who happens just now to remember A
    Peeling an apple somewhere far away.

—1958

Richard Wilbur (b. 1921) *will be remembered by posterity as perhaps the most skillful metricist and exponent of wit that American poetry has produced. His highly polished poetry—against the grain of much contemporary writing—is a monument to his craftsmanship and intelligence. Perhaps the most honored of all living American poets, Wilbur served as poet laureate of the United States in 1987. His translations of the verse dramas of Molière and Racine are regularly performed throughout the world.*

Richard Wilbur

Junk

> Huru Welandes
>
>   wore ne geswiceσ
>
> monna a'nigum
>
>   σara σe Mimming can
>
> heardne gehealdan.
>
>   —Waldere°

An axe angles

        from my neighbor's ashcan;
It is hell's handiwork,

        the wood not hickory,
The flow of the grain

        not faithfully followed.
The shivered shaft

        rises from a shellheap
Of plastic playthings,

        paper plates,   5
And the sheer shards

        of shattered tumblers
That were not annealed

        for the time needful.
At the same curbside,

        a cast-off cabinet
Of wavily-warped

        unseasoned wood
Waits to be trundled

        in the trash-man's truck.   10
Haul them off! Hide them!

        The heart winces

The epigraph, taken from a fragmentary Anglo-Saxon poem, concerns the legendary smith Wayland, and may roughly be translated: "Truly, Wayland's handiwork—the sword Mimming which he made—will never fail any man who knows how to use it bravely. [Wilbur's note]

For junk and gimcrack,
                    for jerrybuilt things
And the men who make them
                         for a little money,

Bartering pride
              like the bought boxer
Who pulls his punches,
                     or the paid-off jockey   15
Who in the home stretch
                       holds in his horse.

Yet the things themselves
                        in thoughtless honor
Have kept composure,
                    like captives who would not
Talk under torture.
                   Tossed from a tailgate
Where the dump displays
                        its random dolmens,   20
Its black barrows
                and blazing valleys,
They shall waste in the weather
                              toward what they were.

The sun shall glory
                   in the glitter of glass-chips,
Foreseeing the salvage
                      of the prisoned sand,
And the blistering paint
                        peel off in patches,   25
That the good grain
                   be discovered again.

Then burnt, bulldozed,
                      they shall all be buried
To the depth of diamonds,
                         in the making dark
Where halt Hephaestus
                     keeps his hammer
And Wayland's work
                  is worn away.   30

                                        —1961

Playboy

High on his stockroom ladder like a dunce
The stock-boy sits, and studies like a sage
The subject matter of one glossy page,
As lost in curves as Archimedes° once.

Sometimes, without a glance, he feeds himself.   5
The left hand, like a mother-bird in flight,
Brings him a sandwich for a sidelong bite,
And then returns it to a dusty shelf.

What so engrosses him? The wild décor
Of this pink-papered alcove into which   10
A naked girl has stumbled, with its rich
Welter of pelts and pillows on the floor,

Amidst which, kneeling in a supple pose,
She lifts a goblet in her farther hand,
As if about to toast a flower-stand   15
Above which hovers an exploding rose

Fired from a long-necked crystal vase that rests
Upon a tasseled and vermillion cloth
One taste of which would shrivel up a moth?
Or is he pondering her perfect breasts?   20

Nothing escapes him of her body's grace
Or of her floodlit skin, so sleek and warm
And yet so strangely like a uniform,
But what now grips his fancy is her face.

And how the cunning picture holds her still   25
At just that smiling instant when her soul,
Grown sweetly faint, and swept beyond control,
Consents to his inexorable will.

—1969

---

4 Archimedes Greek mathematician (287–212 B.C.)

The Writer

In her room at the prow of the house
Where light breaks, and the windows are tossed with linden,
My daughter is writing a story.

I pause in the stairwell, hearing
From her shut door a commotion of typewriter-keys   5
Like a chain hauled over a gunwale.

Young as she is, the stuff
Of her life is a great cargo, and some of it heavy:
I wish her a lucky passage.

But now it is she who pauses,   10
As if to reject my thought and its easy figure.
A stillness greatens, in which

The whole house seems to be thinking,
And then she is at it again with a bunched clamor
Of strokes, and again is silent.   15

I remember the dazed starling
Which was trapped in that very room, two years ago;
How we stole in, lifted a sash

And retreated, not to affright it;
And how for a helpless hour, through the crack of the door,   20
We watched the sleek, wild, dark

And iridescent creature
Batter against the brilliance, drop like a glove
To the hard floor, or the desk-top.

And wait then, humped and bloody,   25
For the wits to try it again; and how our spirits
Rose when, suddenly sure,

It lifted off from a chair-back,
Beating a smooth course for the right window
And clearing the sill of the world.   30

It is always a matter, my darling,
Of life or death, as I had forgotten. I wish
What I wished you before, but harder.

—1976

Year's End

Now winter downs the dying of the year,
And night is all a settlement of snow;
From the soft street the rooms of houses show
A gathered light, a shapen atmosphere,
Like frozen-over lakes whose ice is thin   5
And still allows some stirring down within.

I've known the wind by water banks to shake
The late leaves down, which frozen where they fell
And held in ice as dancers in a spell
Fluttered all winter long into a lake;   10
Graved on the dark in gestures of descent,
They seemed their own most perfect monument.

There was perfection in the death of ferns
Which laid their fragile cheeks against the stone
A million years. Great mammoths overthrown   15
Composedly have made their long sojourns,
Like palaces of patience, in the gray
And changeless lands of ice. And at Pompeii°

The little dog lay curled and did not rise
But slept the deeper as the ashes rose   20
And found the people incomplete, and froze
The random hands, the loose unready eyes
Of men expecting yet another sun
To do the shapely thing they had not done.

---

18 Pompeii Roman city destroyed by volcanic eruption in A.D. 79

These sudden ends of time must give us pause. 25
We fray into the future, rarely wrought
Save in the tapestries of afterthought.
More time, more time. Barrages of applause
Come muffled from a buried radio.
The New-year bells are wrangling with the snow. 30

—1950

Philip Larkin (1922–1985) *was perhaps the last British poet to establish a significant body of readers in the United States. The general pessimism of his work is mitigated by a wry sense of irony and brilliant formal control. For many years he was a librarian at the University of Hull, and he was also a dedicated fan and critic of jazz.*

Philip Larkin
Next, Please

Always too eager for the future, we
Pick up bad habits of expectancy.
Something is always approaching; every day
Till then we say,

Watching from a bluff the tiny, clear, 5
Sparkling armada of promises draw near.
How slow they are! And how much time they waste,
Refusing to make haste!

Yet still they leave us holding wretched stalks
Of disappointment, for, though nothing balks 10
Each big approach, leaning with brasswork prinked,
Each rope distinct,

Flagged, and the figurehead with golden tits
Arching our way, it never anchors; it's
No sooner present than it turns to past. 15
Right to the last

We think each one will heave to and unload
All good into our lives, all we are owed
For waiting so devoutly and so long.
But we are wrong: 20

Only one ship is seeking us, a black-
Sailed unfamiliar, towing at her back
A huge and birdless silence. In her wake
No waters breed or break.

—*1951*

Aubade

I work all day, and get half drunk at night.
Waking at four to soundless dark, I stare.
In time the curtain-edges will grow light.
Till then I see what's really always there:
Unresting death, a whole day nearer now,   5
Making all thought impossible but how
And where and when I shall myself die.
Arid interrogation: yet the dread
Of dying, and being dead,
Flashes afresh to hold and horrify.   10

The mind blanks at the glare. Not in remorse
—The good not done, the love not given, time
Torn off unused—nor wretchedly because
An only life can take so long to climb
Clear of its wrong beginnings, and may never;   15
But at the total emptiness for ever,
The sure extinction that we travel to
And shall be lost in always. Not to be here,
Not to be anywhere,
And soon; nothing more terrible, nothing more true. 20

This is a special way of being afraid
No trick dispels. Religion used to try,
That vast moth-eaten musical brocade

Created to pretend we never die,
And specious stuff that says *No rational being*   25
Can fear a thing it will not feel, not seeing
That this is what we fear—no sight, no sound,
No touch or taste or smell, nothing to think with,
Nothing to love or link with,
The anaesthetic from which none come round.   30

And so it stays just on the edge of vision,
A small unfocused blur, a standing chill
That slows each impulse down to indecision.
Most things may never happen: this one will,
And realization of it rages out   35
In furnace-fear when we are caught without
People or drink. Courage is no good:
It means not scaring others. Being brave
Lets no one off the grave.
Death is no different whined at than withstood.   40

Slowly light strengthens, and the room takes shape.
It stands plain as a wardrobe, what we know,
Have always known, know that we can't escape,
Yet can't accept. One side will have to go.
Meanwhile telephones crouch, getting ready to ring   45
In locked-up offices, and all the uncaring
Intricate rented world begins to rouse.
The sky is white as clay, with no sun.
Work has to be done.
Postmen like doctors go from house to house.   50

—1977

This Be The Verse

They fuck you up, your mum and dad.
    They may not mean to, but they do.
They fill you with the faults they had
    And add some extra, just for you.

But they were fucked up in their turn
    By fools in old-style hats and coats, 5
Who half the time were soppy-stern
    And half at one another's throats.

Man hands on misery to man.
    It deepens like a coastal shelf. 10
Get out as early as you can,
    And don't have any kids yourself.

—1971

James Dickey (1923–1997) became a national celebrity with the success of his novel Deliverance (1970) and the celebrated film version. There was a long background to Dickey's success, with years spent in the advertising business before he devoted himself fully to writing. Born in Atlanta and educated at Clemson, Vanderbilt, and Rice Universities, Dickey rarely strayed long from the South and taught at the University of South Carolina for over two decades.

James Dickey
The Heaven of Animals

Here they are. The soft eyes open
If they have lived in a wood
It is a wood.
If they have lived on plains
It is grass rolling
Under their feet forever. 5

Having no souls, they have come,
Anyway, beyond their knowing.
Their instincts wholly bloom
And they rise.
The soft eyes open. 10

To match them, the landscape flowers,
Outdoing, desperately
Outdoing what is required:

The richest wood,
The deepest field.   *15*

For some of these,
It could not be the place
It is, without blood.
These hunt, as they have done,
But with claws and teeth grown perfect,   *20*

More deadly than they can believe.
They stalk more silently,
And crouch on the limbs of trees,
And their descent
Upon the bright backs of their prey   *25*

May take years
In a sovereign floating of joy.
And those that are hunted
Know this as their life,
Their reward: to walk   *30*

Under such trees in full knowledge
Of what is in glory above them,
And to feel no fear,
But acceptance, compliance.
Fulfilling themselves without pain   *35*

At the cycle's center,
They tremble, they walk
Under the tree,
They fall, they are torn,
They rise, they walk again.   *40*
                                                    —1962

Alan Dugan (b. 1923) received the 1961 Yale Younger Poets Award, leading to the publication of his first collection as he neared forty. His plainspoken poetic voice, often with sardonic overtones, is appropriate for the anti-romantic stance of his most characteristic poems. For many years Dugan has been associated with the Fine Arts Work Center in Provincetown, Massachusetts, on Cape Cod.

Alan Dugan

Love Song: I and Thou

Nothing is plumb, level or square:
    the studs are bowed, the joists
are shaky by nature, no piece fits
    any other piece without a gap
or pinch, and bent nails 5
    dance all over the surfacing
like maggots. By Christ
    I am no carpenter. I built
the roof for myself, the walls
    for myself, the floors 10
for myself, and got
    hung up in it myself. I
danced with a purple thumb
    at this house-warming, drunk
with my prime whiskey: rage. 15
    Oh I spat rage's nails
into the frame-up of my work:
    it held. It settled plumb,
level, solid, square and true
    for that great moment. Then 20
it screamed and went on through,
    skewing as wrong the other way.
God damned it. This is hell,
    but I planned it, I sawed it,
I nailed it, and I 25
    will live in it until it kills me.
I can nail my left palm
    to the left-hand cross-piece but

I can't do everything myself.
    I need a hand to nail the right,   30
a help, a love, a you, a wife.

—*1961*

Anthony Hecht (b. 1923) is most often linked with Richard Wilbur as one of the American poets of the postwar era who have most effectively utilized traditional poetic forms. The brilliance of Hecht's technique, however, must be set beside the powerful moral intelligence that informs his poetry. The Hard Hours, *his second collection, won the Pulitzer Prize in 1968.*

Anthony Hecht
"More Light! More Light!"°

For Heinrich Blücher and Hannah Arendt°

Composed in the Tower before his° execution
These moving verses, and being brought at that time
Painfully to the stake, submitted, declaring thus:
"I implore my God to witness that I have made no crime."

Nor was he forsaken of courage, but the death was horrible,   5
The sack of gunpowder failing to ignite.
His legs were blistered sticks on which the black sap
Bubbled and burst as he howled for the Kindly Light.

And that was but one, and by no means one of the worst;
Permitted at least his pitiful dignity;   10
And such as were by made prayers in the name of Christ,
That shall judge all men, for his soul's tranquillity.

"More Light! More Light!" reputed last words of Johann Wolfgang von Goethe (1749–1832), greatest German poet **Heinrich Blücher and Hannah Arendt** husband and wife who escaped from Germany in 1941; Arendt wrote several books on the Holocaust **1 his** a fictional English religious martyr (c. 1550), a composite of several actual cases

We move now to outside a German wood.°
Three men are there commanded to dig a hole
In which the two Jews are ordered to lie down   15
And be buried alive by the third, who is a Pole.

Not light from the shrine at Weimar° beyond the hill
Nor light from heaven appeared. But he did refuse.
A Lüger° settled back deeply in its glove.
He was ordered to change places with the Jews.   20

Much casual death had drained away their souls.
The thick dirt mounted toward the quivering chin.
When only the head was exposed the order came
To dig him out again and to get back in.

No light, no light in the blue Polish eye.   25
When he finished a riding boot packed down the earth.
The Lüger hovered lightly in its glove.
He was shot in the belly and in three hours bled to death.

No prayers or incense rose up in those hours
Which grew to be years, and every day came mute   30
Ghosts from the ovens, sifting through crisp air,
And settled upon his eyes in a black soot.

—*1967*

13 **German wood** Buchenwald ("beechen wood") was the site of a concentration camp.   **17 shrine
at Weimar** Goethe's home   **19 Lüger** German military pistol

Denise Levertov (1923–1999) was as an outspoken opponent of U.S. involvement in the Vietnam War, an activity that has tended to overshadow her accomplishments as a lyric poet. Born of Jewish and Welsh parents in England, she emigrated to the United States during World War II.

Denise Levertov
The Ache of Marriage

The ache of marriage:

thigh and tongue, beloved,
are heavy with it,
it throbs in the teeth

We look for communion   5
and are turned away, beloved,
each and each

It is leviathan° and we
in its belly
looking for joy, some joy   10
not to be known outside it

two by two in the ark of
the ache of it.

—*1964*

---

8 leviathan great sea-creature mentioned in book of Job

Louis Simpson (b. 1923) was born in Jamaica to a colonial lawyer father and an American mother. Simpson came to the United States in his teens and served in the U.S. Army in World War II. He won the Pulitzer Prize in 1964 for At the End of the Open Road, *a volume that attempts to reexamine Walt Whitman's nineteenth-century definitions of the American experience. Subsequent collections have continued to demonstrate Simpson's unsentimental view of American suburban life.*

Louis Simpson
American Classic

It's a classic American scene—
a car stopped off the road
and a man trying to repair it.

The woman who stays in the car
in the classic American scene 5
stares back at the freeway traffic.

They look surprised, and ashamed
to be so helpless . . .
let down in the middle of the road!

To think that their car would do this! 10
They look like mountain people
whose son has gone against the law.

But every night they set out food
and the robber goes skulking back to the trees.
That's how it is with the car . . . 15

it's theirs, they're stuck with it.
Now they know what it's like to sit
and see the world go whizzing by.

In the fume of carbon monoxide and dust
they are not such good Americans 20
as they thought they were.

The feeling of being left out
through no fault of your own, is common.
That's why I say, an American classic.

—*1980*

My Father in the Night Commanding No

My father in the night commanding No
Has work to do. Smoke issues from his lips;
  He reads in silence.
The frogs are croaking and the street lamps glow.

And then my mother winds the gramophone: *5*
The Bride of Lammermoor° begins to shriek—
  Or reads a story
About a prince, a castle, and a dragon.

The moon is glittering above the hill.
I stand before the gateposts of the King—   *10*
  So runs the story—
Of Thule, at midnight when the mice are still.

And I have been in Thule! It has come true—
The journey and the danger of the world,
  All that there is   *15*
To bear and to enjoy, endure and do.

Landscapes, seascapes . . . Where have I been led?
The names of cities—Paris, Venice, Rome—
  Held out their arms.
A feathered god, seductive, went ahead.   *20*

Here is my house. Under a red rose tree
A child is swinging; another gravely plays.
  They are not surprised
That I am here; they were expecting me.

And yet my father sits and reads in silence,   *25*
My mother sheds a tear, the moon is still,
  And the dark wind
Is murmuring that nothing ever happens.

---

6 Bride of Lammermoor *Lucia di Lammermoor*, opera by Donizetti

Beyond his jurisdiction as I move,
Do I not prove him wrong? And yet, it's true
    They will not change
There, on the stage of terror and of love.

The actors in that playhouse always sit
In fixed positions—father, mother, child
    With painted eyes.
How sad it is to be a little puppet!

Their heads are wooden. And you once pretended
To understand them! Shake them as you will,
    They cannot speak.
Do what you will, the comedy is ended.

Father, why did you work? Why did you weep,
Mother? Was the story so important?
    "Listen!" the wind
Said to the children, and they fell asleep.

              —*1963*

Vassar Miller (1924–1997) *was a lifelong resident of Houston born with cerebral palsy. Miller published both traditional devotional verse and a large body of autobiographical poetry in open forms.* If I Had Wheels or Love, *her collected poems, appeared in 1990.*

Vassar Miller
Subterfuge

I remember my father, slight,
staggering in with his Underwood,°
bearing it in his arms like an awkward bouquet

for his spastic child who sits down
on the floor, one knee on the frame
of the typewriter, and holding her left wrist

2 Underwood popular brand of manual typewriter

with her right hand, in that precision known
to the crippled, pecks at the keys
with a sparrow's preoccupation.

Falling by chance on rhyme, novel and curious bubble   10
blown with a magic pipe, she tries them over and over,
spellbound by life's clashing in accord or against itself,

pretending pretense and playing at playing,
she does her childhood backward as children do,
her fun a delaying action against what she knows.   15

My father must lose her, his runaway on her treadmill,
will lose the terrible favor that life has done him
as she toils at tomorrow, tensed at her makeshift toy.

—*1981*

Donald Justice (b. 1925) has published more selectively than most of his contemporaries. His Pulitzer Prize–winning volume of selected poems displays considerable literary sophistication and reveals the poet's familiarity with the traditions of contemporary European and Latin American poetry. As an editor, he is responsible for rescuing the important work of Weldon Kees from obscurity.

Donald Justice
Counting the Mad

This one was put in a jacket,
This one was sent home,
This one was given bread and meat
But would eat none,
And this one cried No No No No   5
All day long.

this one looked at the window
As though it were a wall,
This one saw things that were not there,
This one things that were,   10
And this one cried No No No No
All day long.

This one thought himself a bird,
This one a dog,
And this one thought himself a man,
An ordinary man,
And this one cried No No No No
All day long.

15

—1960

Carolyn Kizer (b. 1925) has led a fascinating career that includes a year's study in Taiwan and another year in Pakistan, where she worked for the U.S. State Department. Her first collection, The Ungrateful Garden *(1961), demonstrates an equal facility with formal and free verse, but her subsequent books (including the Pulitzer Prize–winning* Yin *of 1985) have tended more toward the latter. A committed feminist, Kizer anticipated many of today's women's issues as early as the mid-1950s, just as the poem "The Ungrateful Garden" was published a decade before "ecology" became a household word.*

Carolyn Kizer

The Ungrateful Garden

Midas watched the golden crust
That formed over his streaming sores,
Hugged his agues, loved his lust,
But damned to hell the out-of-doors

Where blazing motes of sun impaled
The serried° roses, metal-bright.
"Those famous flowers," Midas wailed,
"Have scorched my retina with light."

5

This gift, he'd thought, would gild his joys,
Silt up the waters of his grief;
His lawns a wilderness of noise,
The heavy clang of leaf on leaf.

10

Within, the golden cup is good
To heft, to sip the yellow mead.

6 serried crowded in rows

Outside, in summer's rage, the rude   15
Gold thorn has made his fingers bleed.

"I strolled my halls in golden shift,
As ruddy as a lion's meat.
Then I rushed out to share my gift,
And golden stubble cut my feet."   20

Dazzled with wounds, he limped away
To climb into his golden bed.
Roses, roses can betray.
"Nature is evil," Midas said.

—1961

Maxine Kumin (b. 1925) was born in Philadelphia and educated at Radcliffe. Kumin was an early literary ally and friend of Anne Sexton, with whom she co-authored several children's books. The winner of the 1973 Pulitzer Prize, Kumin has preferred a rural life raising horses for some years. Her increased interest in the natural world has paralleled the environmental awareness of many of her readers.

Maxine Kumin
Noted in the *New York Times*

Lake Buena Vista, Florida, June 16, 1987

Death claimed the last pure dusky seaside sparrow
today, whose coastal range was narrow,
as narrow as its two-part buzzy song.
From hummocks lost to Cape Canaveral
this mouselike skulker in the matted grass,   5
a six-inch bird, plain brown, once thousands strong,
sang *toodle-raeee azhee*, ending on a trill
before the air gave way to rocket blasts.

It laid its dull white eggs (brown specked) in small
neat cups of grass on plots of pickleweed,   10
bulrushes, or salt hay. It dined

on caterpillars, beetles, ticks, the seeds
of sedges. Unremarkable
the life it led with others of its kind.

Tomorrow we can put it on a stamp, 15
a first-day cover with Key Largo rat,
Schaus swallowtail, Florida swamp
crocodile, and fading cotton mouse.
How simply symbols replace habitat!
The tower frames of Aerospace 20
quiver in the flush of another shot
where, once indigenous, the dusky sparrow
soared trilling twenty feet above its burrow.

—1989

Robert Creeley (b. 1926) *was educated at Harvard, and is one of several important contemporary poets (Denise Levertov is another) to be associated with Black Mountain College, a small experimental school in North Carolina that attracted writers and artists during the 1950s.*

Robert Creeley
I Know a Man

As I sd to my
friend, because I am
always talking,—John, I

sd, which was not his
name, the darkness sur- 5
rounds us, what

can we do against
it, or else, shall we &
why not, buy a goddamn big car,

drive, he sd, for 10
christ's sake, look
out where yr going.

—1962

Oh No

If you wander far enough
you will come to it
and when you get there
they will give you a place to sit

for yourself only, in a nice chair,   5
and all your friends will be there
with smiles on their faces
and they will likewise all have places.

—1962

---

*Allen Ginsberg (1926–1997) became the chief poetic spokesman of the Beat
Generation. He was a force — as poet and celebrity — who continued to outrage and
delight four decades after the appearance of* Howl, *the monumental poem describing
how Ginsberg saw: "the best minds of my generation destroyed by madness."
Ginsberg's poems are cultural documents that provide a key to understanding the radical changes in American life, particularly among youth, that began in the mid-1950s.*

Allen Ginsberg
A Supermarket in California

What thoughts I have of you tonight, Walt Whitman, for I walked
down the sidestreets under the trees with a headache self-conscious
looking at the full moon.

In my hungry fatigue, and shopping for images, I went into
the neon fruit supermarket, dreaming of your enumerations!

What peaches and what penumbras?° Whole families shopping at
night! Aisles full of husbands! Wives in the avocados, babies
in the tomatoes!—and you, García Lorca,° what were you doing down
by the watermelons?

---

3 penumbras shadows   **3 García Lorca** Federico García Lorca, Spanish poet (1899–1936)

I saw you, Walt Whitman, childless, lonely old grubber, poking among the meats in the refrigerator and eyeing the grocery boys.

I heard you asking questions of each: Who killed the pork chops? What price bananas? Are you my Angel?   5

I wandered in and out of the brilliant stacks of cans following you, and followed in my imagination by the store detective.

We strode down the open corridors together in our solitary fancy tasting artichokes, possessing every frozen delicacy, and never passing the cashier.

Where are we going, Walt Whitman? The doors close in an hour. Which way does your beard point tonight?

(I touch your book and dream of our odyssey in the supermarket and feel absurd.)

Will we walk all night through solitary streets? The trees add shade to shade, lights out in the houses, we'll both be lonely.   10

Will we stroll dreaming of the lost America of love past blue automobiles in driveways, home to our silent cottage?

Ah, dear father, graybeard, lonely old courage-teacher, what America did you have when Charon° quit poling his ferry and you got out on a smoking bank and stood watching the boat disappear on the black waters of Lethe?°

—1956

---

12 Charon ferryman of Hades   **Lethe** river in Hades, means forgetfulness

James Merrill (1926–1995) wrote "The Changing Light at Sandover," a long poem that resulted from many years of sessions with a Ouija board. The book became his major work and, among many other things, a remarkable memoir of a long-term gay relationship. Merrill's shorter poems, collected in 2001, reveal meticulous crafts-manship and a play of wit unequaled among contemporary American poets.

James Merrill

Casual Wear

Your average tourist: Fifty. 2.3
Times married. Dressed, this year, in Ferdi Plinthbower°
Originals. Odds 1 to 9¹⁰°
Against her strolling past the Embassy

Today at noon. Your average terrorist: *5*
Twenty-five. Celibate. No use for trends,
At least in clothing. Mark, though, where it ends.
People have come forth made of colored mist

Unsmiling on one hundred million screens
To tell of his prompt phone call to the station,   *10*
"Claiming responsibility"—devastation
Signed with a flourish, like the dead wife's jeans.

                             —1984

Charles on Fire

Another evening we sprawled about discussing
Appearances. And it was the consensus
That while uncommon physical good looks
Continued to launch one, as before, in life
(Among its vaporous eddies and false calms),   *5*
Still, as one of us said into his beard,
"Without your intellectual and spiritual
Values, man, you are sunk." No one but squared

---

2 Ferdi Plinthbower a fictional designer   **3 1 to 9¹⁰** pronounced "one to nine to the tenth power"

The shoulders of his own unloveliness.
Long-suffering Charles, having cooked and served the meal,   *10*
Now brought out little tumblers finely etched
He filled with amber liquor and then passed.
"Say," said the same young man, "in Paris, France,
They do it this way"—bounding to his feet
And touching a lit match to our host's full glass.   *15*
A blue flame, gentle, beautiful, came, went
Above the surface. In a hush that fell
We heard the vessel crack. The contents drained
As who should step down from a crystal coach.
Steward of spirits, Charles's glistening hand   *20*
All at once gloved itself in eeriness.
The moment passed. He made two quick sweeps and
Was flesh again. "It couldn't matter less,"
He said, but with a shocked, unconscious glance
Into the mirror. Finding nothing changed,   *25*
He filled a fresh glass and sank down among us.

—1966

W. D. Snodgrass (b. 1926) *won the Pulitzer Prize for his first collection,* Heart's Needle *(1959), and is generally considered one of the first important confessional poets. However, in his later career he has turned away from autobiographical subjects, writing, among other poems, a long sequence of dramatic monologues spoken by leading Nazis during the final days of the Hitler regime.*

W. D. Snodgrass
Mementos, I

Sorting out letters and piles of my old
    Canceled checks, old clippings, and yellow note cards
That meant something once, I happened to find
    Your picture. *That* picture. I stopped there cold,
Like a man raking piles of dead leaves in his yard   *5*
    Who has turned up a severed hand.

Still, that first second, I was glad: you stand
    Just as you stood—shy, delicate, slender,
In that long gown of green lace netting and daisies
    That you wore to our first dance. The sight of you stunned   *10*
Us all. Well, our needs were different, then,
        And our ideals came easy.

Then through the war and those two long years
    Overseas, the Japanese dead in their shacks
Among dishes, dolls, and lost shoes; I carried   *15*
    This glimpse of you, there, to choke down my fear,
Prove it had been, that it might come back.
        That was before we got married.

—Before we drained out one another's force
    With lies, self-denial, unspoken regret   *20*
And the sick eyes that blame; before the divorce
    And the treachery. Say it: before we met. Still,
I put back your picture. Someday, in due course,
        I will find that it's still there.

—1968

Frank O'Hara (1926–1966) suffered an untimely death in a dune buggy accident on Fire Island that robbed American poetry of one its most refreshing talents. An authority on modern art, O'Hara incorporates many of the spontaneous techniques of abstract painting in his own poetry, which was often written as an immediate reaction to the events of his daily life.

Frank O'Hara
The Day Lady° Died

It is 12:20 in New York a Friday
three days after Bastille day,° yes
it is 1959 and I go get a shoeshine
because I will get off the 4:19 in Easthampton

Lady Billie Holiday (1915–1959), blues singer **2 Bastille day** July 14

at 7:15 and then go straight to dinner   *5*
and I don't know the people who will feed me

I walk up the muggy street beginning to sun
and have a hamburger and a malted and buy
an ugly NEW WORLD WRITING to see what the poets
in Ghana are doing these days   *10*
                                 I go on to the bank
and Miss Stillwagon (first name Linda I once heard)
doesn't even look up my balance for once in her life
and in the GOLDEN GRIFFIN I get a little Verlaine
for Patsy with drawings by Bonnard although I do   *15*
think of Hesiod, trans. Richard Lattimore or
Brendan Behan's new play or *Le Balcon* or *Les Nègres*
of Genet, but I don't, I stick with Verlaine
after practically going to sleep with quandariness

and for Mike I just stroll into the PARK LANE   *20*
Liquor Store and ask for a bottle of Strega and
then I go back where I came from to 6th Avenue
and the tobacconist in the Ziegfeld Theatre and
casually ask for a carton of Gauloises and a carton
of Picayunes, and a NEW YORK POST with her face on it   *25*

and I am sweating a lot by now and thinking of
leaning on the john door in the 5 SPOT
while she whispered a song along the keyboard
to Mal Waldron° and everyone and I stopped breathing.

                                                        —1964

---

29 Mal Waldron Holiday's accompanist.

John Ashbery (b. 1927) was born in upstate New York and educated at Harvard University. His first full-length book, Some Trees, *was chosen by W. H. Auden as winner of the Yale Younger Poets Award in 1956. His enigmatic poems have intrigued readers for so long that much contemporary literary theory seems to have been created expressly for explicating his poems. Impossible to dismiss, Ashbery is now seen as the chief inheritor of the symbolist tradition brought to American locales by Wallace Stevens.*

John Ashbery
Farm Implements and Rutabagas in a Landscape

The first of the undecoded messages read: "Popeye sits in thunder,
Unthought of. From that shoebox of an apartment,
From livid curtain's hue, a tangram emerges: a country."
Meanwhile the Sea Hag was relaxing on a green couch: "How
    pleasant
To spend one's vacation *en la casa de Popeye*," she scratched   5
Her cleft chin's solitary hair. She remembered spinach

And was going to ask Wimpy if he had bought any spinach.
"M'love," he intercepted, "the plains are decked out in thunder
Today, and it shall be as you wish." He scratched
The part of his head under his hat. The apartment   10
Seemed to grow smaller. "But what if no pleasant
Inspiration plunge us now to the stars? *For this is my country.*"

Suddenly they remembered how it was cheaper in the country.
Wimpy was thoughtfully cutting open a number 2 can of
    spinach
When the door opened and Swee'pea crept in. "How
    pleasant!"   15
But Swee'pea looked morose. A note was pinned to his bib.
    "Thunder
And tears are unavailing," it read. "Henceforth shall Popeye's
    apartment
Be but remembered space, toxic or salubrious, whole or scratched."

Olive came hurtling through the window; its geraniums scratched
Her long thigh. "I have news!" she gasped. "Popeye, forced as you
    know to flee the country
One musty gusty evening, by the schemes of his wizened, duplicate
    father, jealous of the apartment
And all that it contains, myself and spinach
In particular, heaves bolts of loving thunder
At his own astonished becoming, rupturing the pleasant
20

Arpeggio of our years. No more shall pleasant
Rays of the sun refresh your sense of growing old, nor the scratched
Tree-trunks and mossy foliage, only immaculate darkness and thunder."
She grabbed Swee'pea. "I'm taking the brat to the country."
"But you can't do that—he hasn't even finished his spinach,"
Urged the Sea Hag, looking fearfully around at the apartment.
25

30

But Olive was already out of earshot. Now the apartment
Succumbed to a strange new hush. "Actually it's quite pleasant
Here," thought the Sea Hag. "If this is all we need fear from spinach
Then I don't mind so much. Perhaps we could invite Alice the Goon
    over"—she scratched
One dug pensively—"but Wimpy is such a country
Bumpkin, always burping like that." Minute at first, the thunder
35

Soon filled the apartment. It was domestic thunder,
The color of spinach. Popeye chuckled and scratched
His balls: it sure was pleasant to spend a day in the country.

—1966

Paradoxes and Oxymorons

The poem is concerned with language on a very plain level.
Look at it talking to you. You look out a window
Or pretend to fidget. You have it but you don't have it.
You miss it, it misses you. You miss each other.

The poem is sad because it wants to be yours, and cannot.
What's a plain level? It is that and other things,
5

Bringing a system of them into play. Play?
Well, actually, yes, but I consider play to be

A deeper outside thing, a dreamed role-pattern,
As in the division of grace these long August days   10
Without proof. Open-ended. And before you know
It gets lost in the steam and chatter of typewriters.

It has been played once more. I think you exist only
To tease me into doing it, on your level, and then you aren't there
Or have adopted a different attitude. And the poem   15
Has set me softly down beside you. The poem is you.

—1981

*W. S. Merwin (b. 1927) often displays environmental concerns that have moti-
vated much poetry in recent years. Even in earlier work his fears of the results of un-
controlled destruction of the environment are presented allegorically. Born in New
York City, he currently resides in Hawaii.*

W. S. Merwin
For the Anniversary of My Death

Every year without knowing it I have passed the day
When the last fires will wave to me
And the silence will set out
Tireless traveller
Like the beam of a lightless star   5

Then I will no longer
find myself in life as in a strange garment
surprised at the earth
And the love of one woman
And the shamelessness of men   10
As today writing after three days of rain
Hearing the wren sing and the falling cease
And bowing not knowing to what

—1969

The Last One

Well they'd make up their minds to be everywhere because why not.
Everywhere was theirs because they thought so.
They with two leaves they whom the birds despise.
In the middle of stones they made up their minds.
They started to cut.   5

Well they cut everything because why not.
Everything was theirs because they thought so.
It fell into its shadows and they took both away.
Some to have some for burning.

Well cutting everything they came to the water.   10
They came to the end of the day there was one left standing.
They would cut it tomorrow they went away.
The night gathered in the last branches.
The shadow of the night gathered in the shadow on the water.
The night and the shadow put on the same head.   15
And it said Now.

Well in the morning they cut the last one.
Like the others the last one fell into its shadow.
It fell into its shadow on the water.
They took it away its shadow stayed on the water.   20

Well they shrugged they started trying to get the shadow away.
They cut right to the ground the shadow stayed whole.
They laid boards on it the shadow came out on top.
They shone lights on it the shadow got blacker and clearer.
They exploded the water the shadow rocked.   25
They built a huge fire on the roots.
They sent up black smoke between the shadow and the sun.
The new shadow flowed without changing the old one.
They shrugged they went away to get stones.

They came back the shadow was growing.   30
They started setting up stones it was growing.
They looked the other way it went on growing.
They decided they would make a stone out of it.
They took stones to the water they poured them into the shadow.

They poured them in they poured them in the stones vanished.   35
The shadow was not filled it went on growing.
That was one day.

The next day was just the same it went on growing.
They did all the same things it was just the same.
They decided to take its water from under it.   40
They took away water they took it away the water went down.
The shadow stayed where it was before.
It went on growing it grew onto the land.
They started to scrape the shadow with machines.
When it touched the machines it stayed on them.   45
They started to beat the shadow with sticks.
Where it touched the sticks it stayed on them.
They started to beat the shadow with hands.
Where it touched the hands it stayed on them.
That was another day.   50

Well the next day started about the same it went on growing.
They pushed lights into the shadow.
Where the shadow got onto them they went out.
They began to stomp on the edge it got their feet.
And when it got their feet they fell down.   55
It got into eyes the eyes went blind.
The ones that fell down it grew over and they vanished.
The ones that went blind and walked into it vanished.
The ones that could see and stood still
It swallowed their shadows.   60
Then it swallowed them too and they vanished.
Well the others ran.

The ones that were left went away to live if it would let them.
They went as far as they could.
The lucky ones with their shadows.   65

—1969

James Wright (1927–1980) showed compassion for losers and underdogs of all types, an attitude evident everywhere in his poetry. A native of Martins Ferry, Ohio, he often described lives of quiet desperation in the blue-collar towns of his youth. Like many poets of his generation, Wright wrote formal verse in his early career and shifted to open forms during the 1960s.

James Wright
A Blessing

Just off the highway to Rochester, Minnesota,
Twilight bounds softly forth on the grass.
And the eyes of those two Indian ponies
Darken with kindness.
They have come gladly out of the willows   5
To welcome my friend and me.
We step over the barbed wire into the pasture
Where they have been grazing all day, alone.
They ripple tensely, they can hardly contain their happiness
That we have come.   10
They bow shyly as wet swans. They love each other.
There is no loneliness like theirs.
At home once more,
They begin munching the young tufts of spring in the darkness.
I would like to hold the slenderer one in my arms,   15
For she has walked over to me
And nuzzled my left hand.
She is black and white,
Her mane falls wild on her forehead,
And the light breeze moves me to caress her long ear   20
That is delicate as the skin over a girl's wrist.
Suddenly I realize
That if I stepped out of my body I would break
Into blossom.

—1963

Saint Judas

When I went out to kill myself, I caught
A pack of hoodlums beating up a man.
Running to spare his suffering, I forgot
My name, my number, how my day began,
How soldiers milled around the garden stone   5
And sang amusing songs; how all that day
Their javelins measured crowds; how I alone
Bargained the proper coins, and slipped away.

Banished from heaven, I found this victim beaten,
Stripped, kneed, and left to cry. Dropping my rope   10
Aside, I ran, ignored the uniforms:
Then I remembered bread my flesh had eaten,
The kiss that ate my flesh. Flayed without hope,
I held the man for nothing in my arms.

—1959

---

*Philip Levine (b. 1928) was born in Detroit, Michigan. He is one of many con-
temporary poets to hold a degree from the University of Iowa Writers' Workshop.
The gritty urban landscapes and characters trapped in dead-end industrial jobs that
provide Levine subjects for many poems match exactly with his unadorned, informal
idiom. Like the deceptively simple William Carlos Williams, Levine has influenced
many younger poets.*

Philip Levine
Genius

Two old dancing shoes my grandfather
gave the Christian Ladies,
an unpaid water bill, the rear license
of a dog that messed on your lawn,
a tooth I saved for the good fairy   5
and which is stained with base metals

and plastic filler. With these images
and your black luck and my bad breath
a bright beginner could make a poem
in fourteen rhyming lines about the purity   10
of first love or the rose's many thorns
or dew that won't wait long enough
to stand my little gray wren a drink.

—1981

Anne Sexton (1928–1974) lived a tortured life of mental illness and family troubles, becoming the model of the confessional poet. A housewife with two small daughters, she began writing poetry as the result of a program on public television, later taking a workshop from Robert Lowell in which Sylvia Plath was a fellow student. For fifteen years until her suicide, she was a vibrant, exciting presence in American poetry. A controversial biography of Sexton by Diane Wood Middlebrook appeared in 1991.

Anne Sexton
Cinderella

You always read about it:
the plumber with twelve children
who wins the Irish Sweepstakes.
From toilets to riches.
That story.   5

Or the nursemaid,
some luscious sweet from Denmark
who captures the oldest son's heart.
From diapers to Dior.
That story.   10

Or a milkman who serves the wealthy,
eggs, cream, butter, yogurt, milk,
the white truck like an ambulance
who goes into real estate
and makes a pile.   15
From homogenized to martinis at lunch.

Or the charwoman
who is on the bus when it cracks up
and collects enough from the insurance.
From mops to Bonwit Teller.   20
That story.

Once
the wife of a rich man was on her deathbed
and she said to her daughter Cinderella:
Be devout. Be good. Then I will smile   25
down from heaven in the seam of a cloud.
The man took another wife who had
two daughters, pretty enough
but with hearts like blackjacks.
Cinderella was their maid.   30
She slept on the sooty hearth each night
and walked around looking like Al Jolson.
Her father brought presents home from town,
jewels and gowns for the other women
but the twig of a tree for Cinderella.   35
She planted that twig on her mother's grave
and it grew to a tree where a white dove sat.
Whenever she wished for anything the dove
would drop it like an egg upon the ground.
The bird is important, my dears, so heed him. 40

Next came the ball, as you all know.
It was a marriage market.
The prince was looking for a wife.
All but Cinderella were preparing
and gussying up for the big event.   45
Cinderella begged to go too.
Her stepmother threw a dish of lentils
into the cinders and said: Pick them
up in an hour and you shall go.
The white dove brought all his friends;   50
all the warm wings of the fatherland came,
and picked up the lentils in a jiffy.
No, Cinderella, said the stepmother,

you have no clothes and cannot dance.
That's the way with stepmothers.

Cinderella went to the tree at the grave
and cried forth like a gospel singer:
Mama! Mama! My turtledove,
send me to the prince's ball!
The bird dropped down a golden dress
and delicate little gold slippers.
Rather a large package for a simple bird.
So she went. Which is no surprise.
Her stepmother and sisters didn't
recognize her without her cinder face
and the prince took her hand on the spot
and danced with no other the whole day.

As nightfall came she thought she'd
better get home. The prince walked her home
and she disappeared into the pigeon house
and although the prince took an axe and broke
it open she was gone. Back to her cinders.
These events repeated themselves for three days.
However on the third day the prince
covered the palace steps with cobbler's wax
And Cinderella's gold shoe stuck upon it.
Now he would find whom the shoe fit
and find his strange dancing girl for keeps.
He went to their house and the two sisters
were delighted because they had lovely feet.
The eldest went into a room to try the slipper on
but her big toe got in the way so she simply
sliced it off and put on the slipper.
The prince rode away with her until the white dove
told him to look at the blood pouring forth.
That is the way with amputations.
They don't just heal up like a wish.
The other sister cut off her heel
but the blood told as blood will.
The prince was getting tired.

55

60

65

70

75

80

85

90

He began to feel like a shoe salesman.
But he gave it one last try.
This time Cinderella fit into the shoe
like a love letter into its envelope.

At the wedding ceremony   95
the two sisters came to curry favor
and the white dove pecked their eyes out.
Two hollow spots were left
like soup spoons.

Cinderella and the prince   100
lived, they say, happily ever after,
like two dolls in a museum case
never bothered by diapers or dust,
never arguing over the timing of an egg,
never telling the same story twice,   105
never getting a middle-aged spread,
their darling smiles pasted on for eternity
Regular Bobbsey Twins.
That story.

                                                            —1970

The Truth the Dead Know

For my mother, born March 1902, died March
1959, and my father, born February 1900, died
June 1959

Gone, I say and walk from church,
refusing the stiff procession to the grave,
letting the dead ride alone in the hearse.
It is June. I am tired of being brave.

We drive to the Cape. I cultivate   5
myself where the sun gutters from the sky,
where the sea swings in like an iron gate
and we touch. In another country people die.

My darling, the wind falls in like stones
from the whitehearted water and when we touch   10
we enter touch entirely. No one's alone.
Men kill for this, or for as much

And what of the dead? They lie without shoes
in their stone boats. They are more like stone
than the sea would be if it stopped. They refuse   15
to be blessed, throat, eye and knucklebone.

—*1962*

Thom Gunn (b. 1929) is a British expatriate who has lived in San Francisco for over four decades. Gunn has managed to retain his ties to the traditions of British literature while writing about motorcycle gangs, surfers, gay bars, and drug experiences. The Man with Night Sweats, *his 1992 collection, contains a number of forthright poems on AIDS, of which "Terminal" is one.*

Thom Gunn
From the Wave

It mounts at sea, a concave wall
    Down-ribbed with shine,
And pushes forward, building tall
    Its steep incline.

Then from their hiding rise to sight   5
    Black shapes on boards
Bearing before the fringe of white
    It mottles towards.

Their pale feet curl, they poise their weight
    With a learn'd skill.   10
It is the wave they imitate
    Keeps them so still.

The marbling bodies have become
    Half wave, half men,

Grafted it seems by feet of foam   15
    Some seconds, then,

Late as they can, they slice the face
    In timed procession:
Balance is triumph in this place,
    Triumph possession.   20

The mindless heave of which they rode
    A fluid shelf
Breaks as they leave it, falls and, slowed,
    Loses itself.

Clear, the sheathed bodies slick as seals   25
    Loosen and tingle;
And by the board the bare foot feels
    The suck of shingle.

They paddle in the shallows still;
    Two splash each other;   30
Then all swim out to wait until
    The right waves gather.

    —*1971*

Terminal

The eight years difference in age seems now
Disparity so wide between the two
That when I see the man who armoured stood
Resistant to all help however good
Now helped through day itself, eased into chairs,   5
Or else led step by step down the long stairs
With firm and gentle guidance by his friend,
Who loves him, through each effort to descend,
Each wavering, each attempt made to complete
An arc of movement and bring down the feet   10
As if with that spare strength he used to enjoy,
I think of Oedipus, old, led by a boy.

    —*1992*

John Hollander (b. 1929) *is a prolific author of poetry and criticism. Hollander's wit and formal originality mark him as one of the chief contemporary heirs of W. H. Auden. A native of New York City, he was educated at Columbia University and served as a Junior Fellow at Harvard University. He has taught at Yale University for many years.*

John Hollander
Adam's Task

> "And Adam gave names to all cattle, and to
> the fowl of the air, and to every beast of the
> field . . ."—*Genesis 2:20*

Thou, paw-paw-paw; thou, glurd; thou, spotted
    Glurd; thou, whitestap, lurching through
The high-grown brush; thou, pliant-footed,
    Implex; thou, awagabu.

Every burrower, each flier   5
    Came for the name he had to give:
Gay, first work, ever to be prior,
    Not yet sunk to primitive.

Thou, verdle; thou, McFleery's pomma;
    Thou; thou; thou—three types of grawl;   10
Thou, flisket; thou, kabasch; thou, comma-
    Eared mashawk; thou, all; thou, all.

Were, in a fire of becoming,
    Laboring to be burned away,
Then work, half-measuring, half-humming,   15
    Would be as serious as play.

Thou, pambler; thou, rivarn; thou, greater
    Wherret, and thou, lesser one;
Thou, sproal; thou, zant; thou, lily-eater.
    Naming's over. Day is done.   20

—1971

X. J. Kennedy (b. 1929) is one the few contemporary American poets who has not been attracted by free verse, preferring to remain what he calls a "dinosaur," one of those poets who continue to write in meter. He is also rare among his contemporaries in his commitment to writing poems with strong ties to song. Kennedy is also the author of Literature: An Introduction to Fiction, Poetry, and Drama, *perhaps the most widely used college literature text ever written.*

X. J. Kennedy
In a Prominent Bar in Secaucus One Day

To the tune of "The Old Orange Flute" or the
tune of "Sweet Betsy from Pike"

In a prominent bar in Secaucus one day
Rose a lady in skunk with a topheavy sway,
Raised a knobby red finger—all turned from their beer—
While with eyes bright as snowcrust she sang high and clear:

"Now who of you'd think from an eyeload of me   5
That I once was a lady as proud as could be?
Oh I'd never sit down by a tumbledown drunk
If it wasn't, my dears, for the high cost of junk.

"All the gents used to swear that the white of my calf
Beat the down of the swan by a length and a half.   10
In the kerchief of linen I caught to my nose
Ah, there never fell snot, but a little gold rose.

"I had seven gold teeth and a toothpick of gold,
My Virginia cheroot° was a leaf of it rolled
And I'd light it each time with a thousand in cash—   15
Why the bums used to fight if I flicked them an ash.

"Once the toast of the Biltmore, the belle of the Taft,
I would drink bottle beer at the Drake, never draft,

14 cheroot a thin cigar

And dine at the Astor on Salisbury steak
With a clean tablecloth for each bite I did take.   20

"In a car like the Roxy I'd roll to the track,
A steel-guitar trio, a bar in the back,
And the wheels made no noise, they turned over so fast,
Still it took you ten minutes to see me go past.

"When the horses bowed down to me that I might choose,   25
I bet on them all, for I hated to lose.
Now I'm saddled each night for my butter and eggs
And the broken threads race down the backs of my legs.

"Let you hold in mind, girls, that your beauty must pass
Like a lovely white clover that rusts with its grass.   30
Keep your bottoms off barstools and marry you young
Or be left—an old barrel with many a bung.

"For when time takes you out for a spin in his car
You'll be hard-pressed to stop him from going too far
And be left by the roadside, for all your good deeds,   35
Two toadstools for tits and a face full of weeds."

All the house raised a cheer, but the man at the bar
Made a phonecall and up pulled a red patrol car
And she blew us a kiss as they copped her away
From that prominent bar in Secaucus, N.J.   40

—*1961*

Adrienne Rich Adrienne Rich's most recent books of poetry are Dark Fields of the Republic (Poems 1991–1995) *and* Midnight Salvage (Poems 1995–1998). *A new selection of her essays,* Art of the Possible: Essays and Conversations, *and a new volume of poems,* Fox (Poems 1998–2000), *will be published in 2001. She has recently been the recipient of the Dorothea Tanning Prize and of the Lannan Foundation Lifetime Achievement Award. She lives in California.*

Adrienne Rich
Aunt Jennifer's Tigers

Aunt Jennifer's tigers prance across a screen,
Bright topaz denizens of a world of green.
They do not fear the men beneath the tree;
They pace in sleek chivalric certainty.

Aunt Jennifer's fingers fluttering through her wool   5
Find even the ivory needle hard to pull.
The massive weight of Uncle's wedding band
Sits heavily upon Aunt Jennifer's hand.

When Aunt is dead, her terrified hands will lie
Still ringed with ordeals she was mastered by.   10
The tigers in the panel that she made
Will go on prancing, proud and unafraid.

—1950

Diving into the Wreck

First having read the book of myths,
and loaded the camera,
and checked the edge of the knife-blade,
I put on
the body-armor of black rubber   5
the absurd flippers
the grave and awkward mask.
I am having to do this

not like Cousteau° with his
assiduous team   10
aboard the sun-flooded schooner
but here alone.

There is a ladder.
The ladder is always there
hanging innocently   15
close to the side of the schooner.
We know what it is for,
we who have used it.
Otherwise
it is a piece of maritime floss   20
some sundry equipment.

I go down.
Rung after rung and still
the oxygen immerses me
the blue light   25
the clear atoms
of our human air.
I go down.
My flippers cripple me,
I crawl like an insect down the ladder   30
and there is no one
to tell me when the ocean
will begin.

First the air is blue and then
it is bluer and then green and then   35
black I am blacking out and yet
my mask is powerful
it pumps my blood with power
the sea is another story
the sea is not a question of power   40
I have to learn alone

---

9 Cousteau Jacques-Yves Cousteau (1910–1997), underwater explorer and inventor of the scuba
tank

to turn my body without force
in the deep element.

And now: it is easy to forget
what I came for   45
among so many who have always
lived here
swaying their crenellated fans
between the reefs
and besides   50
you breathe differently down here.

I came to explore the wreck.
The words are purposes.
The words are maps.
I came to see the damage that was done   55
and the treasures that prevail.
I stroke the beam of my lamp
slowly along the flank
of something more permanent
than fish or weed   60

the thing I came for:
the wreck and not the story of the wreck
the thing itself and not the myth
the drowned face always staring
toward the sun   65
the evidence of damage
worn by salt and sway into this threadbare beauty
the ribs of the disaster
curving their assertion
among the tentative haunters.   70

This is the place.
And I am here, the mermaid whose dark hair
streams black, the merman in his armored body.
We circle silently
about the wreck   75
we dive into the hold.
I am she: I am he

whose drowned face sleeps with open eyes
whose breasts still bear the stress
whose silver, copper, vermeil cargo lies   *80*
obscurely inside barrels
half-wedged and left to rot
we are the half-destroyed instruments
that once held to a course
the water-eaten log   *85*
the fouled compass

We are, I am, you are
by cowardice or courage
the one who find our way
back to this scene   *90*
carrying a knife, a camera
a book of myths
in which
our names do not appear.

—1972

Rape

There is a cop who is both prowler and father:
he comes from your block, grew up with your brothers,
had certain ideals.
You hardly know him in his boots and silver badge,
on horseback, one hand touching his gun.   *5*

You hardly know him but you have to get to know him:
he has access to machinery that could kill you.
He and his stallion clop like warlords among the trash,
his ideals stand in the air, a frozen cloud
from between his unsmiling lips.   *10*

And so, when the time comes, you have to turn to him,
the maniac's sperm still greasing your thighs,
your mind whirling like crazy. You have to confess
to him, you are guilty of the crime
of having been forced.   *15*

And you see his blue eyes, the blue eyes of all the family
whom you used to know, grow narrow and glisten,
his hand types out the details
and he wants them all
but the hysteria in your voice pleases him best.   20

You hardly know him but now he thinks he knows you:
he has taken down your worst moment
on a machine and filed it in a file.
He knows, or thinks he knows, how much you imagined;
he knows, or thinks he knows, what you secretly wanted.   25

He has access to machinery that could get you put away;
and if, in the sickening light of the precinct,
and if, in the sickening light of the precinct,
your details sound like a portrait of your confessor,
will you swallow, will you deny them, will you lie your way home?30

—*1972*

Ted Hughes (1930–1998) was a native of Yorkshire, England. Hughes never ventured far from the natural world of his childhood for his subject matter. Hughes was married to Sylvia Plath until her death in 1963; Birthday Letters, *a book of poems about their troubled relationship, appeared in 1998. At the time of his death, Hughes was the British poet laureate.*

Ted Hughes
Pike

Pike, three inches long, perfect
Pike in all parts, green tigering the gold.
Killers from the egg: the malevolent aged grin.
They dance on the surface among the flies.

Or move, stunned by their own grandeur,   5
Over a bed of emerald, silhouette
Of submarine delicacy and horror.
A hundred feet long in their world.

In ponds, under the heat-struck lily pads—
Gloom of their stillness:
Logged on last year's black leaves, watching upwards. *10*
Or hung in an amber cavern of weeds

The jaw's hooked clamp and fangs
Not to be changed at this date;
A life subdued to its instrument;
The gills kneading quietly, and the pectorals. *15*

Three we kept behind glass,
Jungled in weed: three inches, four,
And four and a half: fed fry to them—
Suddenly there were two. Finally one *20*

With a sag belly and the grin it was born with.
And indeed they spare nobody.
Two, six pounds each, over two feet long,
High and dry and dead in the willow-herb—

One jammed past its gills down the other's gullet: *25*
The outside eye stared: as a vice locks—
The same iron in this eye
Though its film shrank in death.

A pond I fished, fifty yards across,
Whose lilies and muscular tench° *30*
Had outlasted every visible stone
Of the monastery that planted them—

Stilled legendary depth:
It was as deep as England. It held
Pike too immense to stir, so immense and old *35*
That past nightfall I dared not cast

But silently cast and fished
With the hair frozen on my head
For what might move, for what eye might move.
The still splashes on the dark pond, *40*

30 tench European freshwater fish

Owls hushing the floating woods
Frail on my ear against the dream
Darkness beneath night's darkness had freed,
That rose slowly towards me, watching.

—1960

Gary Snyder (b. 1930) *was deeply involved in poetic activity in his hometown, San Francisco, when that city became the locus of the Beat Generation in the mid-1950s. Yet Snyder, whose studies in Zen Buddhism and Oriental cultures preceded his acquaintance with Allen Ginsberg and Jack Kerouac, has always exhibited a seriousness of purpose that sets him apart from his peers. His long familiarity with the mountains of the Pacific Northwest dates from his jobs with logging crews during his college days.*

Gary Snyder
A Walk

Sunday the only day we don't work:
Mules farting around the meadow,
   Murphy fishing,
The tent flaps in the warm
Early sun: I've eaten breakfast and I'll   5
    take a walk
To Benson Lake. Packed a lunch,
Goodbye. Hopping on creekbed boulders
Up the rock throat three miles
   Piute Creek—   10
In steep gorge glacier-slick rattlesnake country
Jump, land by a pool, trout skitter,
The clear sky. Deer tracks.
Bad place by a falls, boulders big as houses,
Lunch tied to belt,   15
I stemmed up a crack and almost fell
But rolled out safe on a ledge
   and ambled on.
Quail chicks freeze underfoot, color of stone

Then run cheep! away, hen quail fussing.   20
Craggy west end of Benson Lake—after edging
Past dark creek pools on a long white slope—
Lookt down in the ice-black lake
        lined with cliff
From far above: deep shimmering trout.   25
A lone duck in a gunsightpass
        steep side hill
Through slide-aspen and talus, to the east end
Down to grass, wading a wide smooth stream
Into camp. At last.   30
    By the rusty three-year-
Ago left-behind cookstove
Of the old trail crew,
Stoppt and swam and ate my lunch.

                                              —1968

Derek Walcott (b. 1930) is a native of the tiny Caribbean island of St. Lucia in the West Indies. Walcott combines a love of the tradition of English poetry with the exotic surfaces of tropical life. In many ways, his life and career have constituted a study in divided loyalties, which are displayed in his ambivalent poems about life in the United States, where he has lived and taught for many years. Walcott was awarded the Nobel Prize in 1992.

Derek Walcott
Central America

Helicopters are cutlassing the wild bananas.
Between a nicotine thumb and forefinger
brittle faces crumble like tobacco leaves.
Children waddle in vests, their legs bowed,
little shrimps curled under their navels.
The old men's teeth are stumps in a charred forest.   5
Their skins grate like the iguana's.
Their gaze like slate stones.
Women squat by the river's consolations

where children wade up to their knees,   10
and a stick stirs up a twinkling of butterflies.
Up there, in the blue acres
of forest, flies circle their fathers.
In spring, in the upper provinces
of the Empire, yellow tanagers   15
float up through the bare branches.
There is no distinction in these distances.

—1987

Miller Williams (b. 1930) won the Poets' Prize in 1990 for Living on the
Surface, *a volume of selected poems. A skillful translator of both Giuseppe Belli, a
Roman poet of the early nineteenth century, and of Nicanor Parra, a contemporary
Chilean, Williams has written many poems about his travels throughout the world
yet has retained the relaxed idiom of his native Arkansas. He read a poem at the
1997 presidential inauguration.*

Miller Williams
The Book

I held it in my hands while he told the story.

He had found it in a fallen bunker,
a book for notes with all the pages blank.
He took it to keep for a sketchbook and diary.

He learned years later, when he showed the book   5
to an old bookbinder, who paled, and stepped back
a long step and told him what he held,
what he had laid the days of his life in.
It's bound, the binder said, in human skin.

I stood turning it over in my hands,   10
turning it in my head. Human skin.

What child did this skin fit? What man, what woman?
Dragged still full of its flesh from what dream?

Who took it off the meat? Some other one
who stayed alive by knowing how to do this?   15

I stared at the changing book and a horror grew,
I stared and a horror grew, which was, which is,
how beautiful it was until I knew.

—*1989*

Linda Pastan (b. 1932) served as poet laureate of Maryland, where she has lived and taught for many years. Her first book, A Perfect Circle of Sun, *appeared in 1971, and five more collections have been published since.*

Linda Pastan
Crocuses

They come
by stealth, spreading
the rumor of spring—
near the hedge . . .
by the gate . . .   5
at our chilly feet . . .
mothers of saffron, fathers
of insurrection, purple
and yellow scouts
of an army still massing   10
just to the south.

—*1991*

Sylvia Plath (1932–1963), whose troubled personal life is often difficult to separate from her poetry, is almost always read as an autobiographical and confessional poet. Brilliant and precocious, she served a long apprenticeship to the tradition of modern poetry before attaining her mature style in the final two years of her life. Only one collection, The Colossus, *appeared in her lifetime, and her fame has mainly rested on her posthumous books of poetry and the success of her lone novel,* The Bell Jar. *She committed suicide in 1963. Plath has been the subject of a half-dozen biographical studies, reflecting the intense interest that readers, especially women, have in her life and work.*

Sylvia Plath

Daddy

You do not do, you do not do
Any more, black shoe
In which I have lived like a foot
For thirty years, poor and white,
Barely daring to breathe or Achoo.   5

Daddy, I have had to kill you.
You died before I had time—
Marble-heavy, a bag full of God,
Ghastly statue with one gray toe
Big as a Frisco seal   10

And a head in the freakish Atlantic
Where it pours bean green over blue
In the waters off beautiful Nauset.
I used to pray to recover you.
Ach, du.°   15

In the German tongue, in the Polish town
Scraped flat by the roller
Of wars, wars, wars.
But the name of the town is common.
My Polack friend   20

---

15 Ach, du "Oh, you"

Says there are a dozen or two.
So I never could tell where you
Put your foot, your root,
I never could talk to you.
The tongue stuck in my jaw.   *25*

It stuck in a barb wire snare.
Ich, ich, ich, ich,°
I could hardly speak.
I thought every German was you.
And the language obscene   *30*

An engine, an engine
Chuffing me off like a Jew.
A Jew to Dachau, Auschwitz, Belsen.°
I began to talk like a Jew.
I think I may well be a Jew.   *35*

The snows of the Tyrol, the clear beer of Vienna
Are not very pure or true.
With my gypsy ancestress and my weird luck
And my Taroc pack and my Taroc pack
I may be a bit of a Jew.   *40*

I have always been scared of *you*,
With your Luftwaffe,° your gobbledygoo.
And your neat mustache
And your Aryan eye, bright blue.
Panzer-man, panzer-man, O You—   *45*

Not God but a swastika
So black no sky could squeak through.
Every woman adores a Fascist,
The boot in the face, the brute
Brute heart of a brute like you.   *50*

---

27 Ich, ich, ich, ich "I, I, I, I"   **33 Dachau, Auschwitz, Belsen** German concentration camps
42 Luftwaffe German Air Force

You stand at the blackboard, daddy,
In the picture I have of you,
A cleft in your chin instead of your foot
But no less a devil for that, no not
Any less the black man who   55

Bit my pretty red heart in two.
I was ten when they buried you.
At twenty I tried to die
And get back, back, back to you.
I thought even the bones would do.   60

But they pulled me out of the sack,
And they stuck me together with glue.
And then I knew what to do.
I made a model of you,
A man in black with a Meinkampf° look   65

And a love of the rack and the screw.
And I said I do, I do.
So daddy, I'm finally through.
The black telephone's off at the root,
The voices just can't worm through.   70

If I've killed one man, I've killed two—
The vampire who said he was you
And drank my blood for a year,
Seven years, if you want to know.
Daddy, you can lie back now.   75

There's a stake in your fat black heart
And the villagers never liked you.
They are dancing and stamping on you.
They always *knew* it was you.
Daddy, daddy, you bastard, I'm through.   80

—*1966*

---

65 **Meinkampf** title of Hitler's autobiography ("My Struggle")

Edge

The woman is perfected.
Her dead

Body wears the smile of accomplishment,
The illusion of a Greek necessity

Flows in the scrolls of her toga,   5
Her bare

Feet seem to be saying:
We have come so far, it is over.

Each dead child coiled, a white serpent,
One at each little   10

Pitcher of milk, now empty.
She has folded

Them back into her body as petals
Of a rose close when the garden

Stiffens and odors bleed   15
From the sweet, deep throats of the night flower.

The moon has nothing to be sad about,
Staring from her hood of bone.

She is used to this sort of thing.
Her blacks crackle and drag.   20

—*1965*

Metaphors

I'm a riddle in nine syllables,
An elephant, a ponderous house,
A melon strolling on two tendrils.
O red fruit, ivory, fine timbers!
This loaf's big with its yeasty rising.   5

Money's new-minted in this fat purse.
I'm a means, a stage, a cow in calf.
I've eaten a bag of green apples,
Boarded the train there's no getting off.

—1960

Gerald Barrax (b. 1933) served as the editor of Obsidian II: Black Literature
in Review, *one of the most influential journals of African-American writing. The
author of five collections of poetry, he taught at North Carolina State University.*

Gerald Barrax
Strangers Like Us: Pittsburgh, Raleigh, 1945–1985

The sounds our parents heard echoing over
housetops while listening to evening radios
were the uninterrupted cries running and cycling
we sent through the streets and yards, where spring summer
fall we were entrusted to the night, boys   5
and girls together, to send us home for bath
and bed after the dark had drifted down and eased
contests between pitcher and batter, hider and seeker.

Our own children live imprisoned in light.
They are cycloned into our yards and hearts,   10
whose gates flutter shut on unfamiliar smiles.
At the rumor of a moon, we call them in
before the monsters who hunt, who hurt, who haunt
us, rise up from our own dim streets.

—1992

Anne Stevenson (b. 1933) *is perhaps best known as the author of a controversial biography of Sylvia Plath. Stevenson was born in England of American parents and educated at the University of Michigan. She has lived in England since her twenties. Her* Selected Poems *appeared in 1987.*

Anne Stevenson
Sous-Entendu°

Don't think

that I don't know
that as you talk to me
the hand of your mind
is inconspicuously
taking off my stocking,   5
moving in resourceful blindness
up along my thigh.
Don't think
that I don't know
that you know   10
everything I say
is a garment.

—*1969*

Sous-Entendu "hidden meaning"

Mark Strand (b. 1934) *displays a simplicity in his best poems that reveals the influence of Spanish-language poets like Nicanor Parra, the father of "anti-poetry," and Rafael Alberti, whom Strand has translated. Strand was named U.S. poet laureate in 1990.*

Mark Strand
The Tunnel

A man has been standing
in front of my house
for days. I peek at him
from the living room
window and at night,   5
unable to sleep,
I shine my flashlight
down on the lawn.
He is always there.

After a while   10
I open the front door
just a crack and order
him out of my yard.
He narrows his eyes
and moans. I slam   15
the door and dash back
to the kitchen, then up
to the bedroom, then down.

I weep like a schoolgirl
and make obscene gestures   20
through the window. I
write large suicide notes
and place them so he
can read them easily.
I destroy the living   25
room furniture to prove
I own nothing of value.

When he seems unmoved
I decide to dig a tunnel
to a neighboring yard.   *30*
I seal the basement off
from the upstairs with
a brick wall. I dig hard
and in no time the tunnel
is done. Leaving my pick   *35*
and shovel below,

I come out in front of a house
and stand there too tired to
move or even speak, hoping
someone will help me.   *40*
I feel I'm being watched
and sometimes I hear
a man's voice,
but nothing is done
and I have been waiting for days.   *45*

—1968

Mary Oliver (b. 1935) *was born in Cleveland, Ohio, and educated at Ohio State University and Vassar College. She has served as a visiting professor at a number of universities and at the Fine Arts Center in Provincetown, Massachusetts. She has won both the Pulitzer Prize and the National Book Award for her work, which first appeared in* No Voyage and Other Poems *in 1965.*

Mary Oliver
The Black Walnut Tree

My mother and I debate:
we could sell
the black walnut tree
to the lumberman,
and pay off the mortgage.   *5*
Likely some storm anyway

will churn down its dark boughs,
smashing the house. We talk
slowly, two women trying
in a difficult time to be wise.   10
Roots in the cellar drains,
I say, and she replies
that the leaves are getting heavier
every year, and the fruit
harder to gather away.   15
But something brighter than money
moves in our blood—an edge
sharp and quick as a trowel
that wants us to dig and sow.
So we talk, but we don't do   20
anything. That night I dream
of my fathers out of Bohemia
filling the blue fields
of fresh and generous Ohio
with leaves and vines and orchards.   25
What my mother and I both know
is that we'd crawl with shame
in the emptiness we'd made
in our own and our fathers' backyard.
So the black walnut tree   30
swings through another year
of sun and leaping winds,
of leaves and bounding fruit,
and, month after month, the whip-
crack of the mortgage.   35

—1979

Fred Chappell (b. 1936) wrote the epic-length poem Midquest *(1981), and his achievement was recognized when he was awarded the Bollingen Prize in 1985. A four-part poem written over a decade,* Midquest *uses the occasion of the poet's thirty-fifth birthday as a departure for a complex sequence of autobiographical poems that are heavily indebted to Dante for their formal structure. A versatile writer of both poetry and prose, Chappell displays his classical learning brilliantly and in unusual contexts.*

Fred Chappell
Narcissus and Echo°

Shall the water not remember *Ember*
my hand's slow gesture, tracing above *of*
its mirror my half-imaginary *airy*
portrait? My only belonging *longing*
is my beauty, which I take *ache*   5
away and then return as love *of*
teasing playfully the one being *unbeing.*

whose gratitude I treasure *Is your*
moves me. I live apart *heart*
from myself, yet cannot *not*   10
live apart. In the water's tone, *stone?*
that brilliant silence, a flower *Hour,*
whispers my name with such slight *light,*
moment, it seems filament of air, *fare*
the world become cloudswell. *well.*   15

—*1985*

Narcissus and Echo In the myth, the vain Narcissus drowned attempting to embrace his own reflection in the water. Echo, a nymph who loved him, pined away until only her voice remained.

Lucille Clifton (b. 1936), a native of Depew, New York, was educated at SUNY — Fredonia and Howard University, and has taught at several colleges, including the American University in Washington, D.C. About her own work, she has commented succinctly, "I am a Black woman poet, and I sound like one." Clifton won a National Book Award in 2000.

Lucille Clifton
to my last period

well girl, goodbye,
after thirty-eight years.
thirty-eight years and you
never arrived
splendid in your red dress   5
without trouble for me
somewhere, somehow.

now it is done,
and i feel just like
the grandmothers who,   10
after the hussy has gone,
sit holding her photograph
and sighing, *wasn't she*
beautiful? wasn't she beautiful?

—*1991*

Marge Piercy (b. 1936) was a political radical during her student days at the University of Michigan. Piercy has continued to be outspoken on political, cultural, and sexual issues. Her phrase "to be of use" has become a key measure by which feminist writers and critics have gauged the meaning of their own life experiences.

Marge Piercy

Barbie Doll

This girlchild was born as usual
and presented dolls that did pee-pee
and miniature GE stoves and irons
and wee lipsticks the color of cherry candy.
Then in the magic of puberty, a classmate said: 5
You have a great big nose and fat legs.

She was healthy, tested intelligent
possessed strong arms and back,
abundant sexual drive and manual dexterity.
She went to and fro apologizing.   10
Everyone saw a fat nose on thick legs.

She was advised to play coy,
exhorted to come on hearty,
exercise, diet, smile and wheedle.
Her good nature wore out   15
like a fan belt.
So she cut off her nose and her legs
and offered them up.

In the casket displayed on satin she lay
with the undertaker's cosmetics painted on,   20
a turned-up putty nose,
dressed in a pink and white nightie.
Doesn't she look pretty? everyone said.
Consummation at last.
To every woman a happy ending.   25

—1982

Nancy Willard (b. 1936) *is the author of nine collections of poetry. Willard has also written a novel and an award-winning book of poems for children,* A Visit to William Blake's Inn. *About her whimsical work Donald Hall has said, "She imagines with a wonderful concreteness. But also, she takes real language and by literal-mindedness turns it into the structure of dream."*

Nancy Willard
A Hardware Store as Proof of the Existence of God

I praise the brightness of hammers pointing east
like the steel woodpeckers of the future,
and dozens of hinges opening brass wings,
and six new rakes shyly fanning their toes,
and bins of hooks glittering into bees,   5

and a rack of wrenches like the long bones of horses,
and mailboxes sowing rows of silver chapels,
and a company of plungers waiting for God
to claim their thin legs in their big shoes
and put them on and walk away laughing.   10

In a world not perfect but not bad either
let there be glue, glaze, gum, and grabs,
caulk also, and hooks, shackles, cables, and slips,
and signs so spare a child may read them,
Men, Women, In, Out, No Parking, Beware the Dog.   15

In the right hands, they can work wonders.

—1989

Betty Adcock (b. 1938) *was born in San Augustine, Texas. Adcock has lived for many years in Raleigh, North Carolina, where she is poet-in-residence at Meredith College. Her volume of selected poems,* Interuale, *appeared in 2001.*

Betty Adcock

Digression on the Nuclear Age

In some difficult part of Africa, a termite tribe
builds elaborate tenements that might be called
cathedrals, were they for anything so terminal
as Milton's God. Who was it said
the perfect arch will always separate   5
the civilized from the not? Never mind.

These creatures are quite blind and soft
and hard at labor chemically induced.
Beginning with a dish-like hollow, groups
of workers pile up earthen pellets.   10
A few such piles will reach a certain height;
fewer still, a just proximity.
That's when direction changes, or a change
directs: the correct two bands of laborers
will make their towers bow toward each other.   15
Like saved and savior, they will meet in air.
It is unambiguously an arch and it will serve,
among the others rising and the waste,
an arch's purposes. Experts are sure
a specific moment comes when the very structure   20
triggers the response that will perfect it.

I've got this far and don't know what
termites can be made to mean. Or this poem:
a joke, a play on arrogance, nothing
but language? Untranslated, the world gets on   25

with dark, flawless constructions rising,
rising even where we think we are. And think
how we must hope convergences will fail this time,
that whatever it is we're working on won't work.

—*1988*

Gary Gildner (b. 1938) was born in West Branch, Michigan, and attended Michigan State University. He lives on a ranch in the Clearwater Mountains of Idaho. "First Practice" is the title poem of his first collection, published in 1969, and a volume of Gildner's selected poems appeared in 1984.

Gary Gildner
First Practice

After the doctor checked to see
we weren't ruptured,
the man with the short cigar took us
under the grade school,
where we went in case of attack   5
or storm, and said
he was Clifford Hill, he was
a man who believed dogs
ate dogs, he had once killed
for his country, and if   10
there were any girls present
for them to leave now.
        No one
left. OK, he said, he said I take
that to mean you are hungry   15
men who hate to lose as much
as I do. OK. Then
he made two lines of us
facing each other,
and across the way, he said,   20

is the man you hate most
in the world,
and if we are to win
that title I want to see how.
But I don't want to see   25
any marks when you're dressed,
he said. He said, *Now.*

—*1969*

Robert Phillips (b. 1938) *labored for over thirty years as a New York advertising executive, a remarkable fact when one considers his many books of poetry, fiction, and criticism and the numerous books he has edited. He currently lives in Houston, where he teaches in the creative writing program at the University of Houston.*

Robert Phillips
Compartments

Which shall be final?
  Pine box in a concrete vault,
urn on a mantel?

Last breath a rattle,
  stuffed in a black body bag,   5
he's zipped head to toe.

At the nursing home,
  side drawn to prevent a fall—
in a crib again.

His dead wife's false teeth   10
  underfoot in their bedroom.
Feel the piercing chill.

Pink flamingo lawn,
  a Florida trailer park:
one space he'll avoid.   15

The box they gave him
>   on retirement held a watch
that measures decades.

The new bifocals
>   rest in their satin-lined case,   *20*
his body coffined.

Move to the suburbs.
>   Crowded train at seven-oh-two,
empty head at night.

New playpen, new crib,   *25*
>   can't compete with the newness
of the newborn child.

Oak four-poster bed
>   inherited from family—
Jack Frost defrosted.   *30*

Once he was pink-slipped.
>   Dad helped out: "A son's a son,
Son, from womb to tomb."

Fourteen-foot ceilings,
>   parquet floors, marble fireplace,   *35*
proud first apartment.

The Jack Frost Motel,
>   its very name a portent
for their honeymoon.

Backseat of a car,   *40*
>   cursing the inventor of
nylon pantyhose.

First-job cubicle.
>   Just how many years before
a window office?   *45*

College quad at noon,
>   chapel bells, frat men, coeds,
no pocket money.

his grandfather's barn.
      After it burned to the ground,   *50*
the moon filled its space.

His favorite tree—
      the leaves return to branches?
No, butterflies light.

Closet where he hid   *55*
      to play with himself. None knew?
Mothball orgasms.

Chimney that he scaled
      naked to sweep for his Dad:
Blake's soot-black urchin.   *60*

The town's swimming pool
      instructor, throwing him in
again and again . . .

Kindergarten play
      ground: swings, slides, rings, jungle gym.   *65*
Scraped knees, molester.

Red, blue and green birds
      mobilize over his crib,
its sides a tall fence.

Two months premature,   *70*
      he incubates by light bulbs,
like a baby chick.

He is impatient,
      curled in foetal position,
floating in darkness.   *75*

—2000

Charles Simic (b. 1938) *was born in Yugoslavia and came with his parents to Chicago in 1949. Educated at New York University, he teaches at the University of New Hampshire.* The World Doesn't End, *a collection of prose poems, won the Pulitzer Prize in 1990.*

Charles Simic
Stone

Go inside a stone
That would be my way.
Let somebody else become a dove
Or gnash with a tiger's tooth.
I am happy to be a stone.   5

From the outside the stone is a riddle:
No one knows how to answer it.
Yet within, it must be cool and quiet
Even though a cow steps on it full weight,
Even though a child throws it in a river;   10
The stone sinks, slow, unperturbed
To the river bottom
Where the fishes come to knock on it
And listen.

I have seen sparks fly out   15
When two stones are rubbed,
So perhaps it is not dark inside after all;
Perhaps there is a moon shining
From somewhere, as though behind a hill—
Just enough light to make out   20
The strange writings, the star-charts
On the inner walls.

—1971

Dabney Stuart (b. 1938) has written many poems populated by the supporting cast of the American family romance — parents, wives and ex-wives, and children. A Virginian who has taught for many years at Washington and Lee University, Stuart published Light Years, *a volume of selected poems, in 1995.*

Dabney Stuart
Discovering My Daughter

Most of your life we have kept our separate places:
After I left your mother you knew an island,
Rented rooms, a slow coastal slide northward
To Boston, and, in summer, another island
Hung at the country's tip. Would you have kept going   5
All the way off the map, an absolute alien?

Sometimes I shiver, being almost forgetful enough
To have let that happen. We've come the longer way
Under such pressure, from one person to
Another. Our trip proves again the world is   10
Round, a singular island where people may come
Together, as we have, making a singular place.

—1987

Margaret Atwood (b. 1939) is the leading woman writer of Canada. Atwood excels at both poetry and prose fiction. Among her six novels, The Handmaid's Tale *is perhaps the best known, becoming a bestseller in the United States and the subject of a motion picture. Atwood's* Selected Poems *appeared in 1976.*

Margaret Atwood
Siren° Song

This is the one song everyone
would like to learn: the song
that is irresistible:

Siren in Greek myth, one of the women whose irresistible song lured sailors onto the rocks

the song that forces men
to leap overboard in squadrons   5
even though they see the beached skulls

the song nobody knows
because anyone who has heard it
is dead, and the others can't remember.

Shall I tell you the secret   10
and if I do, will you get me
out of this bird suit?

I don't enjoy it here
squatting on this island
looking picturesque and mythical   15

with these two feathery maniacs,
I don't enjoy singing
this trio, fatal and valuable.

I will tell the secret to you,
to you, only to you.   20
Come closer. This song

is a cry for help: Help me!
Only you, only you can,
you are unique

at last. Alas   25
it is a boring song
but it works every time.

—1974

Stephen Dunn (b. 1939) *is a graduate of the creative writing program at Syracuse University. Dunn teaches at Stockton State College in Pomona, New Jersey. His attempt to blend ordinary experience with larger significance is illustrated in the duality of his book titles like* Full of Lust and Good Usage, Work and Love, *and* Between Angels. *Dunn was awarded the Pulitzer Prize in 2001.*

Stephen Dunn
The Sacred

After the teacher asked if anyone had
    a sacred place
and the students fidgeted and shrank

in their chairs, the most serious of them all
    said it was his car,   5
being in it alone, his tape deck playing

things he'd chosen, and others knew the truth
    had been spoken
and began speaking about their rooms,

their hiding places, but the car kept coming up,   10
    the car in motion,
music filling it, and sometimes one other person

who understood the bright altar of the dashboard
    and how far away
a car could take him from the need   15

to speak, or to answer, the key
    in having a key
and putting it in, and going.

—*1989*

Seamus Heaney (b. 1939) *was born in the troubled country of Northern Ireland. Heaney has largely avoided the type of political divisions that have divided his home- land. Instead, he has chosen to focus on the landscape of the rural Ireland he knew while growing up as a farmer's son. Since 1982, Heaney has taught part of the year at Harvard University. He was awarded the Nobel Prize for Literature in 1995.*

Seamus Heaney
Bogland

for T. P. Flanagan

We have no prairies
To slice a big sun at evening—
Everywhere the eye concedes to
Encroaching horizon,

Is wooed into the cyclops' eye   5
Of a tarn. Our unfenced country
Is bog that keeps crusting
Between the sights of the sun.

They've taken the skeleton
Of the Great Irish Elk   10
Out of the peat, set it up
An astounding crate full of air.

Butter sunk under
More than a hundred years
Was recovered salty and white.   15
The ground itself is kind, black butter

Melting and opening underfoot,
Missing its last definition
By millions of years.
They'll never dig coal here,   20

Only the waterlogged trunks
Of great firs, soft as pulp.
Our pioneers keep striking
Inwards and downwards,

Every layer they strip   25
Seems camped on before.
The bogholes might be Atlantic seepage.
The wet centre is bottomless.

—1969

Digging

Between my finger and my thumb
The squat pen rests; snug as a gun.

Under my window, a clean rasping sound
When the spade sinks into gravelly ground:
My father, digging. I look down   5

Till his straining rump among the flowerbeds
Bends low, comes up twenty years away
Stooping in rhythm through potato drills°
Where he was digging.

The coarse boot nestled on the lug, the shaft   10
Against the inside knee was levered firmly.
He rooted out tall tops, buried the bright edge deep
To scatter new potatoes that we picked
Loving their cool hardness in our hands.

By God, the old man could handle a spade.   15
Just like his old man.

My grandfather cut more turf in a day
Than any other man on Toner's bog.
Once I carried him milk in a bottle
Corked sloppily with paper. He straightened up   20
To drink it, then fell to right away

Nicking and slicing neatly, heaving sods
Over his shoulder, going down and down
For the good turf. Digging.

8 drills furrows

The cold smell of potato mould, the squelch and slap   25
Of soggy peat, the curt cuts of an edge
Through living roots awaken in my head.
But I've no spade to follow men like them.

Between my finger and my thumb
The squat pen rests.   30
I'll dig with it.

—*1980*

Punishment

I can feel the tug
of the halter at the nape
of her neck, the wind
on her naked front.

It blows her nipples   5
to amber beads,
it shakes the frail rigging
of her ribs.

I can see her drowned
body in the bog,   10
the weighing stone,
the floating rods and boughs.

Under which at first
she was a barked sapling
that is dug up   15
oak-bone, brain-firkin:°

her shaved head
like a stubble of black corn,
her blindfold a soiled bandage,
her noose a ring   20

to store
the memories of love.

16 firkin a small barrel

Little adulteress,
before they punished you

you were flaxen-haired,   25
undernourished, and your
tar-black face was beautiful.
My poor scapegoat,

I almost love you
but would have cast, I know,   30
the stones of silence.
I am the artful voyeur

of your brain's exposed
and darkened combs,
your muscles' webbing   35
and all your numbered bones:

I who have stood dumb
when your betraying sisters,
cauled in tar,
wept by the railings,   40

who would connive
in civilized outrage
yet understand the exact
and tribal, intimate revenge.

—*1975*

Tom Disch (b. 1940) *is a science-fiction writer, author of interactive computer fiction, resident critic for magazines as diverse as* Playboy *and* The Nation, *and poet. Disch is possibly the most brilliant satirist in contemporary American poetry.* Yes, Let's, *a collection of his selected poems, appeared in 1989.*

Ballade of the New God ·

I have decided I'm divine.
Caligula and Nero knew
A godliness akin to mine,
But they are strictly hitherto.

They're dead, and what can dead gods do?   5
I'm here and now. I'm dynamite.
I'd worship me if I were you.
A new religion starts tonight!

No booze, no pot, no sex, no swine:
I have decreed them all taboo.   10
My words will be your only wine,
The thought of me your honeydew.
All other thoughts you will eschew
And call yourself a Thomasite
And hymn my praise with loud yahoo.   15
A new religion starts tonight.

But (you might think) that's asinine!
I'm just as much a god as you.
You may have built yourself a shrine
But I won't bend my knee. Who   20
Asked you to be my god? I do,
Who am, as god, divinely right.
Now you must join my retinue:
A new religion starts tonight.

All that I have said is true.   25
I'm god and you're my acolyte.
Surrender's bliss: I envy you
A new religion starts tonight

                                        —*1995*

Florence Cassen Mayers (b. 1940) is a widely published poet and children's author. Her "ABC" books include children's guides to baseball and to the National Basketball Association.

Florence Cassen Mayers
All-American Sestina

One nation, indivisible
two-car garage
three strikes you're out
four-minute mile
five-cent cigar   5
six-string guitar

six-pack Bud
one-day sale
five-year warranty
two-way street   10
fourscore and seven years ago
three cheers

three-star restaurant
sixty-
four-dollar question   15
one-night stand
two-pound lobster
five-star general

five-course meal
three sheets to the wind   20
two bits
six-shooter
one-armed bandit
four-poster

four-wheel drive   25
five-and-dime
hole in one
three-alarm fire

sweet sixteen
two-wheeler   *30*

two-tone Chevy
four rms, hi flr, w/vu
six-footer
high five
three-ring circus   *35*
one-room schoolhouse

two thumbs up, five-karat diamond
Fourth of July, three-piece suit
six feet under, one-horse town

—1996

Pattiann Rogers (b. 1940) *is the foremost naturalist among contemporary American poets. Her poems resound with the rich names of unfamiliar species of plants and animals, most of which she seems to know on intimate terms.* Collected Poems *was published in 2001.*

Pattiann Rogers
Foreplay

When it first begins, as you might expect,
the lips and thin folds are closed, the pouting
layers pressed, lapped lightly,
almost languidly, against one another
in a sealed bud.   *5*

However, with certain prolonged
and random strokings of care
along each binding line, with soft
intrusions traced beneath each pursed
gathering and edge, with inquiring   *10*
intensities of gesture—as the sun
swinging slowly from winter back
to spring, touches briefly,

between moments of moon and masking
clouds, certain stunning points   15
and inner nubs of earth—so
with such ministrations, a slight
swelling, a quiver of reaching,
a tendency toward space,
might be noticed to commence.   20

Then with dampness from the dark,
with moisture from the falling
night of morning, from hidden places
within the hills, each seal begins
to loosen, each recalcitrant clasp   25
sinks away into itself, and every tucked
grasp, every silk tack willingly relents,
releases, gives way, proclaims a turning,
declares a revolution, assumes,
in plain sight, a surging position   30
that offers, an audacious offering
that beseeches, every petal parted wide.

Remember the spiraling, blue
valerian, remember the violet, sucking
larkspur, the laurel and rosebay   35
and pea cockle flung backwards, remember
the fragrant, funnelling lily, the lifted
honeysuckle, the sweet, open pucker
of the ground ivy blossom?

Now even the darkest crease possessed,   40
the most guarded, pulsing, least drop
of pearl bead, moon grain trembling
deep within is fully revealed, fully exposed
to any penetrating wind or shaking fur
or mad hunger or searing, plunging surprise   45
the wild descending sky in delirium
has to offer.

—1994

Robert Hass (b. 1941) was born and reared in San Francisco, and teaches at U. C. Berkeley. His first book, Field Guide, was chosen for the Yale Series of Younger Poets in 1973. Recently he has collaborated with Nobel Prize–winner Czeslaw Milosz on English translations of the latter's poetry. He was appointed U.S. poet laureate in 1995.

Robert Hass

Picking Blackberries with a Friend Who Has Been Reading Jacques Lacan°

August dust is here. Drought
stuns the road,
but juice gathers in the berries.

We pick them in the hot
slow-motion of midmorning.   5
Charlie is exclaiming:

for him it is twenty years ago
and raspberries and Vermont.
We have stopped talking

about *L'Histoire de la vérité,*°   10
about subject and object
and the mediation of desire.

Our ears are stoppered
in the bee-hum. And Charlie,
laughing wonderfully,   15

beard stained purple
by the word *juice,*
goes to get a bigger pot.

—*1979*

Jacques Lacan French psychoanalyst and literary theorist   **10 *L'Histoire de la vérité*** The History *of Truth,* by Lacan

Simon J. Ortiz (b. 1941) *was born in the Pueblo of Acoma, near Albuquerque, New Mexico. Ortiz has explained why he writes: "Because Indians always tell a story. The only way to continue is to tell a story." The author of collections of poetry and prose and of several children's books, Ortiz has taught creative writing and Native American literature at many universities.*

Simon J. Ortiz
The Serenity in Stones

I am holding this turquoise
in my hands.
My hands hold the sky
wrought in this little stone.
There is a cloud   5
at the furthest boundary.
The world is somewhere underneath.

I turn the stone, and there is more sky.
This is the serenity possible in stones,
the place of a feeling to which one belongs.   10
I am happy as I hold this sky
in my hands, in my eyes, and in myself.

—1975

Gibbons Ruark (b. 1941) *is a native of North Carolina. Ruark is the author of five collections of poetry.* Passing through Customs, *a volume of new and selected poems, appeared in 1999. He teaches at the University of Delaware.*

Gibbons Ruark
The Visitor

Holding the arm of his helper, the blind
Piano tuner comes to our piano.
He hesitates at first, but once he finds
The keyboard, his hands glide over the slow
Keys, ringing changes finer than the eye   5

Can see. The dusty wires he touches, row
On row, quiver like bowstrings as he
Twists them one notch tighter. He runs his
Finger along a wire, touches the dry
Rust to his tongue, breaks into a pure bliss   *10*
And tells us, "One year more of damp weather
Would have done you in, but I've saved it this
Time. Would one of you play now, please? I hear
It better at a distance." My wife plays
Stardust. The blind man stands and smiles in her   *15*
Direction, then disappears into the blaze
Of new October. Now the afternoon,
The long afternoon that blurs in a haze
Of music . . . Chopin nocturnes, *Clair de Lune,*
All the old familiar, unfamiliar   *20*
Music-lesson pieces, *Papa's Haydn's*
Dead and gone, gently down the stream . . . Hours later,
After the latest car has doused its beams,
Has cooled down and stopped its ticking, I hear
Our cat, with the grace of animals free   *25*
To move in darkness, strike one key only,
And a single lucid drop of water stars my dream.

—*1971*

---

*Benjamin Alire Sáenz (b. 1954) is a native of New Mexico. Sáenz spoke only
Spanish as a child, a background that lies behind lines like "I want to feel words /
swimming in my throat / like fighting fish / that refuse to be hooked / on a
line." His book,* Dark and Perfect Angels, *contains poems about the landscape of the
Southwest and about Sáenz's three years as a Roman Catholic priest.*

Benjamin Alire Sáenz
To the Desert

I came to you one rainless August night.
You taught me how to live without the rain.
You are thirst and thirst is all I know.

You are sand, wind, sun, and burning sky,
The hottest blue. You blow a breeze and brand   5
Your breath into my mouth. You reach—then *bend*
Your force, to break, blow, burn, and make me new.
You wrap your name tight around my ribs
And keep me warm. I was born for you.
Above, below, by you, by you surrounded.   10
I wake to you at dawn. Never break your
Knot. Reach, rise, blow, *Sálvame, mi dios,*
Trágame, mi tierra. Salva, traga, Break me,
I am bread. I will be the water for your thirst.

—*1995*

---

*Gladys Cardiff (b. 1942) is a member of the Cherokee nation. "Combing" is
taken from her first collection,* To Frighten a Storm, *which was originally published in 1976.*

Gladys Cardiff
Combing

Bending, I bow my head
And lay my hand upon
Her hair, combing, and think
How women do this for
Each other. My daughter's hair   5
Curls against the comb,
Wet and fragrant—orange
Parings. Her face, downcast,
Is quiet for one so young.

I take her place. Beneath   10
My mother's hands I feel
The braids drawn up tight
As a piano wire and singing,
Vinegar-rinsed. Sitting
Before the oven I hear   15

The orange coils tick
The early hour before school.

She combed her grandmother
Mathilda's hair using
A comb made out of bone.   *20*
Mathilda rocked her oak wood
Chair, her face downcast,
Intent on tearing rags
In strips to braid a cotton
Rug from bits of orange   *25*
and brown. A simple act,

Preparing hair. Something
Women do for each other,
Plaiting the generations.

                                                    —1976

Charles Martin (b. 1942) *is a lifelong resident of New York City. Martin has
taught English as a second language for many years at Queensborough College.
"E.S.L." appeared as a prefatory poem to Martin's sequence "Passages from
Friday," an ironic retelling of the Robinson Crusoe story from his servant's point of
view.*

Charles Martin
E.S.L.°

    My frowning students carve
    Me monsters out of prose:
This one—a gargoyle—thumbs its contemptuous nose
At how, in English, subject must agree
With verb—for any such agreement shows   5
    Too great a willingness to serve,
        A docility

E.S.L. English as a Second Language

Which wiry Miss Choi
Finds un-American.
She steals a hard look at me. I wink. Her grin   *10*
Is my reward. *In his will, our peace, our Pass:*
Gargoyle erased, subject and verb now in
    Agreement, reach object, enjoy
        Temporary truce.

    Tonight my students must   *15*
    Agree or disagree:
America is still a land of opportunity.
The answer is always, uniformly, *Yes*—even though
"It has no doubt that here were to much free,"
    As Miss Torrico will insist.   *20*
        She and I both know

    That Language binds us fast,
    And those of us without
Are bound and gagged by those within. Each fledgling
Polyglot must shake old habits: tapping her sneakered feet,   *25*
Miss Choi exorcises incensed ancestors, flout-
    ing the ghosts of her Chinese past.
        Writhing in the seat

    Next to Miss Choi, Mister
    Fedakis, in anguish   *30*
Labors to express himself in a tongue which
Proves *Linear B* to me, when I attempt to read it
Later. They're here for English as a Second Language,
    Which I'm teaching this semester.
        God knows they need it,   *35*

    And so, thank God, do they.
    The night's made easier
By our agreement: I am here to help deliver
Them into the good life they write me papers about.
English is pre-requisite for that endeavor,   *40*
    Explored in their nightly essays
        Boldly setting out

To reconnoiter the fair
New World they would enter:
Suburban Paradise, the endless shopping center   *45*
Where one may browse for hours before one chooses
Some new necessity—gold-flecked magenta
    Wallpaper to re-do the spare
        Bath no one uses,

    Or a machine which can,   *50*
    In seven seconds, crush
A newborn calf into such seamless mush
As a *mousse* might be made of—or our true sublime:
The gleaming counters where frosted cosmeticians brush
    Decades from the allotted span,   *55*
        Abrogating Time

    As the spring tide brushes
    A single sinister
Footprint from the otherwise unwrinkled shore
Of America the Blank. In absolute confusion   *60*
Poor Mister Fedakis rumbles with despair
    And puts the finishing smutches
        To his conclusion

    While Miss Choi erases:
    One more gargoyle routed.   *65*
Their pure, erroneous lines yield an illuminated
Map of the new found land. We will never arrive there,
Since it exists only in what we say about it,
    As all the rest of my class is
        Bound to discover.   *70*

—1987

Sharon Olds (b. 1942) *displays a candor in dealing with the intimacies of family romance covering three generations that has made her one of the chief contemporary heirs to the confessional tradition. A powerful and dramatic reader, she is much in demand on the lecture circuit. Born in San Francisco, she currently resides in New York City.*

Sharon Olds
The One Girl at the Boys Party

When I take my girl to the swimming party
I set her down among the boys. They tower and
bristle, she stands there smooth and sleek,
her math scores unfolding in the air around her.
They will strip to their suits, her body hard and   5
indivisible as a prime number,
they'll plunge into the deep end, she'll subtract
her height from ten feet, divide it into
hundreds of gallons of water, the numbers
bouncing in her mind like molecules of chlorine   10
in the bright blue pool. When they climb out,
her ponytail will hang its pencil lead
down her back, her narrow silk suit
with hamburgers and french fries printed on it
will glisten in the brilliant air, and they will   15
see her sweet face, solemn and
sealed, a factor of one, and she will
see their eyes, two each,
their legs, two each, and the curves of their sexes,
one each, and in her head she'll be doing her   20
wild multiplying, as the drops
sparkle and fall to the power of a thousand from her body.

—*1983*

James Tate (b. 1943) writes a unique brand of comic surrealism that has remained constant throughout his career. The Lost Pilot *won the Yale Younger Poets Award in 1966. Tate's* Selected Poems *was the recipient of the Pulitzer Prize in 1992.*

James Tate
Teaching the Ape to Write Poems

They didn't have much trouble
teaching the ape to write poems:
first they strapped him into the chair,
then tied the pencil around his hand
(the paper had already been nailed down).   5
Then Dr. Bluespire leaned over his shoulder
and whispered into his ear:
"You look like a god sitting there.
Why don't you try writing something?"

—1991

Ellen Bryant Voight (b. 1943) is a native of Virginia. Voight was trained as a concert pianist before earning her creative writing degree from the University of Iowa. She has taught poetry at a number of colleges in New England and the South.

Ellen Bryant Voight
Daughter

There is one grief worse than any other.

When your small feverish throat clogged, and quit,
I knelt beside the chair on the green rug
and shook you and shook you,
but the only sound was mine shouting you back,   5
the delicate curls at your temples,
the blue wool blanket,

your face blue,
your jaw clamped against remedy—

how could I put a knife to that white neck?   10
With you in my lap,
my hands fluttering like flags,
I bend instead over your dead weight
to administer a kiss so urgent, so ruthless,
pumping breath into your stilled body,   15
counting out the rhythm for how long until
the second birth, the second cry
oh Jesus that sudden noisy musical inhalation
that leaves me stunned
by your survival.   20

—1983

Robert Morgan (b. 1944) is a native of the mountains of North Carolina, and
has retained a large measure of regional ties in his poetry. One of his collections,
Sigodlin, takes its title from an Appalachian word for things that are built slightly
out of square. Gap Creek: The Story of a Marriage, a novel of turn-of-the-
century mountain life, was a bestseller in 2000.

Robert Morgan
Mountain Bride

They say Revis found a flatrock
on the ridge just
perfect for a natural hearth,
and built his cabin with a stick

and clay chimney right over it.   5
On their wedding night he lit
the fireplace to dry away the mountain
chill of late spring, and flung on

applewood to dye
the room with molten color while   10

he and Martha that was a Parrish
warmed the sheets between the tick

stuffed with leaves and its feather
cover. Under that wide hearth
a nest of rattlers,   15
they'll knot a hundred together,

had wintered and were coming awake.
The warming rock
flushed them out early.
It was she   20

who wakened to their singing near
the embers and roused him to go look.
Before he reached the fire
more than a dozen struck

and he died yelling her to stay   25
on the big four-poster.
Her uncle coming up the hollow
with a gift bearham two days later

found her shivering there
marooned above a pool   30
of hungry snakes,
and the body beginning to swell.

—1979

Craig Raine (b. 1944) *early in his career displayed a comic surrealism that was responsible for so many imitations that critic James Fenton dubbed him the founder of the "Martian School" of contemporary poetry. Born in Bishop Auckland, England, and educated at Oxford, Raine is an editor with the prestigious publishing firm of Faber & Faber.*

Craig Raine
A Martian Sends a Postcard Home

Caxtons° are mechanical birds with many wings
and some are treasured for their markings—

they cause the eyes to melt
or the body to shriek without pain.

I have never seen one fly, but   5
sometimes they perch on the hand.

Mist is when the sky is tired of flight
and rests its soft machine on ground:

then the world is dim and bookish
like engravings under tissue paper.   10

Rain is when the earth is television.
It has the property of making colours darker.

Model T is a room with the lock inside—
a key is turned to free the world

for movement, so quick there is a film   15
to watch for anything missed.

But time is tied to the wrist
or kept in a box, ticking with impatience.

In homes, a haunted apparatus sleeps,
that snores when you pick it up.   20

1 Caxtons i.e., books; after William Caxton (1422–1491), first English printer

If the ghost cries, they carry it
to their lips and soothe it to sleep

with sounds. And yet, they wake it up
deliberately, by tickling with a finger.

Only the young are allowed to suffer   25
openly. Adults go to a punishment room

with water but nothing to eat.
They lock the door and suffer the noises

alone. No one is exempt
and everyone's pain has a different smell.   30

At night, when all the colours die,
they hide in pairs

and read about themselves—
in colour, with their eyelids shut.

—1978

Enid Shomer *(b. 1944) grew up in Washington, D.C., and lived for a number of
years in Florida. Her first collection,* Stalking the Florida Panther *(1987), ex-
plored both the Jewish traditions of her childhood and her adult attachment to her
adopted state. In recent years she has published* Imaginary Men, *a collection of
short stories, and* Black Drums, *a collection of poetry.*

Enid Shomer
Women Bathing at Bergen-Belsen°

April 24, 1945

Twelve hours after the Allies arrive
there is hot water, soap. Two women bathe
in a makeshift, open-air shower while nearby
fifteen thousand are flung naked into mass graves

Bergen-Belsen German concentration camp in WWII

by captured SS guards. Clearly legs and arms   5
are the natural handles of a corpse. The bathers,
taken late in the war, still have flesh
on their bones, still have breasts. Though nudity was
a death sentence here, they have undressed,
oblivious to the soldiers and the cameras.   10
The corpses push through the limed earth like upended
headstones. The bathers scrub their feet, bending
in beautiful curves, mapping the contours
of the body, that kingdom to which they've returned.

—1987

Alice Walker (b. 1944), *the author of* The Color Purple *and other novels, is a leading African-American writer. Less well known as a poet, she won the Pulitzer Prize for fiction in 1983. Her most recent novels combine her concerns with both racial and feminist issues.*

Alice Walker
Even as I Hold You

Even as I hold you
I think of you as someone gone
far, far away. Your eyes the color
of pennies in a bowl of dark honey
bringing sweet light to someone else   5
your black hair slipping through my fingers
is the flash of your head going
around a corner
your smile, breaking before me,
the flippant last turn   10
of a revolving door,
emptying you out, changed,
away from me.

Even as I hold you
I am letting go.   15

—1979

Wendy Cope (b. 1945) says, "I hardly ever tire of love or rhyme. / That's why I'm Poor and have a rotten time." Her first collection, Making Cocoa for Kingsley Amis (1986), was a bestseller in England. Whether reducing T. S. Eliot's modernist classic "The Waste Land" to a set of five limericks or chronicling the life and loves of Jason Strugnell, her feckless poetic alter-ego, Cope remains one of the wisest and wittiest poets writing today. "I dislike the term 'light verse' because it is used as a way of dismissing poets who allow humor into their work. I believe that a humorous poem can also be 'serious'; deeply felt and saying something that matters." She lives in Winchester, England.

Wendy Cope
Rondeau Redoublé

There are so many kinds of awful men—
One can't avoid them all. She often said
She'd never make the same mistake again:
She always made a new mistake instead.

The chinless type who made her feel ill-bred;   5
The practised charmer, less than charming when
He talked about the wife and kids and fled—
There are so many kinds of awful men.

The half-crazed hippy, deeply into Zen,
Whose cryptic homilies she came to dread;   10
The fervent youth who worshipped Tony Benn—
'One can't avoid them all,' she often said.

The ageing banker, rich and overfed,
who held forth on the dollar and the yen—
Though there were many more mistakes ahead,   15
She'd never make the same mistake again.

The budding poet, scribbling in his den
Odes not to her but to his pussy, Fred;
The drunk who fell asleep at nine or ten—
She always made a new mistake instead.   20

And so the gambler was at least unwed
And didn't preach or sneer or wield a pen
Or hoard his wealth or take the Scotch to bed.

She'd lived and learned and lived and learned but then
There are so many kinds.   *25*

—*1986*

B. H. Fairchild (b. 1945) *grew up in Liberal, Kansas, and his father's machine shop provides the title and the setting for his prize-winning collection,* The Art of the Lathe. *Fairchild teaches at the California State University, San Bernardino. His first two collections of poetry, both from small presses, have recently been published by alicejames books.*

B. H. Fairchild
Body and Soul

Half-numb, guzzling bourbon and Coke from coffee mugs,
our fathers fall in love with their own stories, nuzzling
the facts but mauling the truth, and my friend's father begins
to lay out with the slow ease of a blues ballad a story
about sandlot baseball in Commerce, Oklahoma decades ago.   *5*
These were men's teams, grown men, some in their thirties
and forties who worked together in zinc mines or on oil rigs,
sweat and khaki and long beers after work, steel guitar music
whanging in their ears, little white rent houses to return to
where their wives complained about money and broken
      Kenmores   *10*
and then said the hell with it and sang *Body and Soul*
in the bathtub and later that evening with the kids asleep
lay in bed stroking their husband's wrist tattoo and smoking
Chesterfields from a fresh pack until everything was O.K.
Well, you get the idea. Life goes on, the next day is Sunday,   *15*
another ball game, and the other team shows up one man short.

They say, we're one man short, but can we use this boy,
he's only fifteen years old, and at least he'll make a game.
They take a look at the kid, muscular and kind of knowing
the way he holds his glove, with the shoulders loose,   *20*
the thick neck, but then with that boy's face under
a clump of angelic blonde hair, and say, oh, hell, sure,

let's play ball. So it all begins, the men loosening up,
joking about the fat catcher's sex life, it's so bad
last night he had to hump his wife, that sort of thing,   25
pairing off into little games of catch that heat up into
throwing matches, the smack of the fungo bat, lazy jogging
into right field, big smiles and arcs of tobacco juice,
and the talk that gives a cool, easy feeling to the air,
talk among men normally silent, normally brittle and a little   30
angry with the empty promise of their lives. But they chatter
and say rock and fire, babe, easy out, and go right ahead
and pitch to the boy, but nothing fancy, just hard fastballs
right around the belt, and the kid takes the first two
but on the third pops the bat around so quick and sure   35
that they pause a moment before turning around to watch
the ball still rising and finally dropping far beyond
the abandoned tractor that marks left field. Holy shit.
They're pretty quiet watching him round the bases,
but then, what the hell, the kid knows how to hit a ball,   40
so what, let's play some goddamned baseball here.
And so it goes. The next time up, the boy gets a look
at a very nifty low curve, then a slider, and the next one
is the curve again, and he sends it over the Allis Chalmers,
high and big and sweet. The left fielder just stands there,
      frozen.   45
As if this isn't enough, the next time up he bats left-handed.
They can't believe it, and the pitcher, a tall, mean-faced
man from Okarche who just doesn't give a shit anyway
because his wife ran off two years ago leaving him with
three little ones and a rusted-out Dodge with a cracked block,   50
leans in hard, looking at the fat catcher like he was the
      sonofabitch
who ran off with his wife, leans in and throws something
out of the dark, green hell of forbidden fastballs, something
that comes in at the knees and then leaps viciously towards
the kid's elbow. He swings exactly the way he did
      right-handed,   55
and they all turn like a chorus line toward deep right field
where the ball loses itself in sagebrush and the sad burnt
dust of dustbowl Oklahoma. It is something to see.

But why make a long story long: runs pile up on both sides,
the boy comes around five times, and five times the pitcher   *60*
is cursing both God and His mother as his chew of tobacco
    sours
into something resembling horse piss, and a ragged and bruised
Spalding baseball disappears into the far horizon. Goodnight,
Irene. They have lost the game and some painful side bets
and they have been suckered. And it means nothing to them   *65*
though it should to you when they are told the boy's name is
Mickey Mantle. And that's the story and those are the facts.
But the facts are not the truth. I think, though, as I scan
the faces of these old men now lost in the innings of their
    youth,
I think I know what the truth of this story is, and I imagine   *70*
it lying there in the weeds behind that Allis Chalmers
just waiting for the obvious question to be asked: why, oh
why in hell didn't they just throw around the kid, walk him,
after he hit the third homer? Anybody would have,
especially nine men with disappointed wives and dirty socks   *75*
and diminishing expectations for whom winning at anything
meant everything. Men who know how to play the game,
who had talent when the other team had nothing except this
    ringer
who without a pitch to hit was meaningless, and they could go
    home
with their little two-dollar side bets and stride into the house   *80*
singing *If You've Got the Money, Honey, I've Got the Time*
with a bottle of Southern Comfort under their arms and grab
Dixie or May Ella up and dance across the gray linoleum
as if it were V-Day all over again. But they did not.
And they did not because they were men, and this was a boy.   *85*
And they did not because sometimes after making love,
after smoking their Chesterfields in the cool silence and
listening to the big bands on the radio that sounded so glamorous,
so distant, they glanced over at their wives and noticed the lines
growing heavier around the eyes and mouth, felt what their
    wives   *90*
felt: that Les Brown and Glenn Miller and all those dancing
    couples

and in fact all possibility of human gaiety and light-heartedness
were as far away and unreachable as Times Square or the Avalon
ballroom. They did not because of the gray linoleum lying there
in the half-dark, the free calendar from the local mortuary   95
that siad one day was pretty much like another, the work gloves
looped over the doorknob like dead squirrels. And they did not
because they had gone through a depression and a war that had left
them with the idea that being a man in the eyes of their fathers
and everyone else had cost them just too goddamned much to
    lay it   100
at the feet of a fifteen year-old boy. And so they did not walk
    him,
and lost, but at least had some ragged remnant of themselves
to take back home. But there is one thing more, though it is not
a fact. When I see my friend's father staring hard into the bottomless
well of home plate as Mantle's fifth homer heads toward
    Arkansas,   105
I know that this man with the half-orphaned children and
worthless Dodge has also encountered for his first and possibly
only time that vast gap between talent and genius, has seen
as few have in the harsh light of an Oklahoma Sunday, the blonde
and blue-eyed bringer of truth, who will not easily be
    forgiven.   110

—1998

Leon Stokesbury (b. 1945), *as an undergraduate at Lamar State College of Technology (now Lamar University), was acquainted with the legendary singer Janis Joplin, the subject of "Evening's End." The author of three collections of poetry, including* Autumn Rhythm: New and Selected Poems, *Stokesbury has also edited anthologies of contemporary Southern poetry and the poetry of World War II.*

Leon Stokesbury
Evening's End 1943–1970

For the first time in what must be
the better part of two years now
I happened to hear Janis

in her glory—
all that tinctured syrup   *5*
dripping off
a razorblade—
on the radio today singing "Summertime."

And it took me back to this girl I knew,
a woman really, my first year   *10*
writing undergraduate poetry
at the Mirabeau B. Lamar
State College of Technology
in Beaumont, Texas,
back in 1966.   *15*

This woman was the latest in a line,
the latest steady
of my friend John Coyle that spring—
and I remember she was plain:
she was short: and plain   *20*
and wore her brown hair up
in a sort of bun in back
that made her plainer still.

I don't know where John met her,
but word went round   *25*
she had moved back in with Mom and Dad
down in Port Arthur
to get her head straight,
to attend Lamar,
to study History,   *30*
after several years in San Francisco
where she had drifted
into a "bad scene"
taking heroin.

I was twenty,   *35*
still lived with Mom and Dad myself,
and so knew nothing
about "bad scenes,"
but I do remember once or twice
each month that spring   *40*

John would give a party
with this woman always there.
And always as the evening's end came on
this woman, silent for hours,
would reveal, from thin air,   45
her guitar,
settle in a chair,
release her long hair
from the bun it was in,
and begin.   50

Her hair flowed over her shoulders,
and the ends of the strands of hair
like tarnished brass in lamplight
would brush and drag across
the sides of the guitar   55
as this woman bent
over it.

How low and guttural, how
slow and torchlit, how
amber her song, how absolutely   60
unlike the tiny nondescript
a few minutes before.

And I remember also,
from later on that spring,
from May of that year,   65
two nights in particular.

The first night was a party
this woman gave
at her parents' home.
Her parents' home   70
was beige:
the bricks the parents' home
was built with
were beige.
The entire house was carpeted   75
in beige.

John's girl greeted everyone at the door,
a martini in one hand
and a lit cigarette
in an Oriental   80
ivory cigarette holder in the other,
laughing
for once, and tossing back
her long brown hair.

All the women wore
black full-length party dresses—
and I remember the young woman's father,
how odd he seemed
in his charcoal suit and tie,
his gray hair—   90
how unamused.

Then John Coyle was drunk.
He spilled his beer
across the beige frontroom carpet:
that darker dampness sinking in,   95
the father vanished
from the scene.

The next week we double-dated.
I convinced John and his girl
to see a double feature,   100
Irma La Douce and *Tom Jones*,
at the Pines Theatre.

And I can recall John's girl
saying just one thing that night.

After the films, John was quizzical,   105
contentious, full of ridicule
for movies I had guaranteed he would enjoy.
He turned and asked her
what she thought—
and in the softest   110
of tones, a vague rumor
of honeysuckle in the air,
she almost whispered,

"I thought they were beautiful."

That was the last time I saw her,   *115*
the last thing that I heard her say.

A few weeks later,
she drove over to John's house
in the middle of the afternoon,
and caught him in bed   *120*
with Suzanne Morain,
a graduate assistant
from the English Department at Lamar.

John told me later
that when she saw them in the bedroom   *125*
she ran into the kitchen,
picked up a broom,
and began to sweep the floor—
weeping.

When John sauntered in   *130*
she threw the broom at him,
ran out the door,
got in her car and drove away.
And from that day on,
no one ever saw that woman   *135*
in Beaumont again.

The next day she moved to Austin.
And later on, I heard,
back to San Francisco.
And I remember when John told me this,   *140*
with a semi-shocked expression
on his face, he turned
and looked up, and said, "You know,
I guess she must have really *loved* me."

I was twenty years old.   *145*
What did I know?
What could I say?

I could not think
of anything to say,
except, "Yes,   *150*
I guess so."

It was summertime.

Thus runs the world away.

—*1996*

Marilyn Nelson (b. 1946) *is the author of* The Homeplace, *a sequence of poems on family history.* The Homeplace *is remarkable for its sensitive exploration of the mixed white and black bloodlines in the poet's family history.* Carver: A Life in Poems, *a poetic biography of George Washington Carver, appeared in 2001.*

Marilyn Nelson
The Ballad of Aunt Geneva

Geneva was the wild one.
Geneva was a tart.
Geneva met a blue-eyed boy
and gave away her heart.

Geneva ran a roadhouse.   5
Geneva wasn't sent
to college like the others:
Pomp's pride her punishment.

She cooked out on the river,
watching the shore slide by,   10
her lips pursed into hardness,
her deep-set brown eyes dry.

They say she killed a woman
over a good black man
by braining the jealous heifer   15

with an iron frying pan.

They say, when she was eighty,
she got up late at night
and sneaked her old, white lover in
to make love, and to fight.   *20*

First, they heard the tell-tale
singing of the springs,
then Geneva's voice rang out:
I need to buy some things,

So next time, bring more money.   *25*
And bring more moxie, too.
I ain't got no time to waste
on limp white mens like you.

Oh yeah? Well, Mister White Man,
it sure might be stone-white,   *30*
but my thing's white as it is.
And you know damn well I'm right.

Now listen: take your heart pills
and pay the doctor mind.
If you up and die on me,   *35*
I'll whip your white behind.

They tiptoed through the parlor
on heavy, time-slowed feet.
She watched him, from her front door,
walk down the dawnlit street.   *40*

Geneva was the wild one.
Geneva was a tart.
Geneva met a blue-eyed boy
and gave away her heart.

—1990

Ai (b. 1947) has written a number of realistic dramatic monologues that often reveal the agonies of characters trapped in unfulfilling or even dangerous lives. With her gallery of social misfits, she is the contemporary heir to the tradition begun by Robert Browning.

Ai
Child Beater

Outside, the rain, pinafore of gray water, dresses the town
and I stroke the leather belt,
as she sits in the rocking chair,
holding a crushed paper cup to her lips.
I yell at her, but she keeps rocking;   5
back, her eyes open, forward, they close.
Her body, somehow fat, though I feed her only once a day,
reminds me of my own just after she was born.
It's been seven years, but I still can't forget how I felt.
How heavy it feels to look at her.   10

I lay the belt on a chair
and get her dinner bowl.
I hit the spoon against it, set it down
and watch her crawl to it,
pausing after each forward thrust of her legs   15
and when she takes her first bite,
I grab the belt and beat her across the back
until her tears, beads of salt-filled glass, falling,
shatter on the floor.

I move off. I let her eat,   20
while I get my dog's chain leash from the closet.
I whirl it around my head.
O daughter, so far, you've only had a taste of icing,
are you ready now for some cake?

—1973

> **Jim Hall (b. 1947)** *is one of the most brilliantly inventive comic poets in recent years. He has also written a successful series of crime novels set in his native south Florida, beginning with* Under Cover of Daylight *in 1987.*

Jim Hall
Maybe Dats Your Pwoblem Too

All my pwoblems,
who knows, maybe evwybody's pwoblems
is due to da fact, due to da awful twuth
dat I am SPIDERMAN.

I know, I know. All da dumb jokes: 5
No flies on you, ha ha,
and da ones about what do I do wit all
doze extwa legs in bed. Well, dat's funny yeah.
But you twy being
SPIDERMAN for a month or two. Go ahead.   10

You get doze cwazy calls fwom da
Gubbener askin you to twap some booglar who's
only twying to wip off color T.V. sets.
Now, what do I cawre about T.V. sets?
But I pull on da suit, da stinkin suit,   15
wit da sucker cups on da fingers,
and get my wopes and wittle bundle of
equipment and den I go flying like cwazy
acwoss da town fwom woof top to woof top.

Till der he is. Some poor dumb color T.V. slob   20
and I fall on him and we westle a widdle

until I get him all woped. So big deal.

You tink when you SPIDERMAN
der's sometin big going to happen to you.
Well, I tell you what. It don't happen dat way.   25
Nuttin happens. Gubbener calls, I go.
Bwing him to powice, Gubbener calls again,
like dat over and over.

I tink I twy sometin diffunt. I tink I twy
sometin excitin like wacing cawrs. Sometin to make   30
my heart beat at a difwent wate.
But den you just can't quit being sometin like
SPIDERMAN.
You SPIDERMAN for life. Fowever. I can't even
buin my suit. It won't buin. It's fwame wesistent.   35
So maybe dat's youwr pwoblem too, who knows.
Maybe dat's da whole pwoblem wif evwytin.
Nobody can buin der suits, dey all fwame wesistent.
Who knows?

—1980

Yusef Komunyakaa (b. 1947) is a native of Bogulusa, Louisiana. Komunyakaa has written memorably on a wide range of subjects, including jazz and his service during the Vietnam War. Neon Vernacular: New and Selected Poems *(1993) won the Pulitzer Prize in 1994, and* Pleasure Dome: New and Collected Poems *appeared in 2001.*

Yusef Komunyakaa
Facing It

My black face fades,
hiding inside the black granite.

I said I wouldn't,
dammit: No tears.
I'm stone. I'm flesh.   *5*
My clouded reflection eyes me
like a bird of prey, the profile of night
slanted against morning. I turn
this way—the stone lets me go.
I turn this way—I'm inside   *10*
the Vietnam Veterans Memorial
again, depending on the light
to make a difference.
I go down the 58,022 names,
half-expecting to find   *15*
my own in letters like smoke.
I touch the name Andrew Johnson;
I see the booby trap's white flash.
Names shimmer on a woman's blouse
but when she walks away   *20*
the names stay on the wall.
Brushstrokes flash, a red bird's
wings cutting across my stare.
The sky. A plane in the sky.
A white vet's image floats   *25*
closer to me, then his pale eyes
look through mine. I'm a window.
He's lost his right arm
inside the stone. In the black mirror
a woman's trying to erase names: *30*
No, she's brushing a boy's hair.

—1988

R. S. Gwynn (b. 1948) *is the editor of this volume and (with Dana Gioia) of* The Longman Anthology of Short Fiction. *He teaches at Lamar University*. No Word of Farewell: Selected Poems 1970–2000 *appeared in 2001.*

R. S. Gwynn

Approaching a Significant Birthday, He Peruses *The Norton Anthology of Poetry*

All human things are subject to decay.
Beauty is momentary in the mind.
The curfew tolls the knell of parting day.
If Winter comes, can Spring be far behind?

Forlorn! the very word is like a bell   5
And somewhat of a sad perplexity.
Here, take my picture, though I bid farewell;
In a dark time the eye begins to see

The woods decay, the woods decay and fall—
Bare ruined choirs where late the sweet birds sing.   10
What but design of darkness to appall?
An aged man is but a paltry thing.

If I should die, think only this of me:
Crass casualty obstructs the sun and rain
When I have fears that I may cease to be,   15
To cease upon the midnight with no pain

And hear the spectral singing of the moon
And strictly meditate the thankless muse.
The world is too much with us, late and soon.
It gathers to a greatness, like the ooze.   20

Do not go gentle into the good night.
Fame is no plant that grows on mortal soil.

Again he raised the jug up to the light:
Old age hath yet his honor and his toil.

Downward to darkness on extended wings,   25
Break, break, break, on thy cold gray stones, O Sea,
and tell sad stories of the death of kings.
I do not think that they will sing to me.

—*1990*

Timothy Steele (b. 1948) *has written a successful scholarly study of the rise of
free verse,* Missing Measures, *and is perhaps the most skillful craftsman of the
contemporary New Formalist poets. Born in Vermont, he has lived for a number of
years in Los Angeles, where he teaches at California State University, Los Angeles.*

Timothy Steele
Sapphics° Against Anger

Angered, may I be near a glass of water;
May my first impulse be to think of Silence,
Its deities (who are they? do, in fact, they
            Exist? etc.).

May I recall what Aristotle says of   5
The subject: to give vent to rage is not to
Release it but to be increasingly prone
            To its incursions.

May I imagine being in the Inferno,
Hearing it asked: "Virgilio mio,° who's   10
That sulking with Achilles there?" and hearing
            Virgil say: "Dante,

That fellow, at the slightest provocation,
Slammed phone receivers down, and waved his arms like
A madman. What Attila did to Europe,   15
            What Genghis Khan did

To Asia, that poor dope did to his marriage."
May I, that is, put learning to good purpose,
Mindful that melancholy is a sin, though
        Stylish at present.   *20*

Better than rage is the post-dinner quiet,
The sink's warm turbulence, the streaming platters,
The suds rehearsing down the drain in spirals
        In the last rinsing.

For what is, after all, the good life save that   *25*
Conducted thoughtfully, and what is passion
If not the holiest of powers, sustaining
        Only if mastered.

                                          —*1986*

David Bottoms (b. 1949) *was born in Canton, Georgia. Bottoms is the author both of collections of poetry and successful novels. His first book,* Shooting Rats at Bibb County Dump, *was a winner of the Walt Whitman Award of the Academy of American Poets. He is the co-editor, with Dave Smith, of* The Morrow Anthology of Younger American Poets.

David Bottoms
Sign for My Father, Who Stressed the Bunt

On the rough diamond,
the hand-cut field below the dog lot and barn,
we rehearsed the strict technique
of bunting. I watched from the infield,
the mound, the backstop   *5*
as your left hand climbed the bat, your legs
and shoulders squared toward the pitcher.
You could drop it like a seed
down either base line. I admired your style,

but not enough to take my eyes off the bank   10
that served as our center-field fence.

Years passed, three leagues of organized ball,
no few lives. I could homer
into the garden beyond the bank,
into the left-field lot of Carmichael Motors,   15
and still you stressed the same technique,
the crouch and spring, the lead arm absorbing
just enough impact. That whole tiresome pitch
about basics never changing,
and I never learned what you were laying down.   20

Like a hand brushed across the bill of a cap,
let this be the sign
I'm getting a grip on the sacrifice.

—1983

James Fenton (b. 1949) was born in Lincoln, England, and educated at Oxford. Fenton has worked extensively as a book and drama critic. A brilliant satirical poet, he has also written lyrics for Les Misérables, *the musical version of Victor Hugo's novel, and has served as a journalist in Asia.*

James Fenton
God, a Poem

A nasty surprise in a sandwich,
A drawing-pin caught in your sock,
The limpest of shakes from a hand which
You'd thought would be firm as a rock,

A serious mistake in a nightie,   5
A grave disappointment all around
Is all that you'll get from th'Almighty.

Sapphics stanza form named after Sappho (c. 650 B.C.) **10 Virgilio mio** Dante is addressing Virgil, his guide through hell.

Is all that you'll get underground.

Oh, he *said:* 'If you lay off the crumpet°
I'll see you alright in the end.   10
Just hang on until the last trumpet.
Have faith in me, chum—I'm your friend.'

But if you remind him, he'll tell you:
'I'm sorry, I must have been pissed—°
Though your name rings a sort of a bell. You   15
Should have guessed that I do not exist.

'I didn't exist at Creation,
I didn't exist at the Flood.
And I won't be around for Salvation
To sort out the sheep from the cud—   20

'Or whatever the phrase is. The fact is
In soteriological° terms
I'm a crude existential malpractice
And you are a diet of worms.

'You're a nasty surprise in a sandwich.   25
You're a drawing-pin caught in my sock.
You're the limpest of shakes from a hand which
I'd have thought would be firm as a rock,

'You're a serious mistake in a nightie,
You're a grave disappointment all round—   30
'That's all that you are,' says th'Almighty,
'And that's all that you'll be underground.'

—*1983*

---

9 crumpet vulgar British slang for women   **14 pissed** drunk   **22 soteriological** relation to salvation

Sarah Cortez (b. 1950) grew up in Houston, Texas, and holds degrees in psychology and religion, classical studies, and accounting. She also serves as Visiting Scholar at the University of Houston's Center for Mexican-American Studies. She is a deputy constable in Harris County, Texas.

Sarah Cortez
Tu Negrito

She's got to bail me out,
he says into the phone outside the holding cell.
She's going there tomorrow anyway for Mikey.
Tell her she's got to do this for me.

He says into the phone outside the holding cell,   5
Make sure she listens. Make her feel guilty, man.
Tell her she's got to do this for me.
She can have all my money, man.

Make sure she listens. Make her feel guilty, man.
Tell her she didn't bail me out the other times.   10
She can have all my money, man.
She always bails out Mikey.

Tell her she didn't bail me out the other times.
I don't got no one else to call, cousin.
She always bails out Mikey.   15
Make sure you write all this down, cousin.

I don't got no one else to call, cousin.
I really need her now.
Make sure you write this all down, cousin.
Page her. Put in code 333. That's me.   20

I really need her now.
Write down "Mommie." Change it from "Mom."
Page her. Put in code 333. That's me.
Write down *"Tu Negrito."* Tell her I love her.

Write down "Mommie." Change it from "Mom."   25
I'm her littlest. Remind her.

Write down *"Tu Negrito."*
Tell her I love her. She's got to bail me out.

—2000

Carolyn Forché (b. 1950) *won the Yale Younger Poets Award for her first collection,* Gathering the Tribes *(1975).* The Country Between Us, *Forché's second collection, contains poems based on the poet's experiences in the war-torn country of El Salvador in the early 1980s.*

Carolyn Forché
The Colonel

What you have heard is true. I was in his house.° His wife carried a tray of coffee and sugar. His daughter filed her nails, his son went out for the night. There were daily papers, pet dogs, a pistol on the cushion beside him. The moon swung bare on its black cord over the house. On the television was a cop show. It was in English. Broken bottles were embedded in the walls around the house to scoop the kneecaps from a man's legs or cut his hands to lace. On the windows there were gratings like those in liquor stores. We had dinner, rack of lamb, good wine, a gold bell was on the table for calling the maid. The maid brought green mangoes, salt, a type of bread. I was asked how I enjoyed the country. There was a brief commercial in Spanish. His wife took everything away. There was some talk then of how difficult it had become to govern. The parrot said hello on the terrace. The colonel told it to shut up, and pushed himself from the table. My friend said to me with his eyes: say nothing. The colonel returned with a sack used to bring groceries home. He spilled many human ears on the table. They were like dried peach halves. There is no other way to say this. He took one of them in his hands, shook it in our faces, dropped it into a water glass. It came alive there. I am tired of fooling around he said. As for the rights of anyone, tell your people they can go fuck themselves. He swept the ears to the floor with his arm and held the last of his wine in the air. Something for your poetry, no? he said. Some of the ears on the floor caught this

---

1 his house in El Salvador

scrap of his voice. Some of the ears on the floor were pressed to the ground.

—*1978*

Dana Gioia (b. 1950) *grew up in the suburbs of Los Angeles. He took a graduate degree in English from Harvard but made a successful career in business before devoting his full time to writing. The editor of several textbooks and anthologies, he is also an influential critic whose essay "Can Poetry Matter?" stimulated much discussion when it appeared in* The Atlantic. Interrogations at Noon, *his third collection of poetry, appeared in 2001.*

Dana Gioia
Planting a Sequoia

All afternoon my brothers and I have worked in the orchard,
Digging this hole, laying you into it, carefully packing the soil.
Rain blackened the horizon, but cold winds kept it over the Pacific,
And the sky above us stayed the dull gray
Of an old year coming to an end.   5

In Sicily a father plants a tree to celebrate his first son's birth—
An olive or a fig tree—a sign that the earth has one more life to bear.
I would have done the same, proudly laying new stock into my father's
    orchard,
A green sapling rising among the twisted apple boughs,
A promise of new fruit in other autumns.   10

But today we kneel in the cold planting you, our native giant,
Defying the practical custom of our fathers,
Wrapping in your roots a lock of hair, a piece of an infant's birth cord,
All that remains above earth of a first-born son,
A few stray atoms brought back to the elements.   15

We will give you what we can—our labor and our soil,
Water drawn from the earth when the skies fail,
Nights scented with the ocean fog, days softened by the circuit of bees.
We plant you in the corner of the grove, bathed in western light,
A slender shoot against the sunset.   20

And when our family is no more, all of his unborn brothers dead,
Every niece and nephew scattered, the house torn down,
His mother's beauty ashes in the air,
I want you to stand among strangers, all young and ephemeral to you,
Silently keeping the secret of your birth.   25

                                                                    —*1991*

---

*Rodney Jones (b. 1950) was born in Alabama and received important national
attention when* Transparent Gestures *won the Poets' Prize in 1990. Like many
younger southern poets, he often deals with the difficult legacy of racism and the adjustments that a new era have forced on both whites and blacks.*

Rodney Jones

Winter Retreat: Homage to Martin Luther King, Jr.

There is a hotel in Baltimore where we came together,
we black and white educated and educators,
for a week of conferences, for important counsel
sanctioned by the DOE° and the Carter administration,
to make certain difficult inquiries, to collate notes   5
on the instruction of the disabled, the deprived,
the poor, who do not score well on entrance tests,
who, failing school, must go with mop and pail
skittering across the slick floors of cafeterias,
or climb dewy girders to balance high above cities,   10
or, jobless, line up in the bone cold. We felt
substantive burdens lighter if we stated it right.
Very delicately, we spoke in turn. We walked
together beside the still waters of behaviorism.
Armed with graphs and charts, with new strategies   15
to devise objectives and determine accountability,
we empathetic black and white shone in seminar rooms.

---

4 DOE Department of Education

We enunciated every word clearly and without accent.
We moved very carefully in the valley of the shadow
of the darkest agreement error. We did not digress.   20
We ascended the trunk of that loftiest cypress
of Latin grammar the priests could never
successfully graft onto the rough green chestnut
of the English language. We extended ourselves
with that sinuous motion of the tongue that is half   25
pain and almost eloquence. We black and white
politely reprioritized the parameters of our agenda
to impact equitably on the Seminole and the Eskimo.
We praised diversity and involvement, the sacrifices
of fathers and mothers. We praised the next white   30
Gwendolyn Brooks° and the next black Robert Burns.°
We deep made friends. In that hotel we glistened
over the *pommes au gratin*° and the *poitrine de veau.*°
The morsels of lamb flamed near where we talked.
The waiters bowed and disappeared among the ferns.   35
And there is a bar there, there is a large pool.
Beyond the tables of the drinkers and raconteurs,
beyond the hot tub brimming with Lebanese tourists
and the women in expensive bathing suits doing laps,
if you dive down four feet, swim out far enough,   40
and emerge on the other side, it is sixteen degrees.
It is sudden and very beautiful and colder
than thought, though the air frightens you at first,
not because it is cold, but because it is visible,
almost palpable, in the fog that rises from difference.   45
While I stood there in the cheek-numbing snow,
all Baltimore was turning blue. And what I remember
of that week of talks is nothing the record shows,
but the revelation outside, which was the city
many came to out of the fields, then the thought   50
that we had wanted to make the world kinder,
but, in speaking proudly, we had failed a vision.

                                                          —*1989*

---

31 **Gwendolyn Brooks** black American poet (1917–2000)   **Robert Burns** Scottish poet
(1759–1796)   33 **pommes au gratin** potatoes baked with cheese   **poitrine de veau** brisket of veal

Timothy Murphy (b. 1950), *a former student of Robert Penn Warren at Yale, returned to his native North Dakota to make a career as a venture capitalist in the agricultural field. Unpublished until his mid-forties, Murphy brought four collections to print during the 1990s.*

Timothy Murphy
The Track of a Storm

Bastille Day, 1995

We grieve for the twelve trees we lost last night,
pillars of our community, old friends
and confidants dismembered in our sight,
stripped of their crowns by the unruly winds.
There were no baskets to receive their heads,   5
no women knitting by the guillotines,
only two sleepers rousted from their beds
by fusillades of hailstones on the screens.
Her nest shattered, her battered hatchlings drowned,
a stunned and silent junko watches me   10
chainsawing limbs from corpses of the downed,
clearing the understory of debris
while supple saplings which survived the blast
lay claim to light and liberty at last.

—*1998*

Joy Harjo (b. 1951), a member of the Creek tribe, is one of the leading voices of contemporary Native American poetry. She is a powerful performer and was one of the poets featured on Bill Moyers's television series, The Power of the Word.

Joy Harjo
Song for the Deer and Myself to Return On

This morning when I looked out the roof window
before dawn and a few stars were still caught
in the fragile weft of ebony night
I was overwhelmed. I sang the song Louis taught me:
a song to call the deer in Creek,° when hunting,   5
and I am certainly hunting something as magic as deer
in this city far from the hammock of my mother's belly.
It works, of course, and deer came into this room
and wondered at finding themselves
in a house near downtown Denver.   10
Now the deer and I are trying to figure out a song
to get them back, to get all of us back,
because if it works I'm going with them.
And it's too early to call Louis
and nearly too late to go home.   15

—*1990*

5 **Creek** Native American tribal language

Garrett Hongo (b. 1951), *who is of Japanese ancestry, was born in Hawaii and educated at Pomona College and the University of California at Irvine. His books include* Yellow Light *(1982) and* The River of Heaven *(1988).*

Garrett Hongo

Crossing Ka'ū Desert°

from under the harpstring shade of tree ferns
and the blue trumpets of morning glories
      beside the slick road,
the green creep of davallia and club moss
        (their tiny hammers   5
        staffed quarter-notes
           and fiddlenecks on the forest floor),
spider lilies and ginger flowers like paper cranes
        furling in the tongues of overgrowth,
           in the sapphired arpeggios of rain   10

to the frozen, shale-colored sea,
        froth, swirls, bleak dithyrambs of glass,
a blizzard of cinderrock and singed amulets,
warty spires and pipelines,
        threnodies of surf whirling on the lava land—   15
our blue car the last note of color
driving a black channel
        through hymnless ground

                              —*1988*

Ka'ū Desert on the island of Hawaii

Andrew Hudgins (b. 1951), reared in Montgomery, Alabama, has demonstrated his poetic skills in a wide variety of poems, including a book-length sequence of dramatic monologues, After the Lost War, in the voice of Sidney Lanier, the greatest Southern poet of the late nineteenth century.

Andrew Hudgins

Air View of an Industrial Scene

There is a train at the ramp, unloading people
who stumble from the cars and toward the gate.
The building's shadows tilt across the ground
and from each shadow juts a longer one
and from that shadow crawls a shadow of smoke   5
black as just-plowed earth. Inside the gate
is a small garden and someone on his knees.
Perhaps he's fingering the yellow blooms
to see which ones have set and will soon wither,
clinging to a green tomato as it swells.   10
The people hold back, but are forced to the open gate,
and when they enter they will see the garden
and some, gardeners themselves, will yearn
to fall to their knees there, untangling vines,
plucking at weeds, cooling their hands in damp earth.   15
They're going to die soon, a matter of minutes.
Even from our height, we see in the photograph
the shadow of the plane stamped dark and large
on Birkenau,° one black wing shading the garden.
We can't tell which are guards, which prisoners.   20
We're watchers. But if we had bombs we'd drop them.

—1985

19 **Birkenau** German concentration camp in World War II

Rita Dove (b. 1952) *won the Pulitzer Prize in 1987 for* Thomas and Beulah, *a sequence of poems about her grandparents' lives in Ohio. She is one of the most important voices of contemporary African-American poetry and served as poet laureate of the United States from 1993 to 1995.*

Rita Dove

Adolescence—III

With Dad gone, Mom and I worked
The dusky rows of tomatoes.
As they glowed orange in sunlight
And rotted in shadow, I too
Grew orange and softer, swelling out   5
Starched cotton slips.

The texture of twilight made me think of
Lengths of Dotted Swiss.° In my room
I wrapped scarred knees in dresses
That once went to big-band dances;   10
I baptized my earlobes with rosewater.
Along the window-sill, the lipstick stubs
Glittered in their steel shells.

Looking out at the rows of clay
And chicken manure, I dreamed how it would happen: 15
He would meet me by the blue spruce,
A carnation over his heart, saying,
"I have come for you, Madam;
I have loved you in my dreams."
At his touch, the scabs would fall away.   20
Over his shoulder, I see my father coming toward us:
He carries his tears in a bowl,
And blood hangs in the pine-soaked air.

—*1980*

8 Dotted Swiss type of sheer fabric

Mark Jarman (b. 1952) *was born in Kentucky and has lived in California and Tennessee, where he currently teaches at Vanderbilt University. With Robert McDowell, he edited the* Reaper, *a magazine specializing in narrative poetry. His most recent collection is* Unholy Sonnets, *released in 2000.*

Mark Jarman
After Disappointment

To lie in your child's bed when she is gone
Is calming as anything I know. To fall
Asleep, her books arranged above your head,
Is to admit that you have never been
So tired, so enchanted by the spell   5
Of your grown body. To feel small instead
Of blocking out the light, to feel alone,
Not knowing what you should or shouldn't feel,
Is to find out, no matter what you've said
About the cramped escapes and obstacles   10
You plan and face and have to call the world,
That there remain these places, occupied
By children, yours if lucky, like the girl
Who finds you here and lies down by your side.

—*1997*

Naomi Shihab Nye (b. 1952), a dedicated world traveler and humanitarian, has read her poetry in Bangladesh and the Middle East. Many of her poems are informed by her Palestinian ancestry, and she has translated contemporary Arabic poetry.

Naomi Shihab Nye
The Traveling Onion

It is believed that the onion originally came from
India. In Egypt it was an object of worship—why
I haven't been able to find out. From Egypt the
onion entered Greece and on to Italy, thence into
all of Europe.

—*Better Living Cookbook*

When I think how far the onion has traveled
just to enter my stew today, I could kneel and praise
all small forgotten miracles,
crackly paper peeling on the drainboard,
pearly layers in smooth agreement,   5
the way knife enters onion, straight
and onion falls apart on the chopping block,
a history revealed.

And I would never scold the onion
for causing tears.   10
It is right that tears fall
for something small and forgotten.
How at meal, we sit to eat,
commenting on texture of meat or herbal aroma
but never on the translucence of onion,   15
now limp, now divided,
or its traditionally honorable career:
For the sake of others,
disappear.

—*1986*

Alberto Ríos (b. 1952) was born in Nogales, Arizona, the son of a Mexican-American father and an English-born mother. He won the Walt Whitman Award of the Academy of American Poets for his first book, Whispering to Fool the Wind *(1982). He has also written a collection of short stories,* The Iguana Killer: Twelve Stories of the Heart, *which won the Western States Book Award in 1984.*

Alberto Ríos

The Purpose of Altar Boys

Tonio told me at catechism
the big part of the eye
admits good, and the little
black part is for seeing
evil—his mother told him   5
who was a widow and so
an authority on such things.
That's why at night
the black part gets bigger.
That's why kids can't go out   10
at night, and at night
girls take off their clothes
and walk around their
bedrooms or jump on their
beds or wear only sandals   15
and stand in their windows.
I was the altar boy
who knew about these things,
whose mission on some Sundays
was to remind people of   20
the night before as they
knelt for Holy Communion.
To keep Christ from falling
I held the metal plate under chins,
while on the thick   25
red carpet of the altar
I dragged my feet
and waited for the precise
moment: plate to chin

I delivered without expression   *30*
the Holy Electric Shock,
the kind that produces
a really large swallowing
and makes people think.
I thought of it as justice.   *35*
But on other Sundays the fire
in my eyes was different,
my mission somehow changed.
I would hold the metal plate
a little too hard   *40*
against those certain same
nervous chins, and I
I would look
with authority down
the tops of white dresses.   *45*

                                                  —*1982*

Gary Soto (b. 1952), a professor of Chicano studies at the University of California at Berkeley, grew up in Fresno, California. His poetry collections include The Elements of San Joaquin *(1977) and* The Tale of Sunlight *(1978). A prose book,* Living Up the Street *(1984), is a memoir of his urban childhood.*

Gary Soto
The Skeptics

Pyrrho of Elis and Sextus Empiricus were Skeptics,
Two big-shot thinkers who argued
Over figs, wine, and the loveliness of their sex.
I crowed to my brother about them,
And one evening, with Fig Newton crumbs in our mouths,   *5*
I was Pyrrho and Rick was Sextus,
Both of us skeptical about getting good jobs.
I said, "Brother Sextus, what will you render on the canvas
When you're all grown up?" He chewed
On his Fig Newton and answered, "Pyrrho,   *10*
My young flame, I will draw the reality

Of dead dogs with their feet in the air."
I crowed, "Wow, Rick—I mean Sextus—that's pretty good."
In sandals, we went down to the liquor store,
Each of us in our imaginary Greek robes,   15
And stole a quart of beer. Neither of us was a skeptic
When we swigged on that quart
And walked by the house with a woman hammering walnuts,
The rise and fall of her buttery hand quivering
The two hairs on my chest. We had our figs and wine,   20
And what we Skeptics needed,
Or at least I, was three strokes of that hammering.
I flowed over in my robe and said, "We're Brothers Skeptic,
Ruled by cautious truths." She smiled,
Hammer raised, and said, "Sure you are."   25
Right away we got along, a womanly skeptic
With a nice swing. I sat on the steps,
A young man with his figs, his wine,
And, with my Greek name shed,
A reverent believer in a woman with hammer in hand.   30

—1995

Julia Alvarez (b. 1953) published her first collection, Homecoming, *in 1984. It contained both free verse and "33," a sequence of 33 sonnets on the occasion of the poet's thirty-third birthday. She has gained acclaim for* In the Time of the Butterflies, *a work of fiction, and* The Other Side/El Otro Lado, *a collection of poems.*

Julia Alvarez
Bilingual Sestina

Some things I have to say aren't getting said
in this snowy, blond, blue-eyed, gum-chewing English:
dawn's early light sifting through *persianas* closed
the night before by dark-skinned girls whose words
evoke *cama, aposento, sueños* in *nombres*   5
from that first world I can't translate from Spanish.

Gladys, Rosario, Altagracia—the sounds of Spanish
wash over me like warm island waters as I say
your soothing names: a child again learning the *nombres*
of things you point to in the world before English   10
turned *sol, sierra, cielo, luna* to vocabulary words—
sun, earth, sky, moon. Language closed

like the touch-sensitive *morivivi* whose leaves closed
when we kids poked them, astonished. Even Spanish
failed us back then when we saw how frail a word is   15
when faced with the thing it names. How saying
its name won't always summon up in Spanish or English
the full blown genie from the bottled *nombre.*

Gladys, I summon you back by saying your *nombre.*
Open up again the house of slatted windows closed   20
since childhood, where *palabras* left behind for English
stand dusty and awkward in neglected Spanish.
Rosario, muse of *el patio*, sing in me and through me say
that world again, begin first with those first words

you put in my mouth as you pointed to the world—   25
not Adam, not God, but a country girl numbering
the stars, the blades of grass, warming the sun by saying,
¡Qué calor! as you opened up the morning closed
inside the night until you sang in Spanish,
Estas son las mañanitas, and listening in bed, no English   30

yet in my head to confuse me with translations, no English
doubling the world with synonyms, no dizzying array of words
—the world was simple and intact in Spanish—
luna, sol, casa, luz, flor, as if the *nombres*
were the outer skin of things, as if words were so close   35
one left a mist of breath on things by saying

their names, an intimacy I now yearn for in English—
words so close to what I mean that I almost hear my Spanish
heart beating, beating inside what I say *en inglés.*

—*1995*

David Mason (b. 1954) is best known for the title poem of The Country I Remember, *a long narrative about the life of a Civil War veteran and his daughter. The poem has been performed in a theatrical version. Mason edited, with Mark Jarman,* The Rebel Angels, *an anthology of recent poetry written in traditional forms.*

David Mason
Song of the Powers

Mine, said the stone,
mine is the hour.
I crush the scissors,
such is my power.
Stronger than wishes,   5
my power, alone.

Mine, said the paper,
mine are the words
that smother the stone
with imagined birds,   10
reams of them, flown
from the mind of the shaper.

Mine, said the scissors,
mine all the knives
gashing through paper's   15
ethereal lives;
nothing's so proper
as tattering wishes.

As stone crushes scissors,
as paper snuffs stone   20
and scissors cut paper,
all end alone.
So heap up your paper
and scissor your wishes
and uproot the stone   25
from the top of the hill.
They all end alone
as you will, you will.

—1996

Mary Jo Salter (b. 1954) *has traveled widely with her husband, poet and novelist Brad Leithauser, and has lived in Japan, Italy, and Iceland. A student of Elizabeth Bishop at Harvard, Salter brings to her art a devotion to the poet's craft that mirrors that of her mentor. She has published four collections of poetry and* The Moon Comes Home, *a children's book.*

Mary Jo Salter

Welcome to Hiroshima

is what you first see, stepping off the train:
a billboard brought to you in living English
by Toshiba Electric. While a channel
silent in the TV of the brain

projects those flickering re-runs of a cloud   5
that brims its risen columnful like beer
and, spilling over, hangs its foamy head,
you feel a thirst for history: what year

it started to be safe to breathe the air,
and when to drink the blood and scum afloat   10
on the Ohta River. But no, the water's clear,
they pour it for your morning cup of tea

in one of the countless sunny coffee shops
whose plastic dioramas advertise
mutations of cuisine behind the glass: 15
a pancake sandwich; a pizza someone tops

with a maraschino cherry. Passing by
the Peace Park's floral hypocenter (where
how bravely, or with what mistaken cheer,
humanity erased its own erasure),   20

you enter the memorial museum
and through more glass are served, as on a dish
of blistered grass, three mannequins. Like gloves
a mother clips to coatsleeves, strings of flesh

hang from their fingertips; or as if tied   25
to recall a duty for us, *Reverence*
the dead whose mourners too shall soon be dead,
but all commemoration's swallowed up

in questions of bad taste, how re-created
horror mocks the grim original,   30
and thinking at last *They should have left it all*
you stop. This is the wristwatch of a child.

Jammed on the moment's impact, resolute
to communicate some message, although mute,
it gestures with its hands at eight-fifteen   35
and eight-fifteen and eight-fifteen again

while tables of statistics on the wall
update the news by calling on a roll
of tape, death gummed on death, and in the case
adjacent, an exhibit under glass   40

is glass itself: a shard the bomb slammed in
a woman's arm at eight-fifteen, but some
three decades on—as if to make it plain
hope's only as renewable as pain,

and as if all the unsung   45
debasements of the past may one day come
rising to the surface once again—
worked its filthy way out like a tongue.

                                                    —*1985*

Cathy Song (b. 1955) was born in Honolulu, Hawaii, and holds degrees from Wellesley College and Boston University. Her first book, Picture Bride, *won the Yale Series of Younger Poets Award in 1983.* School Figures, *her third collection, appeared in 1995.*

Cathy Song
Stamp Collecting

The poorest countries
have the prettiest stamps
as if impracticality were a major export
shipped with the bananas, t-shirts, and coconuts.
Take Tonga, where the tourists,   5
expecting a dramatic waterfall replete with birdcalls
are taken to see the island's peculiar mystery:
hanging bats with collapsible wings
like black umbrellas swing upside down from fruit trees.
The Tongan stamp is a fruit.   10
The banana stamp is scalloped like a butter-varnished seashell.
The pineapple resembles a volcano, a spout of green on top,
and the papaya, a tarnished goat skull.

They look impressive,
these stamps of countries without a thing to sell   15
except for what is scraped, uprooted and hulled
from their mule-scratched hills.
They believe in postcards,
in portraits of progress: the new dam;
a team of young native doctors   20
wearing stethoscopes like exotic ornaments;
the recently constructed "Facultad de Medicina,"°
a building as lack-lustre as an American motel.

The stamps of others are predictable.
Lucky is the country that possesses indigenous beauty.   25

22 Facultad de Medicina Medical Faculty (building)

Say a tiger or a queen.
The Japanese can display to the world
their blossoms: a spray of pink on green.
Like pollen, they drift, airborne.
But pity the country that is bleak and stark.   *30*

Beauty and whimsey are discouraged as indiscreet.
Unbreakable as their climate, a monument of ice,
they issue serious statements, commemorating
factories, tramways and aeroplanes;
athletes marbled into statues.   *35*
They turn their noses upon the world, these countries,
and offer this: an unrelenting procession
of a grim, historic profile.

—1988

Janet Holmes (b. 1956) published a first collection, The Physicist at the Mall,
which contained several poems about her work experiences as a technical writer. The
Green Tuxedo, *a second collection, appeared in 1999. Holmes teaches at Boise*
State University in Idaho.

Janet Holmes
Cinquains for Rocky

You want
a word that means
separating two things
by bringing them closer. "What for?"
she asks.   *5*

"Doesn't
make sense." It does,
you tell her, when one speaks
about relationships—about
you two.   *10*

—1993

Catherine Tufariello (b. 1963) *grew up in upstate New York and holds a Ph.D. from Cornell University. Her first two collections of poetry appeared in 2001. A translator of the sonnets of Petrarch, she has taught at the University of Miami.*

Catherine Tufariello
Useful Advice

You're 37? Don't you think that maybe
It's time you settled down and had a baby?

No wine? You're pregnant, aren't you? I knew it!

Hey, are you sure you two know how to do it?

All Dennis has to do is look at me   5
And I'm knocked up.

           Some things aren't meant to be.
It's sad, but try to see this as God's will.

I've heard that sometimes when you take the Pill . . .

Does he wear boxers? Briefs are bad for sperm.

A former partner at my husband's firm   10
Who tried for years got pregnant when she stopped
Working so hard.

          Why don't you two adopt?
You'll have one of your own then, like my niece.

At work I heard about this herb from Greece—

My sister swears by dong quai. Want to try it?   15

Forget the high-tech stuff. Just change your diet.

Yoga is good for that. My cousin Carol—

It's true! Too much caffeine can make you sterile.

They have these ceremonies in Peru—

You mind my asking, is it him or you?   20

Have you tried acupuncture? Meditation?

It's in your head. Relax! Take a vacation
And have some fun. You think too much. Stop trying.

Did I say something wrong? Why are you crying?

—2000

Appendix 1

Poems Grouped by Genre, Technique, or Subject

Because it is possible to classify the poems in the anthology in many different ways, the following appendix is not exhaustive. It should, however, provide suggestions for reading and writing about poems that share some similarities. Some poems appear in more than one category.

Aging (See also Carpe Diem)
"When I Was Fair and Young"
"Sonnet 73" (Shakespeare)
"How Soon Hath Time"
"Ulysses"
"The Love Song of J. Alfred Prufrock"
"What Lips My Lips Have Kissed"
"In a Prominent Bar in Secaucus One Day"
"Compartments"

Allegorical And Symbolic Poetry
"The Burning Babe"
"Redemption"
"John Barleycorn"
"The Haunted Palace"
"Because I Could Not Stop for Death"
"Up-hill"
"Anecdote of the Jar"
"The Snow Man"
"Journey of the Magi"
"Next, Please"
"The Ungrateful Garden"
"Oh No"

"The Last One"
"Diving into the Wreck"

Animals
"Jubilate Agno (selection)"
"The Tyger"
"The Eagle"
"A Narrow Fellow in the Grass"
"The Fish" (Moore)
"r-p-o-p-h-e-s-s-a-g-r"
"The Fish" (Bishop)
"Traveling Through the Dark"
"The Heaven of Animals"
"A Blessing"
"Pike"
"Song for the Deer and Myself to Return On"

Art: Immortality of Art (Ars Longa Vita Brevis)
"Amoretti: Sonnet 75"
"Sonnet 18" (Shakespeare)
"Ozymandias"
"Ode on a Grecian Urn"
"Sailing to Byzantium"
"Anecdote of the Jar"

Ballads and Narratives
"Bonny Barbara Allen"
"Sir Patrick Spens"
"John Barleycorn"
"La Belle Dame Sans Merci"
"Ballad of Birmingham"
"Body and Soul"
"Evening's End"
"The Ballad of Aunt Geneva"

Carpe Diem
"When I Was Fair and Young"
"To the Virgins, to Make Much of Time"
"Song"
"To His Coy Mistress"
"Loveliest of Trees, the Cherry Now"
"Piazza Piece"

Childhood and Adolescence
"The Sacred"
"One Girl at the Boys Party"
"Adolescence—III"
"The Purpose of Altar Boys"

Conceit and Extended Metaphor
"A Valediction: Forbidding Mourning"
"Holy Sonnet 14"
"Easter Wings"
"The Pulley"
"The Author to Her Book"
"Huswifery"
"The Haunted Palace"
"The Arsenal at Springfield"
"Love Song: I and Thou"
"Metaphors"
"Narcissus and Echo"
"Digression on the Nuclear Age"

Conceit: Petrarchan
"Sonnet 130" (Shakespeare)
"There Is a Garden in Her Face"

Death (See also Elegy)
"Holy Sonnet 10"
"When I Have Fears"
"Because I Could Not Stop for Death"
"I Died for Beauty—But Was Scarce"
"I Heard a Fly Buzz—When I Died"
"Ah, Are You Digging on My Grave?"
"Eight O'Clock"
"Home Burial"
"Last Word of My English Grandmother"
"Do Not Go Gentle into That Good Night"
"The Death of the Ball Turret Gunner"
"We Real Cool"
"Next, Please"
"For the Anniversary of My Death"
"Terminal"
"Sea Canes"
"Compartments"

Dramatic Dialogues
"Ah, Are You Digging on My Grave"
"The Ruined Maid"
"Home Burial"
"Piazza Piece"
"Ballad of Birmingham"
"Narcissus and Echo"

Dramatic Monologues and Related Poems
"The Chimney Sweeper"
"The Little Black Boy"
"A Poison Tree"
"Ulysses"
"My Last Duchess"
"Porphyria's Lover"
"The River-Merchant's Wife: A Letter"
"Journey of the Magi"

"The Love Song of J. Alfred
     Prufrock"
"The Death of the Ball Turret
     Gunner"
"We Real Cool"
"Saint Judas"
"In a Prominent Bar in Secaucus
     One Day"
"Siren Song"
"Maybe Dats Your Pwoblem Too"
"*Tu Negrito*"

Duty
"Sir Patrick Spens"
"To Lucasta, Going to the Wars"
"For the Union Dead"

Elegy
"On My First Son"
"Elegy Written in a Country
     Churchyard"
"The Cross of Snow"
"In Memoriam A.H.H., 54"
"Bells for John Whiteside's
     Daughter"
"Sonnet 5" (Millay)
"The Day Lady Died"
"The Truth the Dead Know"
"Terminal"
"Planting a Sequoia"

Fate
"Ballad of Birmingham"
"Design"
"Leda and the Swan"
"The Unknown Citizen"

History
"On the Late Massacre in
     Piedmont"
"Elegy Written in a Country
     Churchyard"
"Ozymandias"
"The Second Coming"
"The Purse-Seine"
"For the Union Dead"
"Year's End"

"Casual Wear"
"Central America"
"Punishment"
"Digression on the Nuclear Age"
"The Colonel"

Holocaust
"'More Light! More Light!'"
"The Book"
"Women Bathing at Bergen-Belsen"
"Daddy"
"Air View of an Industrial Scene"

Humanity
"Crossing Brooklyn Ferry"
"nobody loses all the time"
"Chaplinesque"
"As I Walked Out One Evening"
"Traveling Through the Dark"
"A Primer of the Daily Round"
"Counting the Mad"
"A Supermarket in California"
"Saint Judas"
"Genius"
"Compartments"
"All-American Sestina"
"Sapphics Against Anger"
"The Traveling Onion"
"Stamp Collecting"

Language
"r-p-o-p-h-e-s-s-a-g-r"
"Adam's Task"
"Picking Blackberries with a Friend
     Who Has Been Reading Jacques
     Lacan"
"E.S.L."
"A Martian Sends a Postcard
     Home"
"Bilingual Sestina"

Love
"Sonnet 29" (Shakespeare)
"Sonnet 30" (Shakespeare)
"The Canonization"
"In This Strange Labyrinth How
     Shall I Turn"

"A Red, Red Rose"
"Sonnets from the Portuguese, 43"
"Even As I Hold You"

Love: Loss of

"Western Wind"
"They Flee from Me"
"La Belle Dame sans Merci"
"The Raven"
"Neutral Tones"
"What Lips My Lips Have Kissed"
"One Art"
"Mementos, I"

Love: Marital

"Sonnet 116" (Shakespeare)
"A Valediction: Forbidding
        Mourning"
"My Last Duchess"
"Dover Beach"
"Firelight"
"Home Burial"
"The River-Merchant's Wife: A
        Letter"
"Love Song: I and Thou"
"The Ache of Marriage"
"Aunt Jennifer's Tigers"
"Mountain Bride"

Myth

"To Helen"
"The Oxen"
"Leda and the Swan"
"The Love Song of J. Alfred
        Prufrock"
"Imperial Adam"
"Musée des Beaux Arts"
"Adam's Task"
"Edge"
"Narcissus and Echo"
"Siren Song"

Nature and God

"It Is a Beauteous Evening"
"Ode: Intimations of Immortality"
"To a Waterfowl"

"Each and All"
"A Noiseless Patient Spider"
"Song of Myself, 6"
"When I Heard the Learn'd
        Astronomer"
"God's Grandeur"
"Design"
"The Snow Man"
"Sunday Morning"
"A Hardware Store As Proof of the
        Existence of God"

Nature: Descriptive Poetry

"Description of a City Shower"
"The Wild Honey Suckle"
"I Wandered Lonely As a Cloud"
"Lines (Composed a Few Miles
        Above Tintern Abbey . . .)"
"To the Fringed Gentian"
"Pied Beauty"
"The Need of Being Versed in
        Country Things"
"Stopping by Woods on a Snowy
        Evening"
"Pear Tree"
"Sea Rose"
"Halley's Comet"
"Root Cellar"
"Fern Hill"
"How Everything Happens"
"A Walk"
"To the Desert"
"The Track of a Storm"
"Crossing Ka'u Desert"

Nature: The Environment

"God's Grandeur"
"The Purse-Seine"
"pity this busy monster"
"The Fish" (Bishop)
"Traveling Through the Dark"
"The Ungrateful Garden"
"Noted in *The New York Times*"
"The Last One"
"The Black Walnut Tree"

"Song for the Deer and Myself to
Return On"

Nature: Seasons of the Year
"When Daisies Pied (Spring and
Winter)"
"Ode to the West Wind"
"To the Fringed Gentian"
"Spring and All"
"Reapers"
"Year's End"
"Crocuses"

Parents and Children
"Frost at Midnight"
"Silence"
"My Papa's Waltz"
"Those Winter Sundays"
"Do Not Go Gentle into That Good
Night"
"For My Daughter"
"The Mother"
"The Writer"
"This Be the Verse"
"My Father in the Night
Commanding No"
"The Truth the Dead Know"
"Daddy"
"Digging"
"Daughter"
"*Tu Negrito*"

Physical Handicaps
"When I Consider How My Light Is
Spent"
"Subterfuge"
"The Visitor"

Poetry
"The Author to Her Book"
"Essay on Criticism (selection)"
"Nuns Fret Not at Their Convent's
Narrow Room"
"On First Looking into Chapman's
Homer"
"'Terence, This Is Stupid Stuff'"

"Paradoxes and Oxymorons"
"Digging"
"Teaching the Ape to Write Poems"
"Approaching a Significant
Birthday, He Peruses *The
Norton Anthology of Poetry*"

Poetry: Inspiration
"Astrophel and Stella: Sonnet 1"
"Kubla Khan"
"Ode to a Nightingale"
"Out of the Cradle Endlessly
Rocking"
"The Writer"

Political and Social Themes
"On the Late Massacre in
Piedmont"
"The Chimney Sweeper"
"Eight O'Clock"
"The Mill"
"The Unknown Citizen"
"Dolor"
"The Mother"
"American Classic"
"Casual Wear"
"Central America"
"Child Beater"
"*Tu Negrito*"
"The General"
"Stamp Collecting"

Race and Racism
"The Little Black Boy"
"We Wear the Mask"
"Dream Boogie"
"Theme for English B"
"Incident"
"Yet Do I Marvel"
"Ballad of Birmingham"
"For Malcolm X"
"For the Union Dead"
"Ballad of Aunt Geneva"
"Winter Retreat: Homage to Martin
Luther King, Jr."

Satire
"Description of a City Shower"
"Stanzas"
"The Ruined Maid"
"Disillusionment of Ten O'Clock"
"The Hero"
"The Unknown Citizen"
"Playboy"
"E.S.L."
"Teaching the Ape to Write Poems"
"God, a Poem"

Sexual Themes (See also Carpe Diem)
"Sonnet 20" (Shakespeare)
"The Flea"
"To His Coy Mistress"
"The Ruined Maid"
"The Love Song of J. Alfred Prufrock"
"Playboy"
"Rape"
"Foreplay"
"The Purpose of Altar Boys"

Solitude
"Ode on Solitude"
"The Soul Selects Her Own Society"
"The Lake Isle of Innisfree"
"Acquainted with the Night"
"Stopping by Woods on a Snowy Evening"

Sonnets (See Appendix 2: Traditional Stanza, Fixed, and Nonce Forms

Sports
"To an Athlete Dying Young"
"From the Wave"
"First Practice"
"Body and Soul"
"Sign for My Father, Who Stressed the Bunt"

Suicide
"Bonny Barbara Allen"
"The Mill"
"Richard Cory"
"Résumé"
"Saint Judas"
"Edge"

War
"The Arsenal at Springfield"
"A Sight in Camp in the Daybreak Gray and Dim"
"War Is Kind"
"Dreamers"
"Dulce et Decorum Est"
"The Death of the Ball Turret Gunner"
"Mementos, I"
"Digression on the Nuclear Age"
"Facing It"
"Welcome to Hiroshima"

Women's Issues
"Portrait d'une Femme"
"Oh, Oh, You Will Be Sorry for That Word" (Millay)
"One Perfect Rose"
"Women"
"Playboy"
"Cinderella"
"Aunt Jennifer's Tigers"
"Rape"
"Daddy"
"Metaphors"
"Sous-entendu"
"to my last period"
"Barbie Doll"
"Siren Song"
"Combing"
"The One Girl at the Boys Party"
"Rondeau Redoublé"
"Useful Advice"

Appendix 2

Traditional Stanza, Fixed, and Nonce Forms

Acrostic Verse
Stuart, Dabney: "Discovering My Daughter"

Accentual Meter
Bishop, Elizabeth: "The Fish"
Hardy, Thomas: "The Convergence of the Twain"
Wilbur, Richard: "Junk"
Wilbur, Richard: "The Writer"

Ballad Stanza (and Variants)
Anonymous: "Bonny Barbara Allan"
Anonymous: "Sir Patrick Spens"
Auden, W. H.: "As I Walked Out One Evening"
Burns, Robert: "John Barleycorn"
Fenton, James: "God, a Poem"
Hollander, John: "Adam's Task"
Keats, John: "La Belle Dame sans Merci"
Plath, Sylvia: "Daddy"
Poe, Edgar Allan: "The Haunted Palace"
Roethke, Theodore: "My Papa's Waltz"
Rossetti, Christina: "Up-Hill"
Waniek, Marilyn Nelson: "Ballad of Aunt Geneva, The"

Ballade
Disch, Tom: "Ballade of the New God"

Blank Verse
Coleridge, Samuel Taylor: "Frost at Midnight"
Frost, Robert: "Home Burial"
Hudgins, Andrew: "Air View of an Industrial Scene"
Merrill, James: "Charles on Fire"
Ruark, Gibbons: "Visitor, The"
Stafford, William: "Traveling Through the Dark"
Stevens, Wallace: "Sunday Morning"
Tennyson, Alfred, Lord: "Ulysses"
Wordsworth, William: "Lines (Composed a Few Miles Above Tintern Abbey . . ."
Yeats, William Butler: "Second Coming, The"

Cento
Gwynn, R. S.: "Approaching a Significant Birthday, He Peruses *The Norton Anthology of Poetry*"

Cinquain
Holmes, Janet: "Cinquains for Rocky"

Common Meter
Anonymous: "Western Wind"
Burns, Robert: "Red, Red Rose, A"
Cullen, Countee: "Incident"
Dickinson, Emily: "Because I Could Not Stop for Death"
Dickinson, Emily: "I Died for Beauty—But Was Scarce"
Dickinson, Emily: "I Heard a Fly Buzz—When I Died"
Dickinson, Emily: "My Life Closed Twice Before Its Close"
Dickinson, Emily: "Narrow Fellow in the Grass, A"
Herrick, Robert: "To the Virgins, to Make Much of Time"
Lovelace, Richard: "To Lucasta, Going to the Wars"

Concrete Poetry
cummings, e.e.: "r-p-o-p-h-e-s-s-a-g-r"
Herbert, George: "Easter Wings"
Swenson, May: "How Everything Happens"

Couplets, Short
Blake, William: "Poison Tree, A"
Blake, William: "Tyger, The"
Bryant, William Cullen: "To the Fringed Gentian"
Housman, A. E.: "Loveliest of Trees, the Cherry Now"
Housman, A. E.: "'Terence, This Is Stupid Stuff . . .'"
Housman, A. E.: "To an Athlete Dying Young"
Marvell, Andrew: "To His Coy Mistress"

Couplets, Heroic
Bradstreet, Anne: "Author to Her Book, The"
Browning, Robert: "My Last Duchess"
Dryden, John: "Epigram on Milton"
Dryden, John: "To the Memory of Mr. Oldham"
Jonson, Ben: "On My First Son"
Pope, Alexander: "Essay on Criticism, An (selection)"
Rich, Adrienne: "Aunt Jennifer's Tigers"
Sarton, May: "A Guest"
Swift, Jonathan: "Description of a City Shower, A"
Toomer, Jean: "Reapers"
Tufariello, Catherine: "Useful Advice"

Fourteeners
Southwell, Robert: "Burning Babe, The"

Haiku
Phillips, Robert: "Compartments"

In Memoriam Stanza
Tennyson, Alfred, Lord: "In Memoriam A. H. H., 54"

Long Meter
Frost, Robert: "The Need of Being Versed in Country Things"
Larkin, Philip: "This Be the Verse"

Ode, Irregular
Arnold, Matthew: "Dover Beach"
Coleridge, Samuel Taylor: "Kubla Khan"
Frost, Robert: "After Apple-Picking"
Owen, Wilfred: "Dulce Et Decorum Est"

Sonnet, Italian

Browning, Elizabeth Barrett: "Sonnets from the Portuguese, 43"

Donne, John: "Holy Sonnet 10"

Donne, John: "Holy Sonnet 14"

Frost, Robert: "Design"

Hopkins, Gerard Manley: "God's Grandeur"

Keats, John: "On First Looking into Chapman's Homer"

Longfellow, Henry Wadsworth: "Cross of Snow, The"

Millay, Edna St. Vincent: "What Lips My Lips Have Kissed"

Milton, John: "How Soon Hath Time"

Milton, John: "On the Late Massacre in Piemont"

Milton, John: "When I Consider How My Light Is Spent"

Robinson, Edwin Arlington: "Firelight"

Wordsworth, William: "It Is a Beauteous Evening"

Wordsworth, William: "Nuns Fret Not at Their Narrow Convent Cell"

Sonnet, Nonce

Barrax, Gerald: "Strangers like Us: Pittsburgh, Raleigh, 1945-1985"

Coleridge, Samuel Taylor: "Work Without Hope"

Cullen, Countee: "Yet Do I Marvel"

Cummings, E. E.: "pity this busy monster"

Herbert, George: "Redemption"

Howard, Henry, Earl of Surrey: "Soote Season, The"

Jarman, Mark: "Disappointment"

Kees, Weldon: "For My Daughter"

Ransom, John Crowe: "Piazza Piece"

Shelley, Percy Bysshe: "Ozymandias"

Shomer, Enid: "Women Bathing at Bergen-Belsen"

Sidney, Sir Philip: "Astrophel and Stella: Sonnet 1"

Wright, James: "Saint Judas"

Yeats, William Butler: "Leda and the Swan"

Sonnet, Spenserian

Spenser, Edmund: "Amoretti: Sonnet 75"

Wroth, Mary: "In This Strange Labyrinth How Shall I Turn"

Syllabics

Moore, Marianne: "The Fish"

Plath, Sylvia: "Metaphors"

Thomas, Dylan: "Fern Hill"

Terza Rima

Frost, Robert: "Acquainted with the Night"

Shelley, Percy Bysshe: "Ode to the West Wind"

Triplets

Hardy, Thomas: "The Convergence of the Twain"

Tennyson, Alfred, Lord: "Eagle, The"

Villanelle

Bishop, Elizabeth: "One Art"

Thomas, Dylan: "Do Not Go Gentle into That Good Night"

Acknowledgments

Betty Adcock, "Digression on the Nuclear Age" reprinted by permission of Louisiana State University Press from *Beholdings* by Betty Adcock. Copyright © 1988 by Betty Adcock.

Ai, "Child Beater" from *Cruelty* published by Houghton Mifflin Company. Reprinted by permission of the author.

Julia Alvarez, "Bilingual Sestina" from *The Other Side/El Otro Lado*. Copyright © 1995 by Julia Alvarez. Published by Dutton, a division of Penguin Putnam Inc. Reprinted by permission of Susan Bergholz Literary Services, New York. All rights reserved.

John Ashberry, "Farm Implements and Rutabagas in a Landscape" from *Shadow Train* (New York: Viking, 1981). Reprinted by permission of Georges Borchardt, Inc., for the author. Copyright © 1980, 1981 John Ashberry.

Margaret Atwood, "Siren Song" from *You are Happy. Selected Poems 1965–1975*. Copyright © 1976 by Margaret Atwood. Reprinted by permission of Houghton Mifflin Co. All rights reserved.

W. H. Auden, "As I Walked Out One Evening" "Musee des Beaux Arts" and "The Unknown Citizen" from *W. H. Auden: Collected Poems* by W. H. Auden. Reprinted by permission of Random House, Inc.

Gerald Barrax, "Strangers Like Us: Pittsburgh, Raleigh, 1945–1985" reprinted by permission of Louisiana State University Press from *A Person Sitting in Darkness* by Gerald Barrax. Copyright © 1998 by Gerald Barrax.

Elizabeth Bishop, "One Art" and "The Fish" from *The Complete Poems 1927–1979* by Elizabeth Bishop. Copyright © 1979, 1983 by Alice Helen Methfessel. Reprinted by permission of Farrar, Straus & Giroux, Inc.

Louise Bogan, "Women" from *The Blue Estuaries*. Copyright © 1968 by Louise Bogan. Copyright renewed © 1996 by Ruth Limmer. Reprinted by permission of Farrar, Straus & Giroux, Inc.

David Bottoms, "Sign for My Father, Who Stressed the Bunt" from *Armored Hearts: Selected and New Poems*. Copyright © 1995 by David Bottoms. Reprinted with the permission of Copper Canyon Press, P.O. Box 271, Port Townsend, WA 98368-0271, USA.

Gwendolyn Brooks, "the mother" and "We Real Cool" from *Blacks* by Gwendolyn Brooks. Copyright © 1991 by Gwendolyn Brooks. Reprinted by permission of the author.

Gladys Cardiff, "Combing." Copyright © 1971 by Gladys Cardiff. Reprinted from *To Frighten a Storm* (Copper Canyon Press, 1976) by permission of the author.

Fred Chappell, "Narcissus and Echo" reprinted by permission of Louisiana State University Press from *Source* by Fred Chappell. Copyright © 1985 by Fred Chappell.

Wendy Cope, "Rondeau Redoublé" from *Making Cocoa for Kingsley Amis* by Wendy Cope. Copyright © Wendy Cope 1986. Reproduced by permission of the publishers Faber and Faber Limited.

Hart Crane, "Chaplinesque" from *Complete Poems of Hart Crane* by Marc Simon, editor. Copyright © 1933, © 1958, 1966 by Liveright Publishing Corporation. Copyright © 1986 by Marc Simon. Reprinted by permission of Liveright Publishing Corporation.

Robert Creeley, "I Know a Man" from *Collected Poems of Robert Creeley, 1945–1975*. Copyright © 1983 The Regents of the University of California. Reprinted by permission.

Countee Cullen, "Incident" and "Yet I DO Marvel" published in *On These I Stand* © 1947 Harper & Bros. Renewed 1975 Ida M. Cullen. Copyrights held by The Amistad Research Center Administered by Thompson and Thompson, New York, NY.

E. E. Cummings, "nobody loses all the time" copyright 1926, 1954, © 1991 by the Trustees for the E. E. Cummings Trust. Copyright © 1976 George James Firmage, "pity this busy monster,manunkind" copyright 1944, © 1972, 1991 by the Trustees for the E. E. Cummings Trust, "r-p-o-p-h-e-s-s-a-g-r" copyright 1935, © 1963, 1991 by the Trustees for thee E. E. Cummings Trust. Copyright © 1978 by George James Firmage, from *Complete Poems: 1904–1962* by E. E. Cummings, edited by George J. Firmage. Reprinted by permission of Liveright Corporation.

mission of Farrar, Straus & Giroux, Inc., and Faber & Faber Ltd.

Anthony Hecht, "More Light! More Light!" from *Collected Earlier Poems* by Anthony Hecht, copyright © 1990 by Anthony Hecht. Used by permission of Alfred A. Knopf, a division of Random House, Inc.

John Hollander, "Adam's Task" from *Selected Poetry* by John Hollander, copyright © 1993 by John Hollander. Used by permission of Alfred A. Knopf, a division of Random House, Inc.

Janet Holmes, "Cinquains for Rocky" from *The Physicist at the Mall.* Tallahassee, FL. 1994. Reprinted with permission of Anhinga Press.

Garrett Hongo, "Crossing Ka'u Desert" from *The River of Heaven* by Garrett Hongo, copyright © 1988 by Garrett Hongo. Used by permission of Alfred A. Knopf, a division of Random House, Inc.

A. D. Hope, "Imperial Adam" from *Collected Poems* by A. D. Hope. Copyright © 1968 A. D. Hope. Reprinted by permission of Collins/Angus & Robertson Publishers.

A. E. Housman, "Eight O'Clock" and "Stars, I Have Seen them Fall" by A. E. Housman from *The Collected Poems of A. E. Housman* copyright 1936, © 1950 by Barclays Bank, Ltd. © 1964, 1967, 1968 by Robert E. Symons, © 1922, 1939, 1940, 1965 by Henry Holt and Co. Reprinted by permission of Henry Holt and Company, LLC. "Terence, This Is Stupid Stuff . . . " and "To an Athlete Dying Young" from *Collected Poems of A. E. Housman,* 1939, 1940 © 1965 by Holt, Rinehart, and Winston. Copyright © 1967, 1968 by Robert E. Symons. Reprinted by permission of Henry Holt and Company.

Andrew Hudgins, "Air View of an Industrial Scene" from *Saints and Strangers.* Copyright © 1985 by Andrew Hudgins. Reprinted by permission of Houghton Mifflin Co. All rights reserved.

Langston Hughes, "Dream Boogie" and "Theme for English B" from *The Collected Poems of Langston Hughes* by Langston Hughes, copyright © 1994 by The Estate of Langston Hughes. Used by permission of Alfred A. Knopf, Inc., a division of Random House, Inc.

Ted Hughes, "Pike" and "The Thought-Fox" from *Selected Poems 1957–1981.* Reprinted by permission of HarperCollins and Faber & Faber Ltd.

Mark Jarman, "Questions for Ecclesiates" by Mark Jarman. Copyright © 1997 by Mark Jarman. Reprinted by permission of Story Line Press, Inc., www.storylinepress.com.

Randall Jarrell, "The Death of the Ball Turret Gunner" from *The Complete Poems.* Copyright © 1969 by Mrs. Randall Jarrell. Reprinted by permission of Farrar, Straus & Giroux, Inc.

Robinson Jeffers, "The Purse-Seine" copyright 1938 & renewed 1966 by Donnan & Garth Jeffers, from *The Selected Poems of Robinson Jeffers* by Robinson Jeffers. Used by permission of Random House, Inc.

Rodney Jones, "Winter Retreat: Homage to Martin Luther King, Jr." from *Transparent Gestures.* Copyright © 1989 by Rodney Jones. Reprinted by permission of Houghton Mifflin Co. All rights reserved.

Donald Justice, "Counting the Mad" from *New and Selected Poems* by Donald Justice, copyright © 1995 by Donald Justice. Used by permission of Alfred A. Knopf, a division of Random House, Inc.

Weldon Kees, "For My Daughter" reprinted from *The Collected Poems of Weldon Kees,* edited by Donald Justice, by permission of the University of Nebraska Press. Copyright 1975, by the University of Nebraska Press.

X. J. Kennedy, "In a Prominent Bar in Secaucus One Day." Copyright © 1961 by X. J. Kennedy. Reprinted by permission of Curtis Brown, Ltd.

Caroline Kizer, "The Ungrateful Garden" from *Midnight Was My Cry: New and Selected Poems.* Copyright © 1961. Reprinted by the permission of the author.

Yusef Komunyakaa, "Facing It" from *Dai Cai Dau* by Yusef Komunyakaa. © 1988 by Yusef Komunyakaa. Reprinted by permission of Wesleyan University Press

Maxine Kumin, "Noted in the *New York Times*" from *Nurture* by Maxine Kumin. Copyright © 1989 by Maxine Kumin. Used by permission of Viking Penguin, a division of Penguin Books USA Inc.

Philip Larkin, "Next, Please" from *The Less Deceived.* Reprinted by permission of The Marvell Press, England and Australia. "Aubade" from *Collected Poems* by Philip Larkin. Copyright © 1988, 1989 by the Estate of Philip Larkin. Reprinted by permission of Farrar, Straus & Giroux, Inc. "This Be the Verse" from *High Windows.* Reprinted by permission of Farrar, Straus and Giroux, Inc., and Faber & Faber, Ltd.

Denise Levertov, "The Ache of Marriage" from *Denis Levertov: Poems 1960–1967.* Copyright © 1964 by Denise Levertov Goodman.

Reprinted by permission of New Directions Publishing Corporation.

Robert Lowell, "For the Union Dead" from *For the Union Dead* by Robert Lowell. Copyright © 1959 by Robert Lowell. Copyright renewed © 1987 by Harriet Lowell, Caroline Lowell, and Sheridan Lowell. Reprinted by permission of Farrar, Straus & Giroux, Inc.

David Mason, "Song of the Powers" from *The Country I Remember*, 1996. Story Line Press. No portion of this text may be reprinted without permission.

Florence Cassen Mayers, "All American Sestina." First published in *The Atlantic Monthly*. Reprinted by permission of the author.

James Merrill, "Casual Wear" and "Charles on Fire" from *Selected Poems 1946–1985* by James Merrill, copyright © 1992 by James Merrill. Used by permission of Alfred A. Knopf, Inc., a division of Random House, Inc.

W. S. Merwin, "For the Anniversary of My Death" and "The Last One" from *The Lice*, © 1963, 1964, 1965, 1966, 1967 by W. S. Merwin. No portion of this text may be reprinted without permission of Georges Borchardt, Inc.

Edna St. Vincent Millay, "If I should learn in some quiet casual way," "Not in a Silver Casket," "Oh, Oh, You Will Be Sorry for That Word," and "What Lips My Lips Have Kissed" by Edna St. Vincent Millay. From *Collected Poems*, HarperCollins. Copyright © 1917, 1923, 1931, 1945, 1951, 1958 by Edna St. Vincent Millay and Norma Millay Ellis. All rights reserved. Reprinted by permission of Elizabeth Barnett, Literary Executor.

Vassar Miller, "Subterfuge" from *If I Had Wheels of Love: Collected Poems*. Reprinted by permission of Martha Failing & Co. (Houston, TX).

Marianne Moore, "Silence" and "The Fish" reprinted with the permission of Scribner, a Division of Simon & Schuster, Inc., from *The Collected Poems of Marianne Moore* by Marianne Moore. Copyright © 1935 by Marianne Moore, copyright renewed © 1963 by Marianne Moore and T. S. Eliot.

Robert Morgan, "Mountain Bride" from *Groundwork*, Gnomon Press. Copyright © 1979. Reprinted by permission of the author.

Timothy Murphy, "The Track of a Storm" from *The Dead of Gift* by Timothy Murphy. Copyright © 2001 by Timothy Murphy. Reprinted by permission of Story Line Press, Inc., www.storylinepress.com.

Howard Nemerov, "A Primer of the Daily Round" from *New and Selected Poems* by Howard Nemerov, copyright © 1960 by Howard Nemerov (University of Chicago Press). Reprinted by permission of Margaret Nemerov.

Naomi Shihab Nye, "The Traveling Onion." Reprinted by permission of Naomi Shihab Nye from *Yellow Glove*, Breitenbush Books, Portland, OR. Copyright © 1986 by Naomi Shihab Nye.

Frank O'Hara, "The Day the Lady Died" from *Lunch Poems*. Copyright © 1964 by Frank O'Hara. Reprinted by permission of City Lights Books.

Sharon Olds, "The One Girl at the Boy's Party" from *The Dead and the Living* by Sharon Olds, copyright © 1987 by Sharon Olds. Used by permission of Alfred A. Knopf, a division of Random House, Inc.

Mary Oliver, "The Black Walnut Trees" from *Twelve Moons* by Mary Oliver. Copyright © 1972, 1973, 1974, 1975, 1976, 1977, 1978, 1979 by Mary Oliver; first appeared in *The Ohio Review*. By permission of Little, Brown & Company.

Simon J. Ortiz, "The Serenity in Stones." Permission to reprint given by author Simon J. Ortiz, Copyright 1975.

Wilfred Owen, "Dulce et Decorum Est" from *Wilfred Owen: Collected Poems of Wilfred Owen*. Copyright © 1963 by Chatto & Witndus Ltd. Reprinted by permission of New Directions Publishing Corporation.

Dorothy Parker, "One Perfect Rose" and "Résumé" copyright 1926, renewed © 1954 by Dorothy Parker from *The Portable Dorothy Parker* by Dorothy Parker. Used by permission of Viking Penguin, a division of Penguin Putnam, Inc.

Linda Pastan, "Crocuses." Copyright © 1989 by Linda Pastan, from *Heroes in Disguise* by Linda Pastan. Used by permission of W. W. Norton & Company, Inc.

Robert Phillips, "Compartments" from *Spinach Days*. Copyright © 2000. Reprinted by permission of The Johns Hopkins University Press.

Marge Piercy, "Barbie Doll" from *Circles on the Water* by Marge Piercy, © 1982 by Marge Piercy. Used by permission of Alfred A. Knopf, a division of Random House, Inc.

Sylvia Plath, "Daddy," "Edge" and "Metaphors" from *The Collected Poems of Sylvia Plath*. Reprinted by permission of HarperCollins Publishers and Faber and Faber Ltd.

Ezra Pound, "In the Station at the Metro," "Portrait d'une Femme" and "The River

Wallace Stevens. Used by permission of Alfred A. Knopf, Inc., a division of Random House, Inc.

Anne Stevenson, "Sous-Entendu" (1970). Reprinted from *The Collected Poems of Anne Stevenson 1955–1996* by Anne Stevenson (1996) by permission of Oxford University Press.

Leon Stokesbury, "Evening's End" from *Autumn Rhythm: New & Selected Poems by Leon Stokesbury.* Copyright © 1996. Reprinted by permission of the University of Arkansas Press, Inc.

Mark Strand, "The Tunnel" from *Selected Poems* by Mark Strand, copyright © 1979, 1980 by Mark Strand. Used by permission of Alfred A. Knopf, Inc., a division of Random House.

Dabney Stuart, "Discovering My Daughter" from *Light Years: New and Selected Poems,* 1994. Copyright © 1990, 1991, 1992, 1993, 1994 by Dabney Stuart. Reprinted by permission of Louisiana State University Press.

May Swenson, "How Everything Happens (Based on a Study of the Wave)." Reprinted with permission of Simon & Schuster Books for Young Readers, an imprint of Simon & Schuster Children's Publishing Division for *The Complete Poems to Solve* by May Swenson. Copyright © 1993 by The Literary Estate of May Swenson.

James Tate, "Teaching the Ape to Write Poems." Reprinted by permission of James Tate.

Dylan Thomas, "Do Not Go Gentle Into That Good Night" from *Poems of Dylan Thomas.* Copyright © 1952 by Dylan Thomas. Reprinted by permission of David Hgham Associates, and New Directions Publishing Corporation.

Jean Toomer, "Reapers" from *Cane* by Jean Toomer. Copyright © 1923 by Boni & Liveright, renewed 1951 by Jean Toomer. Used by permission of Liveright Publishing Corporation.

Catherine Tufariello, "Useful Advice" from *Tar River Poetry.* Reprinted by permission.

Ellen Bryant Voigt, "Daughter" from *The Forces of Plenty* by Ellen Voigt. Copyright © 1983 by Ellen Bryant Voigt. Used by permission of W. W. Norton & Company, Inc.

Derek Walcott, "Central America" from *The Arkansas Testament.* Copyright © 1987 by Derek Walcott. Reprinted by permission of Farrar, Straus & Giroux, Inc.

Alice Walker, "Even as I Hold You" from *Good Night Willie Lee, I'll See you in the Morning* by Alice Walker, copyright © 1975, 1976, 1979 by Alice Walker. Used by permission of Doubleday, a Division of Random House, Inc.

Margaret Walker, "For Malcom X" from *This is My Century: New and Selected Poems.* Reprinted by permission of the University of Georgia Press.

Richard Wilbur, "Junk" from *Advice to a Prophet and Other Poems.* Copyright © 1961 and renewed 1989. Reprinted by permission of Harcourt Inc. "Playboy" from *Walking to Sleep: New Poems and Translations,* copyright © 1968 by Richard Wilbur. Reprinted by * permission of Harcourt Brace & Company, Inc. "The Writer" from *The Mind Reader,* copyright © 1971 by Richard Wilbur. Reprinted by permission of Harcourt Brace & Company, Inc. "Year's End" from *Ceremony and Other Poems,* copyright © 1949 and renewed 1977 by Richard Wilbur. Reprinted by permission of Harcourt Brace & Company, Inc.

Nancy Willard, "A Hardware Store as Proof of the Existence of God" from *Water Walker by Nancy Willard,* copyright © 1989 by Nancy Willard. Used by permission of Alfred A. Knopf, a division of Random House, Inc.

Miller Williams, "The Book" from *Living on the Surface: New and Selected Poems.* Copyright © 1989 by Miller Williams. Reprinted by permission of Louisiana State University Press.

William Carlos Williams, "The Last Words of My English Grandmother," "The Red Wheelbarrow" and "Spring and All" from *Collected Poems: 1909–1939, Volume 1,* copyright © 1938 by New Directions Publishing Corp. Reprinted by permission of New Directions Publishing Corp.

James Wright, "A Blessing" from *The Branch Will Not Break* by James Wright. © 1959 by James Wright. "Saint Judas" from *Saint Judas* by James Wright. © 1959 by James Wright. Reprinted by permission of Wesleyan University Press.

William Butler Yeats, "Leda and the Swan," "Sailing to Byzantium," "The Lake Isle of Innesfree," "The Second Coming" and "the Song of Wandering Aengus" reprinted with the permission of Scribner, a Division of Simon & Schuster, Inc., from *The Collected Poems of W. B. Yeats: Revised Second Edition,* edited by Richard J. Finneran. (New York: Scribner, 1996).

Index of Critical Terms

Index of Poets, Titles, and First Lines

Additional Titles of Interest

Note to Instructors: Any of these Penguin-Putnam, Inc. titles can be packaged with this book for a special discount up to 60% off the retail price. Contact your local Allyn & Bacon/Longman sales representative for details on how to create a Penguin-Putnam, Inc. Value Package.

Albee, *The Three Tall Women*
Allison, *Bastard Out of Carolina*
Alvarez, *How the García Girls Lost the Accent*
Austen, *Persuasion*
Austen, *Pride & Prejudice*
Bellow, *The Adventures of Augie March*
Boyle, *Tortilla Curtain*
Cather, *My Antonia*
Cather, *O Pioneers!*
Chopin, *The Awakening*
Conrad, *Nostromo*
DeVantes, *Don Quixote*
DeLillo, *White Noise*
Desal, *Journey to Ithaca*
Douglass, *Narrative of the Life of Frederick Douglass*
Golding, *Lord of the Flies*
Hawthorne, *The Scarlet Letter*
Homer, *Iliad*
Horner, *Odyssey*
Huang, *Madame Butterfly*
Hulme, *Bone People*
Jen, *Typical American*
Karr, *The Liar's Club*
Kerouac, *On The Road*
Kesey, *One Flew Over the Cuckoo's Nest*
King, *Misery*
Larson, *Passing*
Lavin, *In a Cafe*
Marquez, *Love in the time of Cholera*
McBride, *The Color of Water*
Miller, *Death of a Salesman*
Molière, *Tartuffe and Other Plays*

Morrison, *Beloved*
Morrison, *The Bluest Eye*
Morrison, *Sula*
Naylor, *Women of Brewster Place*
Orwell, *1984*
Postman, *Amusing Ourselves to Death*
Rayben, *My First White Friend*
Rose, *Lives on the Boundary*
Rose, *Possible Lives: The Promise of Public*
Rushdie, *Midnight's Children*
Shakespeare, *Four Great Comedies*
Shakespeare, *Four Great Tragedies*
Shakespeare, *Hamlet*
Shakespeare, *Four Histories*
Shakespeare, *King Lear*
Shakespeare, *Macbeth*
Shakespeare, *Othello*
Shakespeare, *Twelfth Night*
Shelley, *Frankenstein*
Silko, *Ceremony*
Solzhenitsyn, *One Day in the Life of Ivan Denisovich*
Sophocles, *The Three Theban Plays*
Spence, *The Death of a Woman Wang*
Steinbeck, *Grapes of Wrath*
Steinbeck, *The Pearl*
Stevenson, *Dr. Jekyll & Mr. Hyde*
Swift, *Gulliver's Travels*
Twain, *Adventures of Huckleberry Finn*
Wilde, *The Importance of Being Earnest*
Wilson, *Joe Turner's Come and Gone*
Wilson, *Fences*
Woolf, *Jacob's Room*